THE

GREAT
BETRAYAL

Other books by Patrick J. Buchanan

Right from the Beginning

Conservative Votes, Liberal Victories

The New Majority

THE

GREAT
BETRAYAL

How American Sovereignty and Social Justice
Are Being Sacrificed
to the Gods of the Global Economy

PATRICK J. BUCHANAN

Little, Brown and Company

Boston New York Toronto London

First Edition

LIBRARY OF CONGRESS CATALOGING-IN-PUBLICATION DATA

Buchanan, Patrick J.
The great betrayal : how American sovereignty and social justice are being sacrificed
to the gods of the global economy / by Patrick J. Buchanan. — 1st ed.
p.   cm.
Includes bibliographical references and index.
ISBN 0-316-11518-5
1. United States — Foreign economic relations.   2. Free trade.
3. Working class — United States.
4. United States — Economic conditions — 1981–   I. Title.
HF1455.B83   1998

337.73 — dc21   97-38818

10   9   8   7   6   5   4   3   2   1

MV-NY

Published simultaneously in Canada by Little, Brown & Company (Canada) Limited
Printed in the United States of America

FOR MY MOTHER AND FATHER

Catherine E. Buchanan

(1911–95)

William B. Buchanan

(1905–88)

CONTENTS

Book Three

THE COUNTERREVOLUTION AND THE COMING OF A NEW POPULISM

Book One

A TALE OF TWO NATIONS

Chapter 1

THE TWO AMERICAS

We are not . . . approaching Socialism at all,
but a very different state of society . . . in
which the Capitalist class shall be even more
powerful and far more secure . . . a society in
which the proletarian mass . . . shall change
their status, lose their present legal freedom,
and be subject to compulsory labor.[1]

— Hilaire Belloc, 1913

It was a bitter cold day in December of 1995.

From New Orleans we took the interstate up through Baton Rouge and over to Lafayette. Acadia Parish is farther on. Our destination: the Fruit of the Loom plant in Rayne.

Acadia is not affluent. In this Catholic and Cajun bayou parish with three pages of Thibodeauxs in the phone book, the average wage in 1993 was only two-thirds of the national average. But things were looking up. Fruit of the Loom — the largest employer in Louisiana, with 7,100 workers — had built a new plant in Rayne. Five hundred Acadiana women had won jobs cutting and sewing T-shirts. The parish had given Fruit of the Loom all the land it wanted for one dollar a year. What did these women do?

"You got there, you start sewing, and you stopped sewing when you leave," said twenty-three-year-old Carolyn Richard. "It got a little pressure on you. You got to make your quota. But if you feel like sewing, you got good pay."[2]

Carolyn's cousin Connie Richard had left school in the tenth grade. She was nineteen with one child when she was hired. Her husband was making $800 a month hanging Sheetrock. "At first, my husband didn't want me to work," Connie told a reporter in her cramped trailer. "But he started seeing how much I was making, and I started helping out with the bills. We could afford a new stove, a washer and dryer. We got used to the money."

Within three years Connie was earning $1,000 a month. With her husband's pay, that came to $21,600 a year. And the benefits were good. When she left work to have two more children, Fruit of the Loom paid her maternity leave, and with the medical benefits, her boy's heart problem was being treated by a specialist.

The work was hard but Connie enjoyed it: "There was a competition among the women to see who could sew more." She usually skipped lunch: food made her sleepy and slowed her down; she would settle for the junk food in the vending machine. Connie was planning to work at the plant "for a long time, maybe so I could buy me a house."

A month before I arrived, Connie Richard's dream had vanished. During work hours a supervisor's voice was piped over the intercom. When the sewing machines stopped, the supervisor announced that the plant was shutting down.

Thelma Alleman had been inspecting T-shirts. When she heard the supervisor's voice, she stopped work and sat down. A production break was unheard of. She had heard the rumors and feared the worst. And the worst happened. "Most of us, we cried," said Thelma.

Five hundred women lost their jobs.

"A Lot of No Christmas"

"This factory meant a lot to these people," said Jonas Breaux, an editor at the *Daily Advertiser* in Lafayette. "When a police officer around here can only make nine hundred dollars a month, a wife could earn a better paycheck from Fruit of the Loom." There was the matter, too, of broken pride. "There's a certain dedication to doing a good job," said Breaux. "People know you here. They know your sister, your cousin, your mama. It's not like walking into a plant in Houston where no one knows you."

Harold Price, director of Louisiana's economic development, saw tough times ahead: "Five hundred layoffs is a big enough number, and for that area of the state, it will hurt. Those jobs were extremely important to Rayne."

"There's going to be a lot of no jobs and a lot of no Christmas," said Agnes Sanchez, manager of the Shop Rite in Rayne. "They're really holding on to their money now."

When I got to Rayne, our tiny motorcade was led through town by the chief of police. Mayor Jim Petitjean introduced me at the plant. I spoke from the back of a pickup; there was not much I could say.

Who killed that plant? Who killed the five hundred jobs of those Acadiana women? The same people who are killing the dreams of millions of working men and women: the government of the United States.

Our own government's policies put these women into a Darwinian competition with Mexican and Honduran women who have to work for fifty cents an hour. Before Fruit of the Loom closed its plant in Rayne, two plants opened in Mexico. With Bill Clinton's North American Free Trade Agreement (NAFTA) deal in 1993 and the devaluation of the peso, which cut in half the dollar wages of Mexican women, Rayne's fate was sealed. Why employ Acadiana women for six dollars an hour when you can hire Mexican women to do the same sewing for fifty cents an hour?

"The jobs that require the least-skilled labor are the easiest to move overseas or to other countries," said Louisiana State University economics professor Loren Scott. "Almost everything from those plants can be packed up in an eighteen-wheeler and trucked to Mexico in no time."

I have visited scores of such plants. The story is always the same: bewildered workers wondering what happened to the good times, what happened to the town they grew up in, what's happening to their country.

AMERICA: AGAIN A HOUSE DIVIDED

After fifteen months of traveling from Alaska to Florida seeking the Republican nomination in 1995–96, I came home convinced that we are losing the country we grew up in. The times when we all sacrificed together, as in World War II, and when we all prospered together, as in the 1950s, are gone. America is no longer one nation indivisible. We are now the "two nations" predicted by the Kerner Commission thirty years ago. Only the dividing line is no longer just race; it is class.

On one side is the new class, Third Wave America — the bankers, lawyers, diplomats, investors, lobbyists, academics, journalists, executives, professionals, high-tech entrepreneurs — prospering beyond their dreams. Buoyant and optimistic, these Americans are full of anticipation about their prospects in the Global Economy.

The children of John Kenneth Galbraith's *The Affluent Society*, they live in spacious homes in tree-lined suburbs, send their kids to schools where parking lots are packed with the latest models, and pore over brochures from the finest colleges. They "Christmas" at Vail and shop at quarter-mile-long malls where the richness and variety of the clothes, shoes, luggage, and leather would have astonished the kings of yesteryear. This is 401K America, where tax-exempt pension funds fatten yearly like cattle and the Dow knows no ceiling. While the good life is now, even better times are just ahead.

On the other side of the national divide is Second Wave America, the forgotten Americans left behind. White-collar and blue-collar, they work for someone else, many with hands, tools, and machines in factories soon to be hoisted onto the chopping block of some corporate downsizer in some distant city or foreign country.

Second Wave America is a land of middle-class anxiety, downsized hopes, and vanished dreams, where economic insecurity is a preexisting condition of life, and company towns become ghost towns overnight. Men in their forties and fifties who have worked for the same company since college come home bewildered to tell shaken wives that they are being let go. People know in their hearts that America will never again be the country they grew up in. The years slide by, family incomes stagnate, wives go to work to make sure their children have the same things as other kids at the public school do. For Middle America, something went wrong. They played by the rules, but the promise was unfulfilled.

This other America is Youngstown, where from the banks of the Mahoning you can gaze across at the cenotaph of a Jones & Laughlin mill that housed 65,000 workers in World War II. For thirty miles up and down the river, there stand the blackened ruins of a dead civilization as the industrial disarmament of the United States proceeds apace. This other America is central Arizona, where you drive through miles of desert, past silent mines, after reading about U.S.-backed loans from the World Bank providing the seed money to open up new copper mines in Chile. This other America is the inner city, where the yellow brick road to the middle class narrows to a single lane.

No site better captures yesterday's America than Detroit, forge and furnace of the arsenal of democracy. Detroit is the burned-out case of American cities. The Empire of the Sun has its revenge. Japanese imports helped kill the city that built the weapons that destroyed the empire. Now grandsons of soldiers of the imperial army work at high-paying manufacturing jobs once held by the fathers of ten-dollar-an-hour retail clerks in Macomb County.

But why blame the Japanese? We did it to ourselves. We Americans constructed a postwar trading regime in which, over twenty-five years, Japan bought 400,000 American cars while selling us 40 million Japanese cars, a ratio of 100:1. One president after another sat still while a third of America's greatest industry was shipped off to Japan. It is not Japan's fault, China's fault, or Mexico's fault that Middle America has been abandoned, that our manufacturing base has shriveled, that foreigners make the things Americans once made for themselves. It is our fault. Like rich and pampered children who never worked for their inheritance, we listened to cloistered academics peddling pet theories and squandered an estate that was the awe of mankind. As we noisily boast of America's "leadership," tough-minded rivals laugh behind our backs and loot us blind on the road to the end of the American Century.

Why should Third Wave America care? With our gross domestic product (GDP) nearing $8 trillion and U.S. companies leading the world in cutting-edge industries, why should they not celebrate the Global Economy? When they inspect their portfolios, pension funds, and bank statements, why should they not believe this is the best of all possible worlds? Third Wave America has much to celebrate:

- The stock market has doubled in value in five years, with a Dow-Jones average that in 1997 crossed the 8000 mark.
- Pension funds are flush, as corporate profits have almost doubled since mid-1992.
- The population of millionaires and billionaires has exploded.
- Between 1980 and 1992, the average income of the top 1 percent of U.S. taxpayers rose 215 percent (from $187,000 to $464,000).
- America's wealthiest 1 percent, which controlled 21 percent of America's wealth in 1949, now controls 40 percent.[3]
- The wealthiest 10 percent of Americans now has 67 percent of America's private wealth.

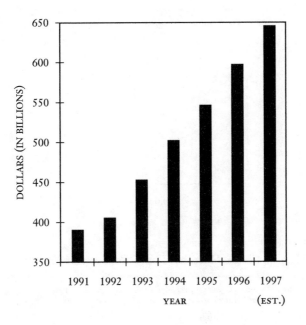

U.S. Corporate Profits (in 1992 Dollars)

Source: U.S. Department of Commerce

- Top CEO salaries — 44 times the average wage of a worker in 1965 — have soared to 212 times the average pay of a worker.[4]

How have the families of Middle America fared?

- Between 1972 and 1994, real wages of working Americans fell 19 percent, the longest slide in three centuries.[5]
- In the spring of 1996 average hourly wages were lower than in 1965.[6]
- In 1970 the price of an average new house was twice a young couple's income; it is now four times that income.[7]
- In real dollars, the after-tax earnings of Americans in retail trade equal earnings in the Depression.
- In 1960 only 18 percent of women with children under the age of six were in the workforce; by 1995 the figure had soared to 63 percent.[8]

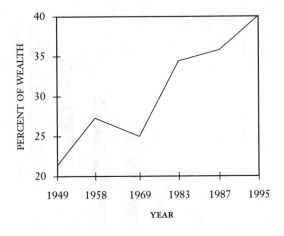

Wealth Share Held by Top 1 Percent of Families

Source: Ravi Batra, *The Great Depression of 1990* (New York: Simon & Schuster, 1987), p. 118; Steven Sass, "Passing the Buck," *Federal Reserve Bank of Boston, Regional Review,* summer 1995, p. 16

- Since 1966 the share of American men with jobs has fallen from 85.4 percent to 76.8 percent. Idle men end up in trouble, often in prison — where 1.1 million American males now reside, with a thousand added weekly to the prison population. Another half a million are in jail.[9]
- In the first six years of the 1990s, the median family income fell 6 percent. During the Depression-era 1930s, it rose 17 percent.[10]
- In the first six years of the 1990s, real earnings of full-time U.S. workers fell .9 percent but rose 10 percent in Germany.[11]
- The federal tax bite, 3 percent of the average family income in 1950, is now 25 percent.
- The wages of U.S. manufacturing workers, once three and four times those in Europe and Japan, are now below Japan's and are only 60% of Germany's.
- Between 1952 and 1988, the constant-dollars earnings of an engineer rose from $30,000 to $75,000 while the earnings of a manufacturing worker rose from $20,000 to $22,000.[12]

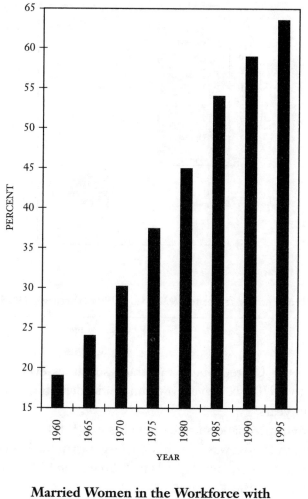

**Married Women in the Workforce with
Children under the Age of Six**

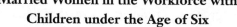

Source: *Statistical Abstract of the United States, 1996*

These are Middle America's rewards, as our elites force-marched the nation into the Global Economy of its dreams. And what has happened to the most productive and self-reliant republic in history?

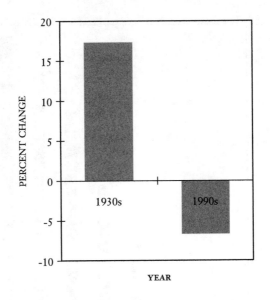

Real Family Income 1930s vs. 1990s (through 1995)

Source: *Economic Report of the President*, 1960, 1996

- Where the United States ran trade surpluses every year from 1900 to 1970, we have now run trade deficits for twenty-six straight years.
- Our total merchandise trade deficit since 1980 is more than $2 trillion. In 1996 it was $191 billion, larger than the budget deficit.
- Imported manufactured goods in 1996 equaled 51 percent of all manufactures MADE IN THE USA.[13]
- The world's greatest creditor nation has become its greatest debtor.
- Since 1970 the dollar has lost two-thirds of its value against the Japanese yen and German mark.[14]
- In 1962 manufacturing accounted for 29 percent of the national income. By 1997 it had fallen to 17 percent, the smallest share of the gross national product (GNP) since the nineteenth century.[15]
- In 1965, 31 percent of our labor force had manufacturing-equivalent jobs. By 1997 that figure was down to 15 percent, also the smallest share since the nineteenth century.[16]

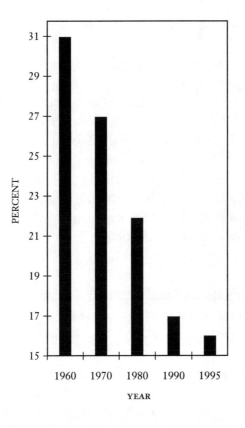

Percent of Workers in Manufacturing

Source: *Statistical Abstract of the United States, 1996*

- Since 1980 the United States has lost 2.6 million manufacturing jobs.
- For the first time, as many Americans work in government as in manufacturing.[17] In twenty-eight states, including California, New York, and Texas, government workers outnumber manufacturing workers.[18]
- Americans no longer make their own cameras, shoes, radios, TVs, toys. A fifth of our steel, a third of our autos, half our machine tools, and two-thirds of our textiles and clothes are made abroad.

- However, jobs at Wal-Mart rose from just 21,000 in 1978 to 628,000 in 1996.[19]
- Foreign interests own 17 percent of the U.S. federal debt. In 1996 foreign purchases of U.S. Treasury bills totaled $122 billion, more than the entire federal budget deficit for all of 1997.[20]
- As of mid-1997, the Treasury's custody account held $628 billion worth of U.S. securities on behalf of foreign central banks, a near doubling since 1993. A hint by Japan's prime minister that Tokyo might sell its share dropped the Dow 192 points in one day.[21]
- Not since Colonial days has America been so vulnerable to foreign regimes. When Mexico threatened to default in 1994, we had to cobble together a $50 billion bailout, lest Mexico's default bring on a financial panic in the United States.

This is the readout of the electrocardiogram of a nation that has begun its descent. As author Pat Choate writes, "A peek behind the glitter of record stock prices and high corporate profits reveals a deepening economic dry rot — a nation that is eating its seed corn and squandering its economic leadership position, here and abroad."[22]

While millions of jobs have been created in retail sales to move the mountains of imports, the manufacturing jobs that enabled Americans with high school diplomas to live the American Dream are being shipped and created overseas. Between 1973 and 1995, the hourly wage of high school dropouts fell 28 percent.[23]

New-class journalists, economists, and academics view all this with cool equanimity. "To make an omelet, one must break eggs," the old Bolsheviks used to say. In building their new world, our elites treat fellow Americans as obsolete equipment. Economic insecurity is here to stay, they say, a condition of the Global Economy we must live with, a growing pain of the new world order. Rarely, however, do they themselves share that pain.

And what is this wondrous new Global Economy? It is but the enlargement of the old international economy of commerce and trade that has existed since before Marco Polo took the Silk Road to China and the "sea dogs" of Elizabeth I raided the Spanish Main for galleons carrying gold and silver back to Aragon and Castile. Today's acolytes of the Global Economy have discovered nothing new; they have simply rewritten the rules of trade to conform to their ideology and to benefit themselves at the expense of their country and their countrymen.

Better the occasional sins of a government acting out of a spirit of charity than the constant omissions of a government frozen in the ice of its own indifference. So it has been said. America's elites, smug and arrogant masters of the "world's last superpower," are frozen in the ice of their own ideology. And the steam is building beneath.

WHO LOST AMERICA?

The decline and fall of Middle America was neither preordained nor inevitable. It was engineered in Washington, D.C. Wages have fallen and the standard of living of American families has stagnated because of a basic law: the law of supply and demand. The price of labor has been dropping because the supply of labor has exploded.

In the Truman and Eisenhower administrations, U.S. markets were thrown open and Europeans and Japanese invited in. What better way to convert them from war-wracked nations into prosperous allies than to give their industries unimpeded access to America's vast and lucrative market — even if that meant low-wage competition for U.S. workers?

The allies responded with enthusiasm, carting off huge slices of America's market while fencing off their own. Our statesmen did not protest; after all, we were the leaders of the free world; we had to set an example. Though the allies had fully recovered by 1960, the unilateral American concessions continued.

Then, with the Immigration Act of 1965, America threw open the "golden door" and tens of millions of immigrants burst through. To their number has been added annual invasions of millions of illegal aliens crossing our southern border to compete with unskilled and semiskilled Americans. Illegal immigrants in the United States now number 5 million, and the U.S. labor supply has grown by more tens of millions in the past twenty-five years than in any other period in history.[24] How could the price of labor *not* fall?

Next came the global trade deals that put American labor into competition with hundreds of millions of Latins, East Asians, Chinese, Eastern Europeans, and Russians. Energetic, talented, hungry, these workers will do the jobs Americans do, for a fraction of the pay an American family needs for a "living wage." Foreign workers, however, do not compete with the children of affluence; they compete with that half of the nation who never graduated from college or never even went to college.

Having declared free trade and open borders to be America's policy, why are we surprised that corporate executives padlocked their plants in the Rust Belt and moved overseas? Why keep your plant here when you can manufacture at a fraction of the cost abroad, ship your goods back, and pocket the windfall profits that come from firing twenty-dollar-an-hour Americans and hiring fifty-cent-an-hour Asians? A pair of Nikes that sells for $150 in the United States costs $5 in wages to make in Indonesia. Any wonder that Nike president Philip Knight is the fifth-richest man in America, with $5.2 billion, while his Indonesian workers make thirty-one cents an hour?[25]

Under both parties, the U.S. government has stacked the deck against the American worker. Take a helicopter up above the Tijuana border at sunset. You will see crowds of Mexicans forming up to dash into the United States, and you will see all the new factories going up on the Mexican side. We export our jobs to Mexico; it exports its jobless to us — the great trade-off of NAFTA.

"Practical men," said John Maynard Keynes, "are usually the slaves of some defunct economist."[26] America's elites are slaves to the ideas of nineteenth-century European scribblers, none of whom ever built a nation. Our industrial base is shrinking and Middle America's standard of living is no longer rising, because we forgot how America became a mighty industrial power and we embraced the myth that it was free trade that made us great. To challenge this myth —

now an article of faith in both parties — is to be treated as imbecilic or immoral. Yet, the lie must be exposed, for more is being sacrificed on the altar of this Moloch than the jobs of our workers and the standard of living of our people. Our politics are being corrupted, our dependency on unstable foreign regimes is growing, and our survival as a self-reliant and independent republic is at risk.

Both parties have collaborated in the sellout. In embracing free trade, Democrats betrayed their workers. In worshiping this golden calf, Republicans turned their back on their history, tradition, and greatest men. Most do not even know it, but they celebrate today what their wisest leaders used to ridicule as the utopian nonsense of the idiots savants of the Paris salons.

It will be no easy task to persuade Americans that these ideas are killing the land we love. Some will never be persuaded. For, to be candid, an end of American independence and sovereignty is what they are about. By increasing our dependence on foreign trade — 10 percent of the GDP in 1950, 23 percent today, 36 percent by 2010 — by shifting power to the institutions of global government, they hope to usher in a day when that chapter in history known as the Age of Nations is ended forever. Thus, their ugliest epithets are reserved for those who unfurl and raise the old banners of patriotism and "America first." It is time to respond not in kind, but in truth.

A PERSONAL JOURNEY

First, an admission. From 1962, when I first began writing editorials exalting John F. Kennedy's Trade Expansion Act, until I left the Reagan White House in 1987, I was a free trader. I believed that free trade was the best policy not only for our country but for all Americans. But something happened along the way.

The first seeds of doubt were planted at the 1976 Republican National Convention in Kansas City. I ran into my Uncle Bob and Aunt Honey, my mother's sister. "Why are you supporting this free trade?" Bob asked. "Don't you know what's happening to the Mon Valley?"

As a boy I had stayed with my grandparents in Charleroi in the heart of that valley of southwestern Pennsylvania, iron and coal country where my mother grew up. I remember being there after the war, when my Uncle Jim would take me down to the veterans hall where he spent the late afternoon sipping beer with his buddies who had come home. That town on the Monongahela always held a special place in my heart. "The Mon Valley is dying," Bob said; imports are killing us.

Still, when I went into Ronald Reagan's White House in 1985, I supported the president's position and oversaw his veto messages killing legislation to protect the shoe and textile industries. I made sure that one referred to the "infamous Smoot-Hawley Tariff."

When I left the White House, I began to change my views. I learned that Toshiba, Japan's industrial giant, had sold silent-propeller technology to Moscow. A treacherous act. But when Congress tried to impose sanctions, U.S. lobbyists (among them people I had worked with in the White House) were all over Capitol Hill, pleading for amnesty — even though Toshiba had put at risk U.S. national security and the lives of American sailors. Did trade trump patriotism?

The more I read of local businesses and factories shutting down, workers being laid off, towns dying as imports soared, the more I began to ask myself, The price of free trade is painful, real, lasting — where is the benefit other than the vast cornucopia of consumer goods at Tysons Corner?

As I began to write skeptically of free trade, I discovered that I was trampling on holy ground. For some conservatives, to question free-trade dogma is heresy punishable by excommunication.

But when did free trade become conservative orthodoxy? Every Republican president from Lincoln to the New Deal had been a high-tariff man. All four presidents on Mount Rushmore — Washington, Jefferson, Lincoln, Theodore Roosevelt — were protectionists. When did unbridled free trade become conservative doctrine and Republican orthodoxy?

I was astonished at the exasperation and rage my deviation provoked. When I went over to the Cato Institute to talk to its scholars about my challenge to President Bush, I suggested that we stay off free trade, as we disagreed. The session had not lasted five minutes before it reached the shouting stage over my "protectionism." I began to realize that free trade is a matter about which it is not acceptable to dissent and remain inside the church.

Another bridge was crossed at Christmas in New Hampshire in 1991. I was at the James River paper mill in the North Country, meeting workers. It was a bad day. Word had gone out that there would be further layoffs. With New Hampshire in the worst economic crisis in decades, there would be no jobs to replace the ones lost. As I waited to shake hands, I noticed half a dozen workers lined up to get their Christmas turkeys. They looked over at me and did not seem friendly. *These men are angry and bitter,* I thought, *let's leave them alone.*

Go over and shake hands, my campaign manager said. I did. As I walked the line, they said nothing. Then I extended my hand to a hard-looking worker about my own age who was staring at the plant floor. I grabbed his hand and told him who I was; he looked up, stared me in the eye, and said in an anguished voice, "Save our jobs!"

It went right through me.

I mumbled something about doing my best. As we drove back down the snow-covered road to Manchester, his face and piercing plea were with me. What could I do? Days later, an aide handed me a clipping from the *Union Leader.* It told of how the U.S. Export-Import Bank was financing a new paper mill — in Mexico!

What are we doing to our own people? I asked myself.

Ever since, I have become convinced that America's elite is oblivious to what is happening to our country, as an older, better America — where we were a community, a nation, a people — slowly dies.

This book is not written, then, by some longtime dissident of U.S. trade policy but by one who, late in life, has come to believe that the policies I helped advance for a quarter of a century are producing what Abraham Lincoln predicted they would — "ruin among our people."

The intellectual architecture of free-trade theory is impressive. But is the theory valid? Does it work as advertised? What did our forefathers believe? How did they build the greatest industrial power on earth out of thirteen rural colonies? How did free trade obtain such a hold on the minds of the American intellectual elite? Is it too late for us to change course?

I have been told a hundred times, "Pat, there is no turning back; it's gone too far; drop it!" I don't believe it. We can restore our country. We can renew the social contract. We can do better by the norms of social justice — for all our people. We can take our country back. And that is why I have written this book.

Chapter 2

TRIUMPH OF THE FREE TRADERS

A FORGOTTEN HERO OF FREE TRADE

When and how did the free traders capture America?

If one year could mark their decisive victory, it would be 1934, with passage of the Reciprocal Trade Agreements Act. And if one year could be cited as the inauguration of the free-trade era, it would be 1967, with completion of the Kennedy Round of trade negotiations. And Woodrow Wilson and Franklin Roosevelt alone excepted, the twentieth century's greatest U.S. champion of free trade was Cordell Hull.

Hull is a forgotten hero of liberalism. As congressman, senator, and secretary of state during a career that spanned a third of a century, he is the statesman most responsible for America's abandonment of economic nationalism. For too long Hull has been ignored by history.

From boyhood Hull shared the vision of the classical liberals who taught that free trade would bind nations together in harmony and peace. He bemoaned the fact that the great tariff battles of his youth were "fought on the home grounds that high tariffs or low tariffs were good or bad for the United States as a purely domestic matter. There was little or no thought of their effect on other countries, little or no thought of their effect on world peace."[1]

A member of the House Committee on Ways and Means in 1913, Hull drafted the nation's first income tax. His idea was to replace tariffs — taxes on foreign imports — with taxes on Americans' income. Hull looked on expanding incomes as "the one great untaxed source of revenue."[2] His particular target was business. Reform was needed, Hull believed, because business had "assisted in building up monopolies and trusts."[3] With the Underwood Tariff of 1913, which slashed tariff rates while imposing the first permanent taxes on personal income, Hull's ideas came together. Liberals now had a practical program, and Hull's belief in the redemptive power of free trade had provided the intellectual and moral foundation.

Here we approach the heart of the "historical conflict between protectionists and free traders." Whom, or what, do we tax? As one student of America's tariff wars has written, "Protectionists prefer taxes on foreign goods, and free traders favor taxes on American incomes."[4]

But to Hull, the issue was about much more than economics.

> Toward 1916 I embraced the philosophy I carried throughout my twelve years as Secretary of State.... From then on, to me, unhampered trade dovetailed with peace; high tariffs, trade barriers, and unfair economic competition, with war.[5]

Ironically, Hull embraced his free-trade philosophy just one year before the first free-trade president, Woodrow Wilson, plunged us into World War I. When peace came, Hull repeatedly drafted legislation calling for a world trade conference. But with Wilson's failure to take the United States into the League of Nations and the GOP sweep of 1920, Hull abandoned his efforts as hopeless.

Twenty years after he authored the Underwood Tariff and fathered the nation's first income tax, however, Cordell Hull was secretary of state. With FDR in power and New Deal Democrats dominant in both houses of Congress, the free traders had it all. A sixty-year era of tariff cuts began. By the 1990s customs duties that once produced 50–90 percent of U.S. revenue would yield 1–2 percent.

In 1934 Congress ceded virtually all power over tariffs and trade to the executive branch. Within two years the State Department had negotiated reciprocal tariff cuts with Cuba, Belgium, Haiti, Sweden, Brazil, Canada, and the Netherlands; by the middle of World War II, thirty bilateral trade agreements were in operation.

Hull served as secretary of state during one of America's crucial decades. Popular in Washington for "his reputation for rugged integrity and because of a Lincolnesque boyhood," Hull was, said one historian, of "extremely mediocre caliber as a diplomat." Self-educated, he knew little of foreign lands, less of foreign languages, and was so given to pompous platitudes that a Washington hostess dubbed him the "hillbilly Polonius."[6] When Hull retired in 1944, FDR gave the portfolio to Edward Stettinius, of whom it was said that he "could not distinguish the Ukraine from a musical instrument."[7] Disparagements aside, Cordell Hull's influence on U.S. trade policy could scarcely have been greater.

The United States in 1945 was at its apogee, determined to succeed, as it had failed to do at the end of World War I, in imposing its vision of a new world order. The visionaries of 1945 created a galaxy of new institutions to give life to their dreams. Under the guidance of Treasury's Harry Dexter White, America had already midwifed the 1944 Bretton Woods agreement, by which Allied currencies were tied to the dollar at fixed rates, and the dollar tied to gold. In 1945 the Americans called into being the United Nations, which would be mother to many children. Among her offspring:

- the International Monetary Fund to assist nations in maintaining the currency-exchange rates, which was given at birth a present of 19.5 million ounces of American gold
- the International Bank for Reconstruction and Development (the World Bank) to repair the ruins of war
- the International Trade Organization (ITO), with power to enforce the rules of international trade, which were no longer to be bilateral but multilateral. While the ITO was winning approval, the General Agreement on Tariffs and Trade (GATT) was to govern international trade.

But in 1946 the tide went out on the New Deal and the "fighting Eightieth" Congress came in. Republicans captured both houses and came to Washington determined to block further transfers of U.S. sovereignty. For House Speaker Joe Martin and Majority Leader Robert Taft, the ITO was a bridge too far. Thus, Cordell Hull, a veteran of three decades of tariff wars, reentered the lists to become honorary chairman of the blue-ribbon Citizens Committee for Reciprocal World Trade. In command of Hull's forces was his executive committee chairman, the rising young diplomatic star who had been at Roosevelt's side at Yalta — Alger Hiss.[8]

"WILL" CLAYTON'S CONCESSION

Hull's hopes for the ITO rested with his fellow Southerner and the millionaire who headed the world's largest cotton brokerage firm and had been won over to the New Deal on free trade: William L. "Will" Clayton. Like Hull, Clayton dreamed of a sister organization to police world trade, the way the new UN was to police world peace. "By training, tradition and conviction Will Clayton is a free trader. Any meddling with the economic machine is, to him, the supreme sin,"[9] wrote *Time* in an August 1936 cover story that painted Clayton as the very model of the progressive new global capitalist. But some felt that he carried free trade too far. For Will Clayton "came under attack for continuing to sell to Nazi Germany and Imperial Japan long after the character of those regimes became obvious."[10]

Still, Clayton's belief in free trade was undiluted. "If we are to bring about world peace . . . and prevent World War III," he said, "[peace] must be based primarily on economic collaboration."[11] Whenever he spoke of liberalizing trade, a daughter said, it appeared as though he were in a trance.[12]

At the Havana conference (November 1947–February 1948) Clayton fought for the ITO like a man possessed. His adversaries were Latin American protectionists and British economic nationalists who wanted to curb imports to deal with their chronic balance-of-payments deficits. Republicans of the Eightieth Congress gave Clayton zero support. To California's Bertrand Gearhart, the U.S. delegation at Havana consisted of "boatloads of smug diplomats, all-wise economists, of experts, theorists, specialists and whatnots, sailing gaily from our shores to barter away . . . the little factory in Wichita, the little shop in Keokuk."[13]

To win over less-developed nations, Clayton made a breathtaking concession: America would accept a one-nation, one-vote formula, with no U.S. veto. America would have the same voting power in the ITO as did Costa Rica. Under the original plan, voting power reflected economic power, which would have given the United States 20 percent of the vote.

Democrats were apathetic, but many Republicans were apoplectic about the ITO. They saw it as an unconstitutional transfer of sovereign power. On March 18, 1948, the House Committee on Ways and Means rejected a resolution endorsing the ITO; in the Committee on Foreign Affairs, the ITO got just two GOP votes, moderate Representative James Fulton of Pennsylvania and liberal Jacob Javits of New York. The Chamber of Commerce also came out against the ITO, seeing in it a supranational governing body and a threat to private enterprise.

With Harry Truman's upset of Thomas Dewey in 1948 and the Democrats' recapturing Congress, the *New York Times* and other liberal newspapers called for resubmission of the ITO to Congress. Public opinion was unmoved. And when the GOP made gains in 1950, Truman threw in his hand, declining even to submit the ITO to Congress. The baby sister of the IMF and World Bank was stillborn.

In the mid-fifties Dwight Eisenhower tried to revive the idea, but his Organization for Trade Cooperation met the same fate. Republicans on Ways and Means issued a 1956 report declaring that the agency "could be likened to a pair of handcuffs fastened around the hands of Congress . . . [and] Congress itself will be throwing away the key."

But Hull's dream, dating back to the days of Wilson, of a world body with the power "to investigate and decide when certain practices were violations of fair trade" was realized in Bill Clinton's gargantuan GATT treaty of 1994. The World Trade Organization (WTO) was born — with Robert J. Dole and Newt Gingrich serving as proud godparents to the new baby.

"A MARSHALL PLAN MENTALITY"

Beyond ideology, another concern impelled America to throw open her markets in the postwar era. The United States needed allies in the Cold War and hoped to help Europe and Japan revive and prosper by letting them feed off America's markets, even if our own industries had to suffer. We adopted what one historian calls a "Marshall Plan mentality."[14]

In the early fifties few were alarmed by America's unilateral trade concessions. Imports amounted to but 4 percent of the GNP, and the notion that America might lose domestic market share was thought preposterous. Truman's Public Advisory Board for Mutual Security in 1953 urged the United States to eliminate "unnecessary" tariffs on automobiles, machinery, and consumer electronics like radios and televisions. These industries had developed such "highly efficient methods of production," said the report, that this country had nothing to fear. "These are types of goods for which American industry needs no protection, or very little protection."[15]

American consul offices were instructed to devote as much attention to servicing foreign exporters as to Americans trying to do business abroad. Under Eisenhower the pressure to open U.S. markets was ratcheted up. "All problems of local industry pale into insignificance in relation to the world crisis," Ike admonished his congressional leaders in 1953.[16] The president was especially worried about Japan: "Japan cannot live, and Japan cannot remain in the free world unless something is done to allow her to make a living,"[17] he told newspaper editors on June 22, 1954.

> Now, if we will not give her any money, if we will not trade with her, if we will not allow her to trade with the Reds, if we will not try to defend in any way the southeast Asian region where she has a partial trade opportunity, what is to happen to Japan? It is going to the Communists.[18]

A soldier and America's preeminent Cold War leader, Dwight Eisenhower had no patience with petty pleas to protect U.S. industry. Such ideas, said the conqueror of Hitler's Reich, represented "shortsightedness bordering upon tragic stupidity."[19] Secretary of State John Foster Dulles was Ike's echo. When the U.S. Tariff Commission unanimously ruled that American mining interests had been seriously injured by tariff concessions to Mexico, Canada, Bolivia, and Peru — and urged corrective relief — the secretary of state vented his exasperation with such small-mindedness. Restoring tariffs to lead and zinc, warned Dulles, could have "grave consequences."

> There would be strong popular resentment in Canada and Mexico, which will make our borders much less secure. The great opportunity to combat Communism in this hemisphere won by the success of Guatemala, would be more than canceled out. Soviet Communist leaders would be elated and would redouble their efforts to divide the free world.[20]

When New England fishermen protested that tons of imports from Canada, Iceland, and Norway were swamping their market, the Tariff Commission agreed. But State did not. Any restrictions on imported fish would have "adverse effects on vital United States political, economic and security interests in Canada, Iceland and Norway." An advisory body warned that a 50 percent duty on fish would strengthen "those elements in Iceland which wish to drive out U.S. NATO troops. As fish goes so goes Iceland."[21]

The threat worked. No duties were imposed. Iceland was saved for NATO, and New England's fishing industry paid the price. Before World War II, groundfish fillets from Canada, Iceland, and Norway had a near-zero share of the U.S. market. By 1952 their share was 20 percent. By the Reagan era it was 80 percent. The New England fishing industry had been sacrificed on the altar of allied solidarity in the Cold War.

Most Republicans yet recalled their tradition as the party that protected U.S. industries and American jobs. Some began to protest. Former president Herbert Hoover warned in 1954 of the ultimate consequences of throwing open U.S. markets: "Thousands of villages and towns would be deprived of their employment. Their schools, churches and skills would be greatly decimated."[22] Trade historian Alfred E. Eckes, Jr., reports that notes of a cabinet meeting reveal that behind closed doors, Treasury Secretary George Humphrey "went completely Neanderthal" and "roared about the trade program." Humphrey said that "not only should there be no tariff reduction for Japan but that the existing tariffs should be raised."[23] Behind his outburst lay Humphrey's belief that

> we were protectionists by history and had been living under a greatly lowered schedule of tariffs in a false sense of security because the world was not in competition. That has changed now and the great wave of world competition from plants we had built for other nations was going to bring vast unemployment to our country.[24]

Humphrey had found an ally in Connecticut's freshman senator, Prescott Bush:

> I never was a free trader. I never felt that we could abolish tariffs and do away with all protective devices, because we would have been flooded with imports which would have hurt our economy, hurt our defense posture, and I felt that these things had to be done gradually, selectively.[25]

TOKYO PLAYS HARDBALL

Republicans lost both houses of Congress in 1954, but Ike was still determined to grant even greater concessions to Japan. The State Department proposed unilateral U.S. concessions on 56 percent of Japanese imports — including glassware, chinaware, optical goods, automobiles, sewing machines, surgical instruments, cameras, and footwear. When the Departments of Agriculture, Commerce, and Labor rose in rebellion, State, with a nod from the Oval Office, played its trump: "the overriding interest of the United States is to strengthen our national security by taking the first step toward binding Japan to the Free World."[26]

National security became the *ultima ratio*, the final argument, in every trade dispute. As the free world leader, America needed allies in the Cold War. The way to bind those allies to the United States and strengthen them for the struggle was through "trade, not aid."

In truth, President Eisenhower had his priorities straight. National security was a compelling — indeed, a conclusive — argument in the early years of the Cold War. But our European and Asian allies did not need to be bribed to enlist in America's cause. They were in far greater and more immediate danger than we were from Communist aggression or subversion. And the trade concessions did not stop when America's allies were back on their feet, competitors and rivals again. A policy pursued out of Cold War necessity would be perpetuated out of peacetime habit. As for the strain on U.S. industries and the discrimination against U.S. exporters, our diplomats could not concern themselves with that. It was not their beat. Their job was to win the Cold War. In every great conflict there must be casualties. If the greatest American industries had to take losses, so be it.

In 1955 the United States undertook across-the-board negotiations with Japan. The U.S. delegation was led by C. Thayer White, the Japanese by one K. Otabe; the two spoke right past each other. As Japan could never compete with the U.S. auto and machine-tool industry, White said, Tokyo should forgo any effort to build up such industries, buy autos and machine tools from the United States, and focus on what Japan might produce more efficiently. Otabe shot back:

(1) If the theory of international trade were pursued to its ultimate conclusion, the United States would specialize in the production of automobiles and Japan in the production of tuna; (2) such a division does not take place . . . because each government encourages and protects those industries which it believes important for reasons of national policy.[27]

Pressed by White to reduce Japan's tariffs on optical equipment, Otabe replied that his government "wished to advance the development of the Japanese optical industry."[28] What about electrical equipment? "The Japanese Government believes that an electronics industry is essential to the development of the Japanese economy, the communications industry and national defense."[29] When the American side asked about tractors, heavy machinery, and petrochemicals, Otabe fired back the same answer and reminded the Americans how the United States had become a mighty industrial nation:

A protective tariff had contributed to the development of new industries in the early history of the United States and . . . that similarly a protective tariff could promote the development of the petrochemical, heavy machinery and other promising industries in Japan.[30]

Japan emerged triumphant.

While U.S. exports to Japan rose 95 percent between 1954 and 1960, most of the growth was in crude materials: mineral fuels and animal and vegetable products. Japan's exports to the United States, however, tripled, with Tokyo's share of America's imported manufactured goods more than doubling — to 15 percent. Unilateral American concessions had laid the cornerstone of Japan, Inc. As one American scholar writes, in the 1960s Japan "was more a trading company than a nation-state."

> The Government . . . fostered strategic industries such as steel and computers by using heavy bureaucratic guidance as well as tariffs, quotas, and informal import prevention policies. And while Japan kept many of its markets shut to imports, the United States, as part of the Cold War bargain, kept world markets open to Japanese products; exports became an engine for Japan's growth.[31]

By 1967 Japan's per capita income was twice what it had been in 1960.[32] Protectionism had created one of the greatest "economic miracles" the world had ever seen. And to what does Japanese scholar Kozo Yamamura attribute his nation's spectacular strides? Protectionism!

> Protection from foreign competition was probably the most important incentive to domestic development that the Japanese government provided. The stronger the home market cushion . . . the smaller the risk and the more likely the Japanese competitor was to increase capacity boldly in anticipation of demand growth. This can give the firm a strategic as well as a cost advantage over a foreign competitor operating in a different environment who must be more cautious.[33]

By 1958 Robert Stevens, president of the textile giant J. P. Stevens, was voicing the concerns of his industry and its millions of workers, demanding higher tariffs in words that echoed Republican platforms of old. We must "preserve our American standard of living . . . we have done all the giving and yielding and losing. . . . The American standard of living is under attack from overseas."[34] Few were listening. For Eisenhower had brought off a revolution; Ike had converted the Republican Party — the nation's citadel of economic nationalism for a century — into an institution whose stance on tariffs and trade was now a mirror image of the party of Wilson, Hull, and FDR.[35]

"Organizing Our Own Decline"

In the 1950s the United States shoveled its wealth abroad in foreign aid, the Korean War, and troop deployments in Europe while throwing open its huge market to allies and neutrals alike. There was no insistence on reciprocal access to foreign markets. Americans proudly boasted of their magnanimity, but a Norwegian historian, Geir Lundestad, dissented. The United States, he wrote, is "organizing its own decline."[36]

By 1960 the Allies, fully recovered from the war, had become rivals in industry after industry. Yet, still the altruistic Americans gave and gave. If Eisenhower was an activist in granting concessions, JFK was a zealot. Though he had pledged in 1960 to protect the textile industry, his trade policy was captured by the State Department, and the franchise given to Undersecretary George Ball, an Adlai Stevenson liberal and ex-lobbyist for foreign interests. From his school days at Northwestern, Ball was a one-worlder, a regular at lunches of the Council on Foreign Relations. In 1946 he had as a client Jean Monnet, future father of the Common Market. Ball also belonged to the transatlantic Bilderberg group, founded by Netherlands Prince Bernhard to tie America and Europe together. By the 1960s and 1970s, Ball was writing and speaking of the need for the world to "evolve units larger than nation-states and better suited to the present day."[37]

Ball relished baiting U.S. textile manufacturers. "For my private and secret gratification," he wrote in his memoirs, he would appear before them, "dressed in a British-made suit, a British-made shirt, shoes made for me in Hong Kong, and a French necktie."[38] The internationalists loved it. Overhearing a textile magnate mutter, "That's the slyest bastard I've seen in years," Ball was delighted: "I found such praise heartwarming."[39]

When Kennedy proposed the Trade Expansion Act (TEA) of 1962 — the most critical legislation he would push through Congress — he compared it to the Marshall Plan. The TEA carried the House, 299–125, and swept the Senate, 78–8. The party of Lincoln, McKinley, Theodore Roosevelt, and Cal Coolidge had been converted to free trade. Among the holdouts was Prescott Bush. This bill, said Bush, will lead straight to the unemployment lines for "hundreds of thousands of American workers." Bush led seven stalwarts, including Barry Goldwater, in principled but futile opposition. The century-old GOP tradition as the party that believed in high tariffs to protect America's manufacturing supremacy and standard of living was dead. Few were more exultant than this twenty-three-year-old editorial writer at the *St. Louis Globe-Democrat*, who congratulated and instructed the president:

> Passage of the trade expansion measure is the most important act of this Congress. . . . It is a thumping administration triumph. . . . This precedent-breaking shift in trade policy can become the most potent cold war weapon in the free Western arsenal — if the President has the wisdom and courage to use it effectively.[40]

Kennedy quickly moved from granting trade concessions to Cold War allies to demanding them for Third World neutrals. The Atlantic community has a moral duty, he declared in Frankfurt in June of 1963, to open "our markets to the developing countries of Africa, Asia, and Latin America."[41]

Americans believed the good times would last forever. Kennedy's "new economics" had unlocked the key to boundless prosperity. To argue that U.S. industries might atrophy or die if too many concessions were made at their expense was taken as a lack of manliness, a lack of confidence that we could "pay any price, bear any burden" in the cause of freedom. This was not the pioneer spirit needed out on the New Frontier.

But by then America's share of world industrial exports was fast falling: from 32 percent in 1950, to 28 percent by 1960, to 20 percent in 1973. Sheltered beneath a U.S. defense umbrella, our allies were invading and capturing U.S. markets. Between 1950 and 1970, Europe's share of world exports rose from 33.1 percent to 43.2 percent. No longer the prostrate, demoralized continent of 1945, Europe now had twice the share of world exports as the United States, which was still bearing the burden of Europe's defense. We were proud to do it.

AMERICA BLINKS AT THE KENNEDY ROUND

After Kennedy's death, grumbling began in the Democratic Party. "This nation in its trade and aid programs has played the role of Andy Gump until it is on the verge of becoming an international Barney Google," said Louisiana senator Russell Long, son of the Kingfish.[42] Senator George Smathers of Florida urged trade negotiator Bill Roth to "stoutly defend our market, the greatest market on earth, from those who are unwilling to strike a fair bargain with us." He admonished Roth:

> Look at the bargain closely and coldly, and agree to it only if we get as much as we give. Don't trade off a horse and accept a rabbit. Don't trade off a barrel of wheat for a biscuit. If agriculture does not get a fair shake there should be no agreement.[43]

"Our economy cannot be dismantled to make the rest of the world happy," said Democratic senator Vance Hartke of Indiana.[44]

In 1967 America arrived at the final crossroad. The Kennedy Round of trade negotiations under GATT was stalled. Europeans were balking at U.S. demands to further open their markets to American agriculture; Japan had given a flat no to greater market access. Fear gripped Washington. The talks were on the verge of collapse.

The U.S. negotiators went to see President Lyndon Johnson. Failure to end the Kennedy Round successfully, they warned, would return global trade to "jungle warfare," risk "spiraling protectionism" in the United States, and "encourage strong forces now at work to make the [European Common Market] into an isolationist, anti-U.S. bloc, while, at the same time, further alienating the poor countries."[45] If America did not make the necessary concessions, disaster was certain.

Again the United States capitulated; and Commerce Secretary Alexander Trowbridge rejoiced. The Kennedy Round, he said,

> represents a very large step toward the thing we've heard so much about in the postwar years: the truly one-world market. . . . The American domestic market — *the greatest and most lucrative market in the world* — *is no longer the private preserve of the American businessman.*[46] (Emphasis added.)

"Viewed from the 1990s," historian Eckes dryly observes, "these words echoed with prescience."[47]

Labor had by then risen in enraged protest. "What the hell good are we doing for this country or for world peace, by exporting jobs to Taiwan or Hong Kong?" said the United Textile Workers' George Baldanzi. With the urban riots in full flame, Baldanzi pointed an accusing finger at the loss of manufacturing jobs. O. R. Strackbein, a leading protectionist, called the deal a "time bomb loosed on the American economy."[48]

On Capitol Hill, both parties — seeing the historic U.S. trade surplus vanishing — began to rebel. Congressman Gerald Ford spoke against the concessions of the Kennedy Round; Senator Hartke called the results "unilateral disarmament." Wrote one observer: "By the end of 1967, no fewer than 729 bills, and 19 in the Senate, proposed quotas on over 20 imports. At one count, 97 of 100 Senators endorsed at least one protectionist bill."[49]

LBJ crushed the uprising with a flat declaration: No quota bill will "become law as long as I am president and can help it."[50] By the end of the sixties, early returns from the Kennedy Round were coming in. America had entered a new era:

> Viewed from a historical perspective, the Kennedy Round marked a watershed. In each of the seventy-four years from 1893 to 1967 the United States ran a merchandise trade surplus (exports of goods exceeded imports). During the 1968–72 implementation period for Kennedy Round concessions, the U.S. trade surplus vanished and a sizable deficit emerged. For twenty of the next twenty-two years, the United States experienced merchandise trade deficits — as much as $160 billion in 1987.[51]

In 1996 the U.S. merchandise trade deficit hit an astounding $191 billion. Never before had an advanced industrial nation recorded such a deficit. If, as Presidents Bush and Clinton have contended, $1 billion in exports equals twenty thousand jobs, America loses between 3.5 million and 4 million manufacturing jobs annually. As manufacturing often pays twice the wages of service-industry jobs, no trade surplus in services can compensate for a deficit in manufacturing. Nor can the taxes paid by ten-dollar-an-hour retail clerks match the Medicare and Social Security contributions of steelworkers and autoworkers. America's trade deficit in merchandise is a primary cause of the coming crisis in Medicare and Social Security.

Adam Smith long ago wrote that capital expended in foreign trade was only half as productive as capital expended in home production. Our $2 trillion trade deficit since 1980 explains why U.S. growth has lost the robustness and vitality it once had. "There is no free lunch," said Milton Friedman.[52] Yes, and free trade is no free lunch.

*   *   *

The Kennedy Round tore down the levees, and floods of imports poured in from low-wage nations. With the tariff collapsed, American companies had a powerful incentive to relocate factories abroad, to take advantage of the low-wage labor and then export back to the United States. Journalists were soon writing excitedly about the Japanese "miracle" and the "tigers" of Asia — Singapore, Hong Kong, Taiwan, South Korea. Few asked at whose expense this sudden Asian prosperity had come.

One after another of the great U.S. industries began to decline, depart, or die. The radio- and television-manufacturing industries disappeared. The antifriction-bearings industry and machine-tool industry were gutted. The mighty auto industry was ravaged. Five years after the Kennedy Round, foreign penetration of the U.S. auto market had doubled, to 16 percent. But in Europe and Japan, internal tariffs, targeted at large American-made cars, kept U.S. exports from making comparable gains.

By 1971 America was spending tens of billions of dollars yearly for the guns of Vietnam, the butter of the Great Society, and the defense of the West. We were running trade deficits, balance-of-payments deficits, and budget deficits. Dollars were pouring out, piling up in foreign treasuries. In the second week of August 1971, our British friends decided to turn in $3 billion of our depreciating dollars for $3 billion in U.S. gold — at the $35-an-ounce price, agreed upon at Bretton Woods in 1944.[53]

Suddenly, the entire U.S. gold supply at Fort Knox was at risk.

On August 15 Richard Nixon slammed the gold window shut, cut the dollar loose, and let it float. The Bretton Woods agreement and the gold exchange standard were dead. The era of U.S. economic hegemony had come to a crashing close. Having "organized its own decline," the United States had masterfully executed the plan. Again, trade historian Eckes:

In the twenty years after 1970 the opportunities Kennedy foresaw vanished for high-paid but relatively low-skilled U.S. workers. *From 1972 to 1992 the United States created 44 million net jobs — particularly in services and government. However, America generated no net jobs in interna-*

tionally traded industries. Japan and many of the other rapidly industrial-izing powers — Taiwan, South Korea, and Brazil among others — en-joyed rapid economic growth, not because they practiced free trade at home, but because they enjoyed access to the open American market. Like nineteenth-century America, they practiced protectionism at home while America's generous market-opening policies provided bountiful export opportunities. Paul Bairoch noted the lesson: "Those who don't obey the rules win."[54] (Emphasis added.)

The impact on America's greatest unions was pronounced and se-vere. Note the losses in union membership from 1979 to 1991 alone:

UNION	MEMBERS LOST
United Steelworkers	505,000
Electrical and electronics workers	178,000
Garment Workers	171,000
Clothing and Textile Workers	154,000
Machinists and Aerospace Workers	154,000
United Automobile Workers (1985–91)	134,000
Oil, Chemical and Atomic Workers	56,000[55]

REAGAN: RHETORIC AND REALITY

No president preached free trade with greater eloquence than Ronald Reagan, and Reagan practiced what he preached. The White House in 1985 refused temporary relief to a shoe industry devastated by imports since the 1960s — even though the U.S. In-ternational Trade Commission had found great injury due to im-ports. Said Reagan, "Protectionism [is a] crippling cure, far more dangerous than any economic illness." To put quotas on shoe im-ports "could invite retaliation" and bring on a "trade war, a war we fought in 1930 with the infamous Smoot-Hawley tariffs and lost."[56]

By the end of the Reagan era, the U.S. shoe industry had lost 88 percent of its home market. Of 205,000 workers making shoes when the Kennedy Round was completed, 47,000 survived the Reagan presidency. When the shoe industry's decline had become evident in the 1970s, President Ford was urged to act. But National Security Adviser Brent Scowcroft warned, "Communists would seize on any U.S. import action against shoes . . . to argue that the U.S. was harming Italy during a time of economic crisis."[57] So the American shoe industry was abandoned while Italy was "saved from communism."

By the time be became president in 1981, Ronald Reagan had been converted to free trade. But, in earlier years, he had apparently been a skeptic. Philosopher Sidney Hook recalled meeting Reagan at the Hoover Institution, when the former governor gave a brief speech assailing the dumping of commodities into the United States. A prize-winning economist interrupted, "What's wrong with dumping, Governor, since it obviously benefits the American consumer?" Reagan retorted that dumping kills American jobs; U.S. factories and workers can't compete against goods sold at below-production cost. A second famous economist interceded, arguing that consumer savings from buying cheaper foreign goods would be invested in other goods whose producers would hire the unemployed Americans. Hook describes Reagan's reaction:

> I have never forgotten the response Reagan made to this lesson in economics. With a puzzled look on his face, he said: "That may very well be. But in the meantime what will happen to the American worker? How will he and his family get along?" I found this response endearing. . . . It manifested an authentic and immediate concern for human beings, rather than a reliance upon laws that operate under ideal conditions, quite different from those in which human beings find themselves.[58]

Reagan was a conservative of the heart with the natural instincts of an economic nationalist. An appeal to what was "best for America" always found in him an attentive audience. Told that Harley-Davidson, builder of the Harley hog of highway legend, was about to go under and that Japanese dumping was the cause, Reagan slapped a 50 percent tariff on the big Japanese motorcycles — to be phased out over five years. Protectionism worked. Harley came roaring back, regained its competitive edge, and within five years was exporting to Japan. In May of 1987 Reagan traveled to York, Pennsylvania, to accept workers' applause for an act of industrial intervention that had saved a company as American as, well, a Harley hog. Reagan straddled a Harley and exulted, "Like America, Harley is back and standing tall." [59] He went on to warn of unilateral American action against unfair traders:

> Where U.S. firms have suffered from temporary surges in foreign competition, we haven't been shy about using our import laws to produce temporary relief. . . . You here at Harley-Davidson are living proof that our laws are working.[60]

Free traders were shocked. This was industrial policy! But Harley was not the only successful example of Reaganite protection. By 1984 the United States was importing almost 5 million cars, with the Japanese shipping 2.7 million vehicles.[61] Detroit was reeling. Reagan demanded and got from Japan a voluntary export restraint (VER) agreement that put a quota on Japanese auto exports to the United States of 1.65 million vehicles a year. Detroit responded. By the mid-1980s investment in new auto plants and equipment was twice the 1975 level, and productivity at the Big Three was rising at an annual rate of 6.5 percent. For the 1980–92 period, industry productivity increased 44.2 percent. The Big Three's share of the U.S. market began to rise.[62] With exports to the United States capped, Japan began building auto-assembly plants in the United States.

Reagan went on to impose import quotas on steel and machine tools. Those industries, too, came roaring back. By 1992 the U.S. machine-tool industry had recaptured more than 50 percent of the U.S. market. With U.S. markets guaranteed to U.S. manufacturers, capital investment soared, executive confidence rose, worker morale shot up — and market share soon followed. Free traders protested, Import quotas violate free trade! But ideology be damned. The American industries came back. Republican protectionism had worked again.

In the early 1980s Hitachi attempted, with the mass dumping of its computer chips, to destroy its U.S. competitors. Word went out from Hitachi to all distributors:

> Win with the 10% rule. . . . Find AMD and Intel sockets. . . . Quote 10 percent below their price. . . . If they requote, go 10 percent again. . . . Don't quit till you win. . . . 25% distributor profit guaranteed.[63]

At a 1985 top-level meeting of national security aides to deal with the semiconductor crisis, Deputy Treasury Secretary Richard Darman reportedly brought discussion to a halt with his Olympian disdain: "Why do we want a semiconductor industry? We don't want some kind of industrial policy in this country. If our guys can't hack it, let 'em go."[64]

Reagan disagreed. He demanded that Tokyo back off and guarantee 20 percent of its own computer-chip market to importers, first among them the Americans. Japan complied. In a few years the U.S. computer chip industry was back on top. Reagan believed in free trade; but he put America first. It is impossible to believe that the patriot who intervened to save Harley would sit still for what is happening to his country today.

In the 1950s U.S. industrial supremacy was a given. America produced all it needed, with the best-rewarded workers on earth. The U.S. industrial heartland, bounded by Canada and the Great Lakes on the north, the Potomac and Ohio on the south, the Atlantic to the east, and the Mississippi and Missouri to the west, produced perhaps a third of the world's goods. From this heartland had come the planes, tanks, and guns that destroyed imperial Japan and reduced the Thousand-Year Reich to rubble in three and a half years. When word came back of his navy's success at Pearl Harbor, Admiral Yamamoto mournfully observed, "I fear we have only awakened a sleeping giant and filled him with a terrible resolve." Educated in the United States, Yamamoto had seen America's awesome industrial power.

Not only were the implements of war forged here, so were the goods of peace that made America the envy of the world. But in a quarter century, manufacturing in the heartland contracted as though this quadrant of the country had been subjected to strategic bombing. Here are the job losses in manufacturing from 1970 to 1992 alone:

Delaware	−8.2%
Missouri	−8.2%
Indiana	−10.1%
Michigan	−16.6%
Maine	−17.5%
Ohio	−25.6%
Rhode Island	−27.6%
Massachusetts	−30.0%
Illinois	−31.3%
Connecticut	−33.6%
Maryland	−33.9%
West Virginia	−34.5%
Pennsylvania	−38.5%
New Jersey	−44.2%
New York	−44.2%[65]

These are the statistics of a nation in an advanced stage of industrial disarmament. While rapid technological change killed some of these jobs, and high state taxes, militant unions, and onerous regulations drove some factory owners to the Sun Belt, this cannot fully explain what happened to America's heartland. *Total* U.S. manufacturing jobs still fell by 7 percent, though our population expanded rapidly.

Where did the jobs go? Farther south than Dixie, farther west than Hawaii: first to Japan, Taiwan, Korea, and Hong Kong; now to Mexico, China, Indonesia, and all across Asia.

Some are unconcerned about losing these "dead-end jobs" in "sunset industries." "I'm a conservative futurist," says Newt Gingrich. "We must accelerate America's entry into the Third Wave Information Age."[66] But not every American belongs to the cognitive elite. Not every American is equipped by nature or nurture to "accelerate" into a "Third Wave Information Age." And when we are rid of all those obsolete industrial jobs, what do we do with the obsolete workers who used to perform them? Who takes care of their families?

Social stability depends on a rising standard of living for all our people, those who work with lathes as well as those who work with laptops. And as we go surfing in Third Wave America, we best not forget those left behind on shore. They, too, are Americans, and they will be heard from. "Social disintegration," writes Harvard's Dani Rodrik, "is not a spectator sport; those on the sidelines get splashed with the mud from the field. Ultimately, the deepening of social fissures can harm all."[67]

Chapter 3

HOW FREE TRADE
IS KILLING AMERICA

> *Free trade is a myth. Foreign countries subsidize their manufacturers, which enables them to undercut United States companies and take the jobs of American workers. . . . This is not competition — it is a stacked deck, stacked against the American worker. . . . If we pursue the policies that have gone on for the last few years, we're going to be a completely service nation.*[1]
>
> — George Meany,
> AFL-CIO PRESIDENT, 1977

Free trade, as Meany said, is a myth. It envisions a future that will never exist and assumes an ideal world that does not exist. True believers, however, will never be dissuaded. To them, free trade is not an economic theory or policy option, it is revealed truth about how the world should work, and it is held to the heart with a devotion that is almost religious. In its economic determinism, its utopianism, and its hold on the imagination, free-trade theory is first cousin to socialism and Marxism.

Yet, if the grip that this myth holds on the minds of America's ruling elite is not broken, we will lose the country the Founding Fathers gave us, and America will separate along class lines. The signs are everywhere, even more visible in Europe, incubator of this dogma. Let us see with concrete examples how free trade is shredding the society we grew up in and selling out America's sovereignty, why free trade is truly a betrayal of Middle America and treason to the vision of the Founding Fathers.

THE PREMIER FALLACY OF ADAM SMITH

Adam Smith's famous quotation is often cited as the core of the free-trade gospel:

> It is the maxim of every prudent master of a family, never to attempt to make at home what it will cost him more to make than to buy. The taylor does not attempt to make his own shoes, but buys them of the shoemaker. The shoemaker does not attempt to make his own clothes, but employs a taylor. . . .
>
> What is prudence in the conduct of every private family, can scarce be folly in that of a great kingdom.[2]

"These words are as true today as they were then," writes Nobel Prize–winning economist Milton Friedman.[3] But Milton Friedman notwithstanding, these words are not true today; they never were. To equate the decisions of a "private family" with those of a "great kingdom" is absurd. A great nation can and will prudently borrow from itself — as America did in two world wars — and go into debt for generations. No family can do that. Families are natural friends, while nations are rivals, antagonists, and often mortal enemies. To compare a family's dependence on a grocer or gas station to a nation's dependence on imported food or OPEC oil is folly for a leader and can be suicidal for a country. No family is self-sufficient, but no superpower can rely on foreign trade for the necessities of national survival — and remain a superpower.

American TV manufacturers once possessed the greatest market on earth, a market Japan coveted. Aided and guided by its Ministry of Industry and Trade, Sony attacked, overran, and captured that U.S. market, destroying its U.S. rivals by dumping TV sets at below-production-cost prices. By 1971 America's domestic TV-manufacturing industry had proved to the satisfaction of judicial officials that Japan was dumping. But the U.S. Treasury waited more than ten years before acting to protect the industry. By the 1980s it was too late. Only one U.S. TV producer was left alive — Zenith — and it is now a subsidiary of a Korean company and has shifted operations to Mexico. The U.S. television-manufacturing industry is history.

In the Global Economy, the relationship of giant corporations like Sony and Zenith is less like the friendly relationship between me and 7-Eleven than it is like the relationship between the U.S. Marines and the Japanese army on Guadalcanal.

In 1946 Japan's steel industry was rubble. Japan had no coal or iron ore. Under free-trade theory, Japan should have purchased its steel from the United States, which could have furnished all it needed. Instead, Japan began to import coal and iron ore and, using government loans, built a steel industry with the most modern technology. Because its wages were a fraction of ours, its exports went untaxed, and its defense was paid for by America, Japan was able to undercut U.S. steel producers and capture America's markets. Now Japan produces far more steel than the United States, though our economy is twice as large.

American steel companies, all privately owned, have for decades been forced to compete in a world where 80 percent of foreign production was government-subsidized or -controlled. Was it fair to U.S. steelmakers, or the United Steelworkers of America, to blithely declare, Let the market work? Steel was not a free market; it was a fixed market. And how wise is it to adopt a laissez-faire attitude toward the foreign capture of a vital industry on which America depends? To how many great industries should we let that apply?

Commercial aircraft has been a crown jewel of U.S. manufacturing and export trade. Yet, consider the fate of the companies that were once America's special pride. Not long ago, McDonnell Douglas and Lockheed helped America dominate a world market in which no European nation could compete with the United States. Europe's answer: a consortium of the aircraft companies of England, Spain, Germany, and France called Airbus Industrie. In its first quarter century this socialist cartel sold 770 planes to 102 airlines but did not make a penny of profit. A U.S. company would have been forced into bankruptcy, but not Airbus. Airbus was backed by the treasuries of European governments, which had a strategic goal unrelated to next year's profits. Europe was determined to capture a huge slice of the Americans' world market, no matter what the initial cost. "If Airbus has to give away planes," warned an executive, "we will do it!"

When Europeans complained of Airbus's subsidies, $26 billion by 1990, German aerospace coordinator Erich Riedl replied, "We don't care about criticism from small-minded pencil-pushers."[4] Boasted Richard Evans of British Aerospace, "Airbus is going to attack the Americans, including Boeing, until they bleed and scream." That is the authentic voice of economic nationalism, a voice an earlier America would have instantly recognized — and known how to deal with.

The Airbus cartel gradually began to squeeze its U.S. rivals to death. Lockheed was the first to give up the ghost. Under an American defense umbrella, our European allies were killing off the very companies that had built the planes that kept Europe free; and American statesmen stood by and watched, like buffalo grazing contentedly on the grass as one after another of their number was cut down.

In late 1996 once-mighty McDonnell Douglas — whose F-15s had swept the skies over Iraq in a war to protect Europe's oil — capitulated, canceling plans to build a 300- to 500-seat passenger jet. The lucrative field of jumbo jets was left exclusively to Boeing and Airbus. McDonnell Douglas had not been defeated in fair competition. It lost because the U.S. government would not tell Europe that the United States would not tolerate a continental cartel running our aircraft companies into the ground.[5]

In the name of "free trade" we let foreign companies — abetted by the regimes that own them — collude and kill U.S. companies, using tactics that would have brought criminal indictments if done by such a conspiracy in the United States. Why did we Americans let this happen?

"It has tried to kill me; I will kill it," said Andrew Jackson when told that Nicholas Biddle's national bank was out to destroy him. What happened to the spirit of Jackson? Only a feckless nation would permit a rival power to rob it of this crown jewel without a ferocious struggle.

In a final abject surrender, when McDonnell Douglas merged with Boeing, the European Union threatened sanctions unless Boeing gave up its exclusive supply contracts with three U.S. airlines. As our government stood by, Boeing capitulated and canceled the contracts.

The corruption of thought begins in the corruption of language. Politicians talk of "trading partners" as though the relationship between the United States and China, or the United States and Japan, is comparable to that between Fred Astaire and Ginger Rogers. Such language does not clarify; it distorts. Toyota and Ford, Boeing and Airbus are not partners; they are adversaries. They may enter into alliances, as even hostile nations do, but added market share for one means diminished market share for the other. Victory for one can mean death of the other.

"All we want is a level playing field," Americans plead. But, as one economic historian has written,

> This term trivializes the issue. This is not some schoolyard game where it doesn't matter who wins or loses. It is a struggle to control the world's wealth and resources, markets and territory; to provide for future generations and for the security of the nation. By defining the issue as one of fairness rather than outcome, the free traders have already steered thought into a dead-end channel.[6]

"The state is a cold monster," said General de Gaulle. Surely, there is more truth in the general's insight than in all our blather about a "family of nations" and "the international community." At a 1981 press conference that horrified the diplomatic community, Ronald Reagan blurted, "The Soviets claim the right to lie, cheat, and steal." Reagan spoke the truth about the Cold War, and there are parallels with today's trade wars. Japan, France, and South Korea may be military allies, but each has a budget for industrial espionage and technology theft. Their principal target: the United States of America. Spies from two dozen countries now operate on U.S. soil, looting the secrets of U.S. industries and targeting high tech, defense, biotechnology, telecommunications, and computer software. Economic espionage, says James Kallstrom of the FBI's New York office, "presents a new set of threats to our national security." The International Trade Commission estimates that in 1988 the United States lost — to economic and industrial espionage — $43 billion and a million American jobs! Foreign governments are now sending students as sleeper agents to take jobs at vital U.S. industries, steal U.S. secrets, and send them back.[7]

FREE TRADE VS. THE FREE MARKET

Some see in the Global Economy simply the natural enlargement of the American economy. They look on free trade as the means to bind the world in a global free market. While the vision is endearing, it is an illusion. For free trade in today's world is not consistent with the U.S. free market; it is at war with it.

In the glossary to *Human Action*, the classic work of the great twentieth-century Austrian economist Ludwig von Mises, four conditions are listed for the operation of a true "market economy": (1) private ownership of the means of production; (2) voluntary exchanges of goods and services; (3) no institutional interference with operation of the market processes that generate prices, wage rates, and interest rates; and (4) a government intent on preserving market processes and protecting peaceful participants from those who would use a threat of force or fraud.[8]

In a U.S.-China trade zone, not one of these conditions for a true free market is met. And the people who pay the price for the absence of those conditions are the people who play by the rules: Americans.

Consider the respective attitudes of Americans and Asians toward what in the United States is a felony: bribery. Most Asian nations engage in bribery, shakedowns, and extortion as the conventional tactics of trade wars. A Boeing contract to sell to China invariably carries Beijing's non-negotiable demand for a transfer of U.S. aircraft technology. The only Americans who routinely do business that way are in organized crime, and the term we use to describe that way of doing business is *racketeering*.

"The U.S. government has documented almost 100 cases between April 1995 and May 1996 in which American firms lost contracts valued at $45 billion to foreign companies that pay bribes," said the *Wall Street Journal* in a recent editorial titled IS CORRUPTION AN ASIAN VALUE?[9]

Now, 45 billion dollars in one year is a lot of lost contracts. But with what weapons do we fight back if we have adopted a free-trade philosophy dictating that in the case of a foreign-inflicted injury or injustice, you do not retaliate because you only hurt yourself?

After passage of the Foreign Corrupt Practices Act in 1977, which outlawed bribery of foreign officials, a study found that the United States had suffered sudden and "unusual" drops in aircraft exports to countries where officials routinely accepted bribes.[10] Who won those contracts? Our European "trading partners," for whom foreign bribery was just a cost of doing business. Let the Americans posture as morally superior, cynical Europeans say; we will take the contracts. In late 1997, the Europeans finally agreed to end the practice of bribing foreign officials — by 1999. But in most European nations these bribes are still tax-deductible.

Louis XIV's finance minister Jean-Baptiste Colbert described trade as "a perpetual and peaceful war of wit and energy among the nations." In that war, free trade amounts to unilateral disarmament. Even Adam Smith knew that his famous metaphor was, at least, inexact. Lest we forget: the "great kingdom" of which Smith was a loyal subject was trying, as he was publishing his great classic, to choke to death its American colonies with a naval blockade. And Adam Smith lived out his days as a commissioner of customs enforcing the Navigation Acts on the American states that had won their liberty from Great Britain.

What's Good for Consumers . . .

> In every country it always is and must
> be the interest of the great body of the
> people to buy whatever they want of those
> who sell it cheapest. The proposition is so
> very manifest, that it seems ridiculous to
> take any pains to prove it; nor could it ever
> have been called in question, had not the interested sophistry of merchants and manufacturers confounded the common sense of
> mankind.[11]
>
> — Adam Smith, 1776

Here is another fallacy of free-trade theory: what's best for its consumers is best for a country. But a nation is more than a consumer cooperative; it is a people, separate and apart, with its own destiny and history, language and faith, institutions and culture. And the national interest must take precedence over any consumer demand for foreign products. Carpe Diem! (Seize the pleasure of the passing day!) has proved as fatal a philosophy to nations as it has to individuals.

George Washington and Alexander Hamilton, entrusted with leadership of the infant republic, rejected the idea of letting consumer preferences shape the national destiny. "A free people . . . should promote such manufactories as tend to render them independent on others for essential, particularly military supplies," said Washington.[12] Nor was James Madison content to entrust America's destiny to consumer whims when he discovered British ships dumping goods in U.S. ports to kill the industries begun during the War of 1812. Madison imposed a protective tariff. The economic nationalists who built America did not permit alien ideologies to prevent them from doing what was best for the nation.

Britain, too, might dissent from the idea that buying cheapest is best for a nation. With the repeal of the Corn Laws in 1846, Britain became so dependent on imported food that she could feed but a fourth of her people by World War I and was almost starved to death by a submarine blockade. On whom did free-trade Britain depend for survival? Protectionist America.

Small nations like Austria or Singapore may never again be self-sufficient. But great nations like America, blessed by Providence with virtually all it needs to stand alone, have no excuse for allowing dependency to grow to the degree it has.

Putting consumption first goes against the grain of common sense, as well as inherited wisdom. Before consumption comes production. Before production, investment. Before investment, savings. And before savings, income — the reward for work. Before a family consumes bread, a farmer must plow the ground, sow the seed, till the field, wait and watch. Before an athlete becomes a champion, he must exercise, train, discipline, and deny himself. No athlete ever consumed his way to an Olympic medal; and no nation ever consumed its way to greatness or prosperity. As Aesop's fable of the ant and the grasshopper teaches: he who puts consumption first has put his foot on the road to ruin.

CAPITAL HAS NO COUNTRY

Adam Smith assured the British people that, as savers of capital naturally seek the best return in their own country, they need not be

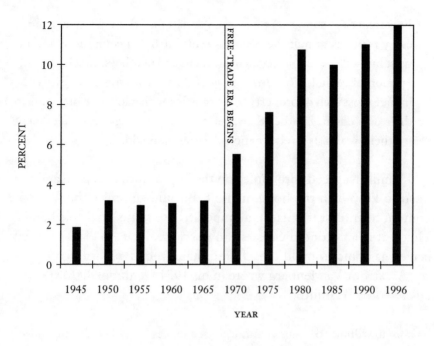

Imports as a Share of GNP/GDP

Source: *Historical Statistics of the United States* and U.S. Department of Trade

concerned about free trade. In a now famous rendering, Smith wrote:

> Upon equal, or nearly equal profits . . . every individual naturally in-
> clines to employ his capital in the manner in which it is likely to afford
> the greatest support to domestic industry, and to give revenue and em-
> ployment to the greatest number of people of his own country. . . . By
> preferring the support of domestic to that of foreign industry, he in-
> tends only his own security . . . he intends only his own gain, and he is
> in this . . . *led by an invisible hand* to promote an end which was no part
> of his intention.[13] (Emphasis added.)

David Ricardo, credited with discovering the theory of comparative advantage, made the same point:

Experience . . . shews . . . that the . . . natural disinclination which every man has to quit the country of his birth and connexions and intrust himself . . . to a strange government and new laws, checks the emigration of capital. *These feelings, which I should be sorry to see weakened,* induce most men of property to be satisfied with a low rate of profits in their own country, rather than seek a more advantageous employment for their wealth in foreign nations.[14] (Emphasis added.)

Hamilton agreed with Smith on the importance of capital and the need to keep it in the home market. But unlike Smith, he was not content to entrust this national imperative to some "invisible hand." He created an economic system to guarantee that America's capital stayed at home to build the United States, not some foreign country. As Arthur Vandenberg wrote in his 1921 testimonial, *The Greatest American,* Hamilton

was unwilling to await natural consequences . . . if beneficent consequences could be guaranteed by government action. He refused to concede that it was best for a thinly settled agricultural nation, like the new America, to buy its manufactured articles in foreign markets wherever cheapest price might seem superficially to beckon to great bargain. He was unwilling to leave the United States at the mercy of "combinations, right or wrong, of foreign policy."[15]

Adam Smith's British empire could afford leaving things to chance; the vulnerable infant republic of Alexander Hamilton could not.

Today, the Global Economy has overtaken the theories of Ricardo and Smith and proved Hamilton right. In the Global Economy, money no longer follows the flag. Money has no flag. Multinational banks, pension funds, and mutual funds move scores of billions of dollars at the speed of light to where the return is greatest, whether it be in Mexican bonds or Japanese yen. When Arab oil producers restricted production to drive up prices, U.S. banks into which the petrodollars poured did not reinvest in America. The big banks lent the money to Mexico, Argentina, and Brazil, confident that these regimes were sounder investments than the old industries of a dying Rust Belt. Economic patriotism? Tell it to Citibank's Thomas Theobald. Asked about his bank's loans to communist regimes, Theobald retorted, "Who knows which political system works? The only test we care about is: Can they pay their bills?"[16]

The transnational corporation does not naturally invest "at home." It has no home. Like the great white shark that calls the entire ocean home, it must swim ceaselessly or sink and die. A transnational has no heart or soul. It is an amoral institution that exists to maximize profits, executive compensation, and stock dividends. If the bottom line commands the cashiering of loyal workers after years of service, it will be done with the same ruthless efficiency with which obsolete equipment is junked.

"Merchants have no country," said Thomas Jefferson. "The mere ground they stand on does not constitute so strong an attachment as that from which they draw their gains."[17] This savage verdict did not apply to all the merchants of the Revolution, but it does apply to the transnational corporation.

How is our world different from that of Adam Smith? Consider Thomas Nelson, Jr. Before the Revolution, Nelson rose in the House of Burgesses to declare, "I am a merchant of Yorktown, but I am a Virginian first. Let my trade perish. I call God to witness that if any British forces are landed in the County of York, of which I am Lieutenant, I will wait no orders, but will summon the militia and drive the invaders into the sea!"[18]

In 1781 Governor Nelson was at Yorktown as the head of Virginia's militia. He was invited by the great Lafayette himself to direct the initial bombardment of the town. As Lafayette wrote in his memoirs:

"To what particular spot would your Excellency direct that we should point the cannon," I asked. "There," promptly replied the noble-minded, patriotic Nelson, "to that house. It is mine, and is, now that the secretary's is nearly knocked to pieces, the best one in town; and there you will be almost certain to find Lord Cornwallis and the British head-quarters. Fire upon it, my dear marquis, and never spare a particle of my property so long as it affords comfort or a shelter to the enemies of my country."[19]

Nelson offered five guineas to the first gunner to hit his house and rode away. His splendid house was destroyed. Compare Thomas Nelson with Thomas Theobald.

The Impact of Exchange Rates

Another feature of the Global Economy unfamiliar to the nine-teenth century is the widespread manipulation of currency values by nation-states. Under a free-trade system, with floating exchange rates, U.S. businesses and workers are at the mercy of foreign central banks. Government-engineered alterations in currency values, done secretly, can have the same impact on trade as an openly imposed tariff.

When NAFTA passed in 1993, the Mexican currency was pegged at 3.5 pesos to the dollar. The United States had a tiny trade surplus with Mexico. A year later the peso sank to seven to the dollar. American goods that Mexicans could buy for 350 pesos in December of 1994 cost 700 by February of 1995. In one year the U.S. trade balance with Mexico went from a surplus to a $15 billion deficit.

For Paul Dimare, devaluation meant disaster. The owner of one of Florida's largest winter tomato farms, Dimare saw his business ravaged by an avalanche of Mexican tomatoes, the dollar price of which had been cut in half by devaluation. In 1995 Dimare was thinking of closing his farm and letting go hundreds of workers, mostly African-American women, few of whom earned much more than minimum wage. By 1988, production at the Dimare farm and processing plant was off two-thirds, and his employees were down to working half days.

Towns on our northern border have also been whipsawed. In

1991 a Canadian dollar was worth 87 cents, and Canadians made 59 million one-day shopping trips to U.S. cities. In 1996 the Canadian dollar had fallen to 73 cents; one-day shopping trips south by Canadians had dropped to 36.4 million. American businesses on the border paid the price as the merchandise trade deficit with Canada in 1996 soared to $23 billion.

The winners in a world of free trade and floating exchange rates are regimes whose central bankers manipulate currency values for national benefit, and a global corporate elite that can shift production from one country to another and calls no country home. Losers are the rooted people, the conservative people tied by the bonds of family, memory, and neighborhood to one community and one country.

ALL INDUSTRIES ARE NOT EQUAL

Behind free-trade theory lies another fallacy: it does not matter which nations produce ships, aircraft, autos, radios, or computers, so long as all can exchange goods freely. *But all industries are not equal.* Had infant America followed free trade, our legendary industrial expansion would never have taken place, and America would never have dominated the twentieth century. The thirteen colonies had almost no industry. Had they followed free-trade theory, we should have stayed with the production and export of cotton, corn, rice, and tobacco, those commodities in which we were most efficient, and imported our manufactured goods from England. America would have become the bakery and tobacconist of Europe. Instead, behind a protective tariff wall, we challenged — and within a century displaced — Great Britain as the greatest industrial nation on earth.

As George Bush was about to go to war in the Persian Gulf over oil, the chairman of his Council of Economic Advisers told a business gathering: "It does not make any difference whether a country makes computer chips or potato chips."[20] But as one critic pointed out, "Patriot missiles won't work with potato chips or chocolate chips or wood chips or buffalo chips."[21] The Patriot depends on computer chips.

Manufacturing is the key to national power. Not only does it pay more than service industries but the rates of productivity growth are higher and the potential of new industry arising is far greater. From radio came television; from television, VCRs and flat-panel screens. From adding machines came calculators and computers. From the electric typewriter came the word processor. Research and development follows manufacturing.

WILL FREE TRADE LEAD TO WORLD PEACE?

It has often struck me that it would be well to try to engraft our free trade agitation upon the peace movement. They are one and the same cause. It has often been to me a matter of surprise that the Friends have not taken up the question of free trade as the means — and I believe the only human means — of effecting universal peace.[22]

How do we answer this most compelling argument, made by the English Quaker Richard Cobden, that free trade is the surest path to world peace?

That claim has echoed through two centuries. "When goods are not allowed to cross borders, soldiers will," warned Frédéric Bastiat.[23] Cordell Hull, as we have seen, declared his faith for the following reason: "Toward 1916 I embraced the philosophy [of free trade]. . . . From then on, to me, unhampered trade dovetailed with peace; high tariffs, trade barriers and unfair economic competition with war."[24] Libertarian Frank Chodorov shared this vision: "The only condition necessary for the growth of Society into One Worldism is the absence of force in the market place, which is another way of saying that politics is a hindrance to, and not an aid of, peace."[25]

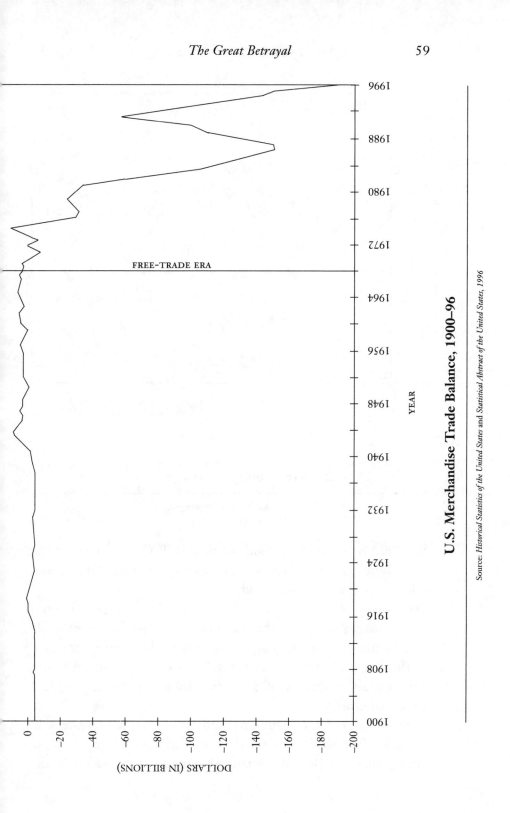

FREE-TRADE ERA

U.S. Merchandise Trade Balance, 1900–96

YEAR

DOLLARS (IN BILLIONS)

Source: *Historical Statistics of the United States and Statistical Abstract of the United States, 1996*

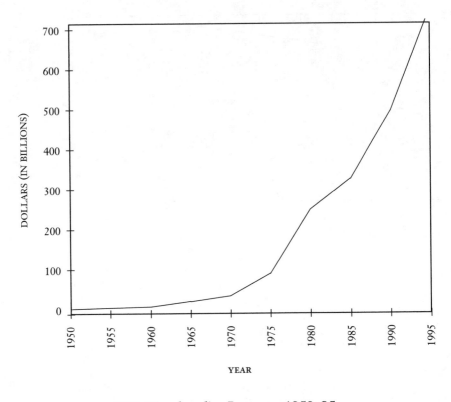

U.S. Merchandise Imports, 1950–95

Source: U.S. Department of Commerce

In his 1997 State of the Union Address, Bill Clinton echoed the theme: "By expanding trade, we can advance the cause of freedom and democracy around the world."[26]

Yet, history seems to contradict them all. The great trading nations of history also seem to have been the most warlike. Free-trade Britain in the nineteenth century was involved in more wars than any other nation, and the nineteenth century's bloodiest war was fought *inside* the world's greatest free-trade zone — the United States of America.

In August 1914 Germany attacked Russia, to whom she sold more goods than to any other nation, and Britain declared war on a Germany that was Britain's greatest Continental customer. In the thirties Japan's principal overseas trade was with China and the United States. Tokyo attacked both. And when Hitler turned on and invaded Stalin's Russia in 1941, he was attacking Germany's principal source of food, oil, and raw materials.

> Free Trade! What is it? Why breaking down the barriers that separate nations; those barriers behind which nestle the feelings of pride, revenge, hatred, and jealousy, which every now and then burst their bounds and deluge whole countries with blood.[27]

So said Cobden. History says otherwise.

THE GLOBAL HIRING HALL

GATT was the Magna Carta of the multinationals.

With Clinton's GATT treaty in 1994, the final scaffolding of the Global Economy was in place. The United States had assured its own Fortune 500 companies that if they shut their plants in Seattle or Salt Lake and opened in Singapore or Shanghai, they could export back to America, free of charge. We gave our greatest companies the most powerful of incentives to pack up and leave; and they responded accordingly.

These global-trade deals added hundreds of millions of Asians and Latin Americans to the labor pool of the industrial democracies. These new entrants into the "global hiring hall" have one thing in common: all are willing to work for a fraction of the wage that an American needs to feed, clothe, house, and educate his or her family. The global hiring hall is the greatest buyer's market in history for human labor. It puts American wage earners into direct competition for production jobs with hundreds of millions of workers all over the world. As labor leader Thomas Donahue says, "The world has become a huge bazaar with nations peddling their work forces in competition with one another, offering the lowest prices for doing business. The customers are . . . the multinational corporations."[28]

What does this mean for American workers? Well, as Ludwig von Mises wrote, "There prevails on the whole earth a tendency toward an equalization of wage rates for the same kind of labor."[29] Equalization of wage rates in the Global Economy means that Americans who produce autos, textiles, and steel will eventually earn the same as Latins and Asians who do the "same kind of labor." But the only way this can happen is for the wages of Asian and Latin workers to rise more rapidly and for the wages of U.S. skilled workers to be slowed, arrested, or fall. And, indeed, this is the stated goal of some American executives. Writes David Morris in his essay "Free Trade: The Great Destroyer":

> The revised version of the American Dream is articulated by Stanley J. Mihelick, executive vice president for production at Goodyear: "Until we get real wage levels down much closer to those of the Brazils and the Koreas, we cannot pass along productivity gains to wages and still be competitive."[30]

And that is what is happening. In the "knowledge industry" — authors, economists, lawyers, journalists, bankers, brokers, entertainers, whose labor foreign workers cannot easily replicate — wages continue to rise. It is Americans who make things with their hands, tools, and machines who are paying the price of free trade.

Not long ago, a worker at a manufacturing job could feed, clothe, and house his family and educate his children. But as wages have stagnated, men are working 140 hours longer each year than they did in 1982, and wives have been forced to enter the labor market in record numbers to maintain the family standard of living.[31] Nearly two-thirds of all women with children under the age of six now work. For today's parents the choice is dreadful. To give children the material blessings of the Affluent Society, many have to deny those same children the security of a young mother's constant presence, love, and care. Thus is free trade antifamily.

Under the Fourteenth Amendment, a state may not "deny [its citizens] . . . the equal protection of the laws." But its intent is violated by such trade deals as NAFTA. A Ford plant in Michigan must meet a higher standard of health, safety, and environmental protection than does a Ford plant in Mexico; it must pay a minimum wage of five dollars an hour, but the Mexican plant can pay as low as fifty cents an hour. Yet, under NAFTA, Fords built in Mexico must be granted the same access to America's market as Fords built in Michigan. Where is the equal protection of the law for American autoworkers who are losing their jobs to Mexican assembly plants?

Americans are the most efficient workers on earth. Given the same rules and regulations, U.S. companies, like U.S. athletes in the Olympics, will win. But if U.S.-owned plants outside the country are exempt from taxes and laws applied to U.S. plants inside America, there is no doubt where manufacturing is headed. With the same weight in its saddlebags, the great thoroughbred Secretariat wins the Derby. But put five hundred pounds in the saddlebags of Secretariat, and he will run third to a Chinese mule and a Mexican burro. Only this is not a horse race, it is a struggle to determine whose century succeeds the American Century.

Dissolving the Bonds of Union

As expanding trade creates new bonds with foreign countries, it dissolves old bonds of patriotism. When Jimmy Carter imposed a grain embargo on Moscow for its invasion of Afghanistan, U.S. farmers, once militantly anticommunist, voted Carter out. Their livelihood was tied, thanks to the grain deals of the Nixon era, to Soviet grain purchases. Self-interest had changed the farmers' perception of national interest.

When the U.S. government sought to impose sanctions on Toshiba for selling silent submarine-propeller technology to Moscow, a treacherous act that imperiled the lives of U.S. sailors, the American hirelings of Japan, Inc. walked the halls of Congress pleading for amnesty for Toshiba.

In 1996, when Congress considered suspending trade privileges

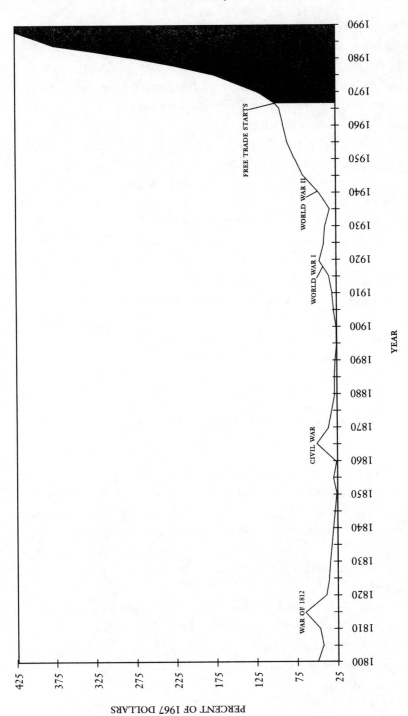

Consumer Price Index, 1800–1995

Source: U.S. Bureau of Labor Statistics

to China for persecuting dissidents, bullying Taiwan, and selling missiles to Iran, America's mightiest defense contractors — Allied Signal, Boeing, GE, Hewlett-Packard, Honeywell, Lockheed-Martin, McDonnell Douglas, Rockwell International, TRW, and United Technologies — lobbied against suspension. If even vital defense contractors are so "hooked" on their China trade that they can no longer see the national interest, then free trade is costing America far more than even the $40 billion annual trade deficit with Beijing.

THE COMING CRISIS OF THE GLOBAL ECONOMY

As Robert Gilpin writes, there are three rival conceptions in political economics. The classical liberal views economics from the standpoint of the individual; the Marxist sees things in terms of classes; the traditionalist has an organic view of society and subordinates economics to the nation.[32]

Classical liberals and advocates of worldwide integration believe that international relations are essentially harmonious. Since the nineteenth century, they have argued that free trade is not a zero-sum game. One nation's gain is not another's loss. All peoples and nations benefit from free trade, and it is the duty of governments to remove all barriers to trade.

Politics, however, *is* a zero-sum game. For every winner there is a loser. GOP congressional victory in 1994 meant the Democrats' defeat. Clinton's reelection doomed Dole's career. "In power terms, international relations is [also] a zero-sum game."[33] One nation's rise entails another's decline. The collapse of the Soviet empire enhanced the power of the United States; and as China grows in power, people speak of the end of the American Century.

In the global arena, politics trumps economics; and it is relative, not absolute, power that counts. As German mercantilist writer Von Hornigk observed three hundred years ago: "Whether a nation be today mighty and rich or not depends not on the abundance or security of its power and riches, but principally on whether its neighbors possess more or less of it."[34]

Nations will abide by the rules of an international system as long as that system works to their advantage. America and Germany rejected Britain's call for free trade in the nineteenth century because they saw their national interest in protectionism. Postwar Japan listened to our discourse on open markets and went its own mercantilist way. As long as Western wealth, technology, and jobs are moving eastward — through foreign aid, loan guarantees, and huge U.S. trade deficits — China will go along. But when wealth and its all-important by-product, power, no longer move eastward, China will walk away from this global system as casually as the Europeans walked away from their war debts. This is the way the world works. Nations are rivals, antagonists, and adversaries, in endless struggle through time to enhance relative power and position. So it has been; so it shall ever be.

COMPARATIVE ADVANTAGE OR COMMON SENSE

Finally, classical free-trade theory fails the test of common sense.

According to Ricardo's law of comparative advantage, the core principle of free-trade dogma, if America makes better computers and textiles than China does, but our advantage in computers is greater than our advantage in textiles, we should (1) focus on computers, (2) let China make textiles, and (3) trade U.S. computers for Chinese textiles. Thus, both nations will do what they do best, and the production of computers and textiles is maximized.

The doctrine begs a question. If Americans are more efficient than Chinese in making clothes — i.e., an American worker with America-made equipment can produce more high-quality goods at less cost than can a Chinese worker, why surrender the more-efficient American industry? Why shift to reliance on a Chinese textile industry that will take years to catch up to where American factories are today?

And if America has an *absolute* advantage over China in producing textiles, what exactly is China's "comparative advantage"? If we contend that China has a "comparative advantage" merely because textiles are its most efficient industry, how can America ever acquire comparative advantage in textiles?

Ricardo's theory is at root not about economics or excellence or more-efficient producers capturing markets. It is a globalist dogma. *It demands that more-efficient producers in advanced countries give up industries to less-efficient producers in less-advanced nations.* Textiles is the perfect example. The U.S. industry, with its high-tech equipment, computerized plants, and well-paid, skilled workers, is the most efficient on earth. Yet, it is being dismantled, piece by piece, and sent off to Third World countries where labor is paid twenty-five cents an hour, where the looms cannot match the modern equipment in U.S. mills, and where the factories operate in conditions rivaling the "satanic mills" of William Blake.

Is child labor or slave labor more efficient than U.S. free labor? Of course not. Are Chinese factories more efficient than U.S. factories? Of course not. What, then, is China's "comparative advantage"? Answer: cheapness. The only advantage China has over the United States lies in its industrial retardation, exploited labor, and utter neglect of health, safety, and environmental concerns. For America to pursue a trade policy that compels our greatest companies to shutter plants here and open them in China pays homage to Ricardian ideology — by rewarding Maoism.

WHY AMERICA SLEPT

Why haven't the harsh consequences of globalism for working Americans persuaded more politicians to take a second look? Because, for many, free trade is a matter of faith. They can no more give it up than Gus Hall can give up his belief in communism or Teddy Kennedy his belief in liberalism. For 150 years the London *Economist* has been preaching free trade. What does *The Economist* care that factories are moving out of the United States? It was not shaken in the faith when factories moved out of Great Britain. When *The Economist* began publishing, Great Britain produced nearly a quarter of the world's goods; now Britain produces about 3 percent. If one's allegiance is to one world, who cares if America is the dominant power? To a citizen of the world, a hollowing out of America's industrial power is an inconsequential, even a positive, development. It matters deeply only to American patriots.

During the Smoot-Hawley Tariff debate, labor leader Matthew Woll suggested a less-flattering reason why it is harder to persuade an economist than an autoworker that free trade is ruinous:

> With few exceptions they [economists] are free traders. They are neither producers nor creators of any commodity or article of trade. They are generally cloistered in the atmosphere of the schoolroom and their mental wares do not enter into the competition with producers where lower wage levels and longer working hours prevail and where standards of living are not only lower but in other respects much inferior to the standards built up in our own country under the American tariff policy. Briefly, these economists and college professors are consumers, not producers.[35]

The same holds for diplomats, bureaucrats, foundation-fed scholars, journalists, professors, and politicians — all of whom tend to be pro–free trade. For them, the policy is not only politically correct, it's cost-free.

A COLONY OF THE WORLD

Another hidden cost of the Global Economy is the slow attrition of our national independence. Trade, as a share of the GDP, has shot up from an average 10 percent before 1970 to 23 percent in 1995, and will rise to an estimated 36 percent by 2010. This startling projection is from the Office of the U.S. Trade Representative.[36] Before

1960 America was self-sufficient in oil. Now we import 10 million barrels a day, half of all the oil we consume, and maintain vast air and naval forces in the Persian Gulf to protect the West's supplies. Out of fear for that supply, the United States had to go to war in 1991. Yet, rather than take alarm at this growing dependency on foreign sources of supply and foreign markets, some conservatives are positively cheerful. Columnist George F. Will writes that it is foolish for America to pursue "the chimera of autarky — national self-sufficiency, independent of the interrelations of trade."[37] But how wise is it for the United States to have a fourth, or a third, of its gross national product tied to trade, and much of that with shaky, unreliable, and even hostile regimes?

Was not the peso crisis of 1994 a fire alarm in the night? When the crisis struck, Michael Camdessus of the International Monetary Fund warned that in the absence of a U.S.-led bailout that could cost $50 billion, potential "world catastrophe" loomed. Sir James Goldsmith, founder of the British Referendum Party, asked a pointed question:

> Financial crises in Latin American countries have been recurring phenomena for many decades. What has suddenly transformed them into potential world catastrophes?
>
> Submarines are built with watertight compartments, so that a leak in one area will not spread and sink the whole vessel. Now that we have globalized the world's economy, the protective compartments no longer exist. Thus, we have globalized problems. A crisis in Mexico has become a "potential world catastrophe."[38]

If a debt crisis in Mexico can bring down the financial house of the United States, what is the benefit to America to justify so incredible a risk?

In the three years after the Mexico City crisis, nothing was done to shelter America from another "potential world catastrophe," and in mid-1997, the pointed warning of Sir James proved prophetic. The Thai stock market began to fall, bringing down the currency, the baht, with it. Within weeks the "contagion" spread to

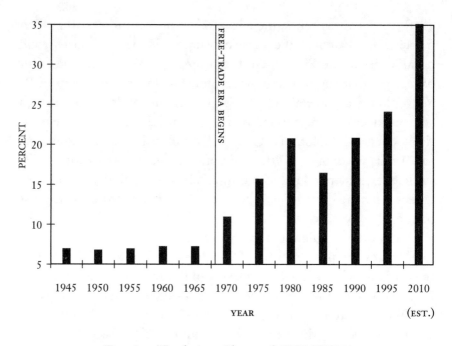

Foreign Trade as a Share of GNP/GDP

Source: *Historical Statistics of the United States* and U.S. Department of Trade

Malaysia, the Philippines, and Indonesia. From there it began to rock the stock markets of North Asia — Taiwan, Hong Kong, South Korea, Japan. By late fall, the South Korean won had lost half of its value; Seoul's stock market was at a ten-year low; the Japanese market was at a two-year low and falling to a level at which Japan's banks were in peril. Almost every Asian currency had collapsed against the U.S. dollar; and the contagion had spread to Brazil, South Africa, Russia, and Eastern Europe.

The year 1998 shaped up as one in which U.S. taxpayers would be put at risk for scores of billions of dollars in IMF bailout money to "trade partners," as these partners were about to flood America with imports and swamp what was left of the U.S. manufacturing base — running U.S. trade deficits and dependency up to levels unseen since the time of Madison.

Is it not time to rebuild those "watertight compartments" that once insulated the U.S. financial system from the chronic monetary collapses of our neighbors south and east?

Again, how farsighted is such global interdependence? During the Bush era it was said that the United States could not take a tough stand in trade talks with Tokyo, lest an angry Japan dump its hoard of U.S. debt onto the world market, forcing up U.S. interest rates and thereby inducing an American recession. In the name of national security, what benefit are we reaping from trade with Japan, to justify this vulnerability to Japanese retribution?

The American Revolution was fought for an economic as well as a political independence. Our Founding Fathers believed, almost to a man, that ending our reliance on foreign trade was a national imperative. They sacrificed mightily to achieve an independence we are now frittering away. We are today reverse-engineering American history, returning to a level of dependency on trade that once put America at the mercy of the predatory powers of the Old World. The most self-sufficient nation of half a century ago is again becoming a colony — a colony of the world.

Pawning America's Soul

In building a global free-trade regime, say its advocates, we shall replicate the U.S. model on a planetary scale. What's good for America is good for mankind! The fallacy here is that the 180-odd nations of the UN are not remotely comparable to the original thirteen states of the Union. Those thirteen states, the building blocks of the U.S. free-trade zone, had been allies in revolution: they shared a common religion, language, history, culture, destiny, and standard of living; they had achieved a high measure of economic integration. Before the Founding Fathers met in Philadelphia in 1787, America was already an embryonic nation. But the political price the states paid in Philadelphia to become a free-trade zone is the price the nations of the world, including America, will have to pay to create a global free-trade zone: the surrender of national sovereignty!

At Philadelphia each state had to yield control of its borders, its tariffs, its trade, and its rights to defend itself and to coin its own money. Under the Constitution, New Yorkers and Virginians could cross each other's territory and settle on each other's land; and the United States would enforce that right with arms if necessary. As the South would discover in 1861, the Constitution was the beginning of the end of state sovereignty.

But to transfer state sovereignty to a national government led by Washington, Adams, Jefferson, and Hamilton is a far cry from transferring U.S. sovereignty to a global regime run by faceless foreign bureaucrats of the WTO or the UN. That would be tantamount to treason. Yet, that is the endgame — as the Europeans have begun to discover.

Global free trade is a Faustian bargain. A nation sells its soul for a cornucopia of foreign goods. First the nation gives up its independence; then its sovereignty, and finally its birthright — nationhood itself. Adam Smith saw the inexorability of the progression: "Were all nations to follow the liberal system of free exportation and free importation, the different states in to which a great continent was divided would so far resemble the provinces of a great empire."[39]

Europe is proving the point, reenacting Philadelphia in 1787. The process has been underway for half a century. The European Coal and Steel Community became the European Economic Community, which evolved into the European Community (EC). Now the EC has become the EU (European Union). The end of the line: a United States of Europe in which Britain and France enjoy the same sovereign rights as Missouri and Mississippi. The process is inexorable, and the nations of Europe are approaching the fail-safe point. Go forward, and there is no turning back; they will cease to be truly independent nations.

Britain is today facing that choice. "Euroskeptics" are imploring conservative comrades not to submit, not to give up the pound for a single European currency. Being part of a new European superstate, they say, is not worth a surrender of British sovereignty. No consumer cooperative is worth a country.

Before the nations of Europe proceed, they should consider Canada. Most of Canada's GNP is now in trade, and 80 percent of that trade is with the United States. Its economic ties now run north-south more strongly than east-west. The TV shows and movies Canadians watch, the magazines they read, are more and more MADE IN THE USA. Canadians today fear the loss of their national identity. Quebec, desperate to retain its French language and culture, is ever on the verge of breaking free. In a recent crisis, a leader in the Maritime Provinces warned that if Quebec broke away, the Maritimes would seek admission to the United States. Said the leader, We now have more in common with New England than with Ontario.

Why is this true? Because of free trade. Many times this century Canadians were warned against joining a U.S. free-trade zone that must result in a dilution and eventual disappearance of Canadian independence. The poet laureate of the British Empire, Rudyard Kipling, asked in 1911:

How can 9 million people enter into such arrangements as are proposed with 90 million strangers on an open frontier of four thousand miles and at the same time preserve their national integrity? It is her own soul Canada risks today. Once that soul is pawned for any consideration Canada must inevitably conform to the commercial, legal, financial, social and ethical standards which will be imposed upon her by the sheer admitted weight of the United States.[40]

When the U.S.-Canada free-trade zone was negotiated, opposition leader John N. Turner challenged Prime Minister Brian Mulroney, echoing the warning of Kipling:

We have built a country, east and west and north, on an infrastructure that resisted the continental pressure of the United States. For 120 years, we've done it, and with one stroke of the pen you've reversed that, thrown us into the north-south pull of the United States. And that will reduce us, I'm sure, to an economic colony of the United States, because when the economic levers go, the political independence is sure to follow.[41]

Turner was right. Watching frustrated Canadians fight a rear-guard action to defend their culture, a traditionalist must empathize. But Canada was warned that the price of economic union with the United States was the loss of its soul. For small nations like Belgium and Holland, losing one's self in a common market may be a necessary sacrifice to keep pace with modernity. But the United States is not some small or middle-sized nation. America is a continent-wide nation that was wholly self-sufficient at the end of World War II, and can become so again. We do not need to trade away our sovereignty for a seat at the table of some global regime. For no great nation can yield its sovereignty and still remain great.

America will soon face the same choice that the nations of Europe now face. NAFTA with Mexico means the gradual merger of the two economies. Eventually there must come a demand for open borders and a single currency. Make no mistake. We are in the betrothal stage of a courtship at the end of which comes a union of America and Mexico — and that is the end of the nation we grew up in.

The transnational elites have seen the brave new world coming and opened their arms. "I believe the nation-state is finished," says Robert Bartley, the editor of the *Wall Street Journal* who champions a five-word amendment to the U.S. Constitution: "There shall be open borders!"

Tear down the border posts! Throw open America's doors to all who wish to shop here, sell here, move here, live here. Nationality means nothing. America is one giant global mall; as Theodore Roosevelt said, a "polyglot boarding house" for the world.

For the United States that is the end of History.

Chapter 4

ANATOMY OF A MURDER

One of the best things that ever happened to America's automobile industry is Japan's automobile industry.[1]

— George F. Will, 1996

To show the devastation that free-trade ideology has wrought on America's industrial heartland, many industries could serve as case studies: radio and television manufacture, in which America once led the world but which is no longer done here; the disappearance of the shoe industry from New England; the abandonment of the textile industry of the South. But to show best what America has sacrificed to this Moloch of free trade, consider that greatest of industries, the one with which this nation has been more closely identified than with any other: automobiles.

For decades the U.S. auto industry employed more workers than any other, consumed more raw materials than any other, paid more taxes than any other, and dominated world production more than any other. Yet, today that industry is contracting, packing, and leaving America, forever, if we do not change our national policy. What happened to the mighty American auto industry? Let's start at the beginning.

Henry Ford was the greatest industrialist of his age. By 1913 the assembly lines he had perfected were turning out a thousand Model Ts a day. With half a million flivvers on America's roads in 1914, Ford announced a legendary decision: he was raising the minimum wage of assembly-line workers to five dollars a day. Ford said he wanted his workers to be able to buy the marvelous machines they were building. While credited with industrial statesmanship, Ford and his partner, James Couzens, acted partly out of desperation. The turnover in their labor force was running at 350 percent a year. Couzens, critics say, came up with the idea of doubling pay to five dollars a day, to put an end to labor strife and keep more highly skilled workers who would not ruin the new machinery in Ford's plants; but Henry took credit for the idea.[2]

By the 1930s General Motors had eclipsed Ford to become the number one corporation in America and the world; and in Detroit GM executives were the new royalty. By the early 1940s Detroit had been converted into the forge and furnace of the arsenal of democracy. Studebaker, which had built the wagons that the pioneers used to cross the Great Plains, built the Weasel armored personnel carrier. Willys-Overland built the jeeps that carried Eisenhower's armies across Europe. Ford built Sherman tanks. Packard produced the engines for PT boats and the P-40s of the Flying Tigers; Buick, the engines for the B-24 Liberator bomber; Chevrolet, the engines for the Flying Boxcar. Oldsmobile built B-25 Mitchell bombers like the planes Colonel "Jimmy" Doolittle used in his 1942 "Thirty Seconds Over Tokyo" raid off the aircraft carrier *Hornet*. Nash-Kelvinator produced the navy Corsair, America's first 400-mph fighter. Hudson helped build the Helldiver attack plane that succeeded the Dauntless, made famous for its heroic exploits in the Battle of Midway, where four Japanese carriers were sent to the bottom of the ocean. And GM led all manufacturers in war production.[3]

When the war ended, Detroit converted its assembly lines with Yankee efficiency and began churning out the powerful, fashionable, and fancy new cars that were the prewar specialty of the United

States. By 1946 hundreds of thousands of new automobiles were rolling off the assembly lines, and Detroit was a thriving, throbbing city of 2 million, its name a synonym for industrial ingenuity and power. The entire world came to Motown to see how the Americans did it.

Half a century later, Detroit had become the symbol and standard of urban decay, a burned-out city of a million where on Devil's Night vandals set fire to trash cans, gutted buildings, and abandoned homes. In 1996 I was driven downtown to an interview with the radio legend J. P. McCarthy. For blocks on end, we silently viewed the hollowed-out ruins and vagrant homeless people. Detroit seemed a city fought over by hostile armies, then abandoned. *This looks like pictures of Beirut,* I thought.

A friend who grew up in Ypsilanti tells of how his father and uncle set out one day to revisit the old Detroit neighborhood. As they came closer to where they had grown up, they grew silent. Within a mile, they turned around. They didn't want to see what had become of the home in which they had been raised.

What happened to Detroit cannot be separated from what happened to the American auto industry, not all of whose wounds were self-inflicted. Indeed, the U.S. auto industry can justifiably claim to have been a victim of abuse, neglect, and abandonment by the government of the United States.

A BEETLE ATTACK

As late as 1983 GM still had 800,000 employees worldwide, with 600,000 in the United States. Including family members, a million and a half U.S. citizens relied on GM for their livelihood. For another 300,000, GM retirement benefits were their principal source of income, which meant that yet another 450,000 Americans depended on GM checks. Two million Americans thus depended directly on GM. How vital an element of the American economy was GM? As retired executive Gus Stelzer writes:

> GM bought more steel than any other firm. It spent more money with hospitals, doctors, dentists, nurses . . . than any other private institution. . . . Dividends paid by GM provided income to over 1,100,000 stockholders, many of whom were widows. . . . In total, in 1983 . . . GM provided all, or a significant share, of income for over 4,000,000 Americans.
>
>   At the same time, GM was, by far, the largest generator of tax revenue for federal, state and local government. In 1983, GM paid $4.9 billion in federal and state income and payroll taxes, property and other taxes. Its employees and retirees were estimated to have paid an additional $4.5 billion in taxes. GM suppliers, and their employees, were estimated to have paid another $10 billion in taxes to thousands of U.S. political agencies. And, finally, it was estimated that GM stockholders paid another $1.2 billion in taxes on dividends they received. Thus, in one year, GM generated over $20 billion in tax revenues, and this made no allowance for a ripple multiplier effect which easily doubled that figure.[4]

Yet, remarkably by the early 1980s, America's greatest company, this strategic national asset, had been under attack for three decades — ever since GM president Charles E. "Engine Charley" Wilson made his famous statement in congressional testimony: "What's good for America is good for General Motors, and vice versa."[5]

The first threat to the once-invincible U.S. auto industry came from the little German car that became omnipresent on America's roads by the early sixties, the Volkswagen Beetle. When one considers its paternity, the Beetle's popularity seems astonishing. For the Beetle's first and greatest patron was Adolf Hitler! Three months after taking power in 1933, Hitler met with young Ferdinand Porsche, an Austrian engineer and disgruntled former employee of Daimler-Benz. Porsche sold the Nazi chancellor on the idea of a car that could "travel more than fourteen kilometers per liter of petrol, seat four passengers, and be priced at around 1,000 reichsmarks (or about $142) compared to the cheapest American car, which cost around $425."[6]

The idea of challenging the Americans — the world's standard for industrial power and technological excellence — appealed to Hitler. He ordered a "people's car" built so Germans could live like Americans, one in five of whom owned a car. In 1933 only one in a hundred Germans could make that boast.

By 1938 Porsche and colleagues had laid the foundation in Lower Saxony for Volkswagen City. The ceremony of incorporation on May 26, 1938, was a gala affair with seventy thousand present, featuring Hitler himself: "I undertake the laying of the cornerstone in the name of the German people. This factory shall arise out of the strength of the entire German people and it shall serve the happiness of the German people."[7]

"The Strength Through Joy Car"[8] it was called, and two hundred SS men were continuously test-driving it on Germany's new autobahns.[9] Dr. Robert Ley, head of the German Labor Front, a former Gauleiter in Cologne, declared, "It is the Führer's will that within a few years no less than 6,000,000 Volkswagens will be on German roads. In ten years' time there will be no working person in Germany who does not own a 'people's car.' "[10]

It was not to be. In 1939 Volkswagen City was turned over to the Nazi warlords and was among the first industrial enterprises to exploit concentration camp labor. Since the new plant had been built in open farmland, however, it was an easy target for British Air Marshal Arthur "Bomber" Harris and U.S. Army Air Corps General Hap Arnold. Two-thirds of Volkswagen City was obliterated. Yet, Volkswagen continued turning out war matériel for Hitler's Reich until it perished in the flames of 1945.[11] When U.S. troops occupied the plant on April 14–15, 1945, they found emaciated Hungarian Jewish slave laborers still there, survivors of thousands sent from Auschwitz, Dachau, and Bergen-Belsen.[12]

And that is the early history of the Volkswagen Beetle.

*   *   *

To American auto executives it was a joke. Small, ugly, noisy, lumpy, underpowered, with its air-cooled engine in the rear and a tiny front trunk, with none of the new conveniences, it seemed no match for the big, sleek American "road hogs" of the 1950s. There was an arrogance in Detroit in those days. "Americans," said young Henry Ford,

> like to blast along over interstate highways at eighty miles an hour in big cars with every kind of power attachment, windows up, air conditioning on, radio going, one finger on the wheel. That's what they want, and that's what they buy, and that's what we manufacture. We build the best cars we can to meet the taste of the American people."[13]

To Ford, small cars were "little shitboxes," and every small car, be it American or foreign-made, was a "g —— m little Volkswagen."[14]

Volkswagen succeeded because it fit the counterculture mood of the era. Driving a Beetle was a form of protest. Beetle drivers honked to one another on the roads. In 1958 one hundred thousand were sold in the United States; four years later a million Beetles were on America's highways.

But Volkswagen had another advantage. Not only was the Beetle a fine, fuel-efficient (34 miles per gallon) little car, the German workers who built it were paid one-fourth the wages of a GM worker and were taxed at one-third the U.S. rate. Germans weren't spending 9 percent of their GNP defending their country. We were, with a large share of that 9 percent going to defend West Germany. Every U.S.-built Chevy or Ford carried in its sticker price the cost of America's defense of the free world. The Beetle, priced at $1,495 in the mid-fifties, $500 below the lowest-priced U.S. car, carried none of this burden.

The Beetle's promoters thought it would cut General Motors down to size. It didn't. The companies crippled or killed by the Beetle were the ones that made small American cars, using American autoworkers: Kaiser Motors and its Henry J., Studebaker and its

Champion, American Motors and its Nash Rambler. A pattern had been set.

> [Volkswagen] was followed by the Renaults, Citroens and Peugots from France, the Saabs and Volvos from Sweden, the Fiats from Italy, the MGs and Jaguars from England, the BMWs, Audis, Porsches and Mercedes from Germany, and the Yugo from Communist Yugoslavia. All were made under conditions that were illegal in America and all were subsidized by their governments who granted tax relief on imports to the U.S.[15]

As Americans were financing the defense of Europe, Europeans were invading and capturing the markets of U.S. auto companies, killing them off one by one and destroying the jobs of American workers. And the U.S. government collaborated with the adversaries of America's greatest industry, with demagogic politicians bullyragging our own auto companies for failing to be "competitive."

THE JAPANESE INVASION

By 1964 Commerce Secretary Luther H. Hodges was confidently reporting that the worst of the foreign invasion was over.

> The U.S. market for foreign cars appears to have leveled off. The imports reached their peak in 1959 when 668,070 cars were brought in. In 1960 and 1961, imports declined when U.S. manufacturers met their competition head-on with a lively line of U.S. compact cars.[16]

Hodges was whistling past the graveyard. For a far better planned and more massive invasion was already being prepared across the Pacific. Before World War II the only cars on Japanese roads were U.S. imports. Japan did not have an auto industry, but Tokyo did have a law on the books restricting foreign companies from building cars in Japan.[17] As late as 1957 Japan produced only 182,000 cars, exporting 6,500.[18] In the early 1960s Japanese cars were considered junk; even at low prices they could not compete with U.S. cars. How did Japan succeed in capturing a huge slice of the U.S. auto market? Hondas, Datsuns, Toyotas, Suzukis, and Mazdas, etc., were all

> made under conditions that violated most U.S. laws. Their labor costs were only 15% of U.S. rates. Their per-capita tax burdens were barely 30% of ours. [Tokyo] gave huge tax rebates to their auto producers who exported to the U.S. in violation of antidumping concepts. The exchange rate was 360 yen to the U.S. dollar. As a result of these highly discriminatory advantages, they were able to price their products 25% to 50% below prices of U.S. cars of comparable size.[19]

With these advantages, the Japanese were selling a million cars a year in the United States by 1970, and "blame America first" journalists and politicians were denouncing U.S. auto companies as too blind or bullheaded to build the small cars that Americans demanded. The charge was unjust and untrue. American companies *had been* building excellent small cars: Corvair, Falcon, Dart, Valiant, Tempest, Chevy II, Nova, Henry J. But American cars, built in U.S. factories that had to abide by U.S. tax and labor laws — and meet environmental, safety, and health standards that foreign factories did not — could not be priced at the same low levels. In Lordstown, Ohio, in 1969 GM put up the most modern assembly plant in the world, using state-of-the-art technology to assemble the new Vega to compete with Japanese imports. The Vega, priced at $1,995, did not even recover GM's costs, many of which had been created by U.S. laws. As the government continued to pile new costs on U.S. companies, it threw open America's doors to foreign cars made in foreign factories that carried none of those costs. In the battle for the U.S. market, the U.S. government had fixed the outcome in favor of the foreign companies.

THE AUTO PACT OF 1965

But we are getting ahead of the story.

In 1965 the United States negotiated the Auto Pact with Canada which declared that for every U.S. car sold in Canada, one would be built in Canada, thus effectively shutting down part of the U.S. industry, packing it up, and shipping it north. Why would the United States do such a thing? Well, the pact was signed at what came to be known to Canadians as the "cultural shock conference" at LBJ Ranch, in a setting that provides an insight into the business acumen of the U.S. government of the era:

> The purpose was the signing of the auto pact, an enormously important trade agreement striking down barriers on automobiles and parts. Johnson signed, knowing practically nothing about it and would soon snap at ambassador Charles Ritchie: "You screwed us on the auto pact!" Secretary of State Dean Rusk, the other powerful presence at the signing, knew nothing about it either. It was part of his aversion to the world of trade and finance. "I still think economics is a dismal science." The result was that the agreement, to [Prime Minister Lester] Pearson's chagrin, became a sidelight to the wild weekend's other fare — booze, gossip, raucous ranch tours, pyjama talk. In Ritchie's phrase, it was a "burlesque circus."[20]

The story is amusing; the consequences are not. In that crucial era America had as leaders men deeply ignorant of industry, trade, and finance who gave away a huge part of the manufacturing base on which millions of America's highest-paid workers depended and which had taken the better part of a century to build. From its birth until the New Deal, America was led mostly by men who knew that nation-states are rivals and antagonists, who understood that manufacturing is a key to national power, and who were familiar with and proud of how America in a single century had developed from thirteen rural colonies into the greatest nation on earth. But since the New Deal, the United States had been led by men ignorant of, or dismissive of, that incredible history. Like prodigal children, they gave away — for reasons of foreign policy, or even foreign popularity — a patrimony that belonged to us all.

As a result of the Auto Pact, "a $657 million automotive products trade surplus with Canada in 1965 turned negative. Over the next twenty-five years the United States experienced automotive deficits with Canada in all but one year."[21] Thirty years later, Canada was producing 2.4 million cars and trucks a year, vehicles that would have been built in the United States. According to a *Wall Street Journal* report filed from Toronto in late 1996,

> under the 1965 Auto Pact between Canada and the U.S., the Big Three auto makers agreed to make at least one vehicle in Canada for every one sold in Canada, in return for duty-free exporting and importing. Because of Canada's advantages for production [including a cheapened Canadian dollar], the U.S. auto makers have built extensive operations here and have easily lived up to the bargain. *The ratio of vehicles produced to vehicles sold in Canada by all auto makers has grown to more than two-to-one today.*[22] (Emphasis added.)

The annual U.S. merchandise trade deficit with Canada is among this nation's largest, reaching $23 billion in 1996, thanks to the Auto Pact.

Under NAFTA, Canada, like Mexico, has become a launching platform for Japan into the U.S. market. By the fall of 1996 Toyota was doubling production at its Corolla plant in Ontario; Honda was building a huge new minivan plant there, and Canada's auto industry accounted for 4 percent of the GDP. "One in every five jobs in Canada depends on the automotive industry," said a proud Canadian economist.[23] Whose jobs did they used to be?

Why did LBJ give away a huge slice of our auto industry? Some say that he was rewarding Canada for supporting us in Vietnam; others, that this was his way of saying thanks for Canada's taking up UN peacekeeping tasks on Cyprus. Whichever is true, part of another great U.S. industry was sacrificed on the altar of Cold War solidarity, and again it was American workers who were making the sacrifices.

When the Yom Kippur War broke out in October 1973, Richard Nixon came to the rescue of a beleaguered Israel. Arab nations retaliated with an oil embargo. Gas prices surged, and U.S. demand for small cars soared. Detroit was now accused of not anticipating that demand. While America was rescuing Israel with a massive air- and sealift, our allies were reaping windfall profits on their smaller cars. And in part because the United States had begun to terminate the tax incentives once given the oil industry, our self-sufficiency in oil was history. Thus, the run-up in imported oil prices proved a double blow.

Hammered constantly by press propaganda, new regulations, rising taxes, and exploding imports, the GM giant began to stumble and falter. As Gus Stelzer writes:

> Between 1990 and 1992 GM lost over $20 billion, even though it had already reduced its work force by more than 100,000 people in the preceding decade. . . . In mid-December, 1991 GM shocked the country by announcing it would close another 21 plants and terminate another 74,000 employees, the ripple effect of which would cause another 200,000 to lose their jobs. It was a tragedy of historic proportions.
>
> No American business institution ever contributed more to the well-being of this nation, yet found itself facing a fight for its very life. But that tragedy was compounded by the cavalier and spiteful manner in which the established press, consistent with a vendetta of more than 30 years, spewed more of its venom to imply that it was all due to inept, bloated management. . . . GM was raped by the policies of its own government.[24]

What "Engine Charley" had said was true, when he said it. In the 1950s what was good for America *was* good for GM, and vice versa.

We see that now as we watch GM "outsourcing" work, closing U.S. plants, and opening factories in Latin America and Asia, as America and GM hand in hand descend the staircase from the industrial zenith they both once knew.

By 1997 GM president John F. Smith, Jr. — his company's share of the U.S. market down to 30 percent — was predicting that half of GM sales after the turn of the century would be outside the United States.[25] Production is leaving as well. "The goal in the very near term is to have fifty percent of our capacity outside of North America," says Mark Hogan, who heads operations in Brazil and Argentina. GM's newest plants are going up in Argentina, Poland, and China. "GM's days of building new plants in North America may be over," says the *Wall Street Journal*. Declares Louis Hughes, head of GM's international expansion: "We are on our way to becoming a transnational corporation."[26] GM executives now openly admit that they prefer to be seen as a global, rather than as an American, company.[27]

It is grossly unfair to damn for a lack of patriotism GM and all the other U.S. companies now siting new plants outside the United States. Not all wanted to leave the land of their birth; not all wanted to be rid of their American workers. Many had no choice: they had to leave, or die. Many of our greatest corporations were driven out of America, whipped into exile by government policies that mandated ever higher costs on production here and by trade policies which told U.S. executives that they could avoid such costs if they moved overseas. For forty years the U.S. government has been stacking the deck against industries that wanted to stay home and hire Americans, and it bears the primary responsibility for the deindustrializaton of this country.

By 1997 even Mexico was running an $11.9 billion automotive trade surplus with the United States, exporting 560,000 cars to America while importing only 46,000, a pro-Mexico ratio of 12:1. Is this because Mexican factories are more efficient, or Mexican employees better workers? Of course not. It is because the policies pursued by the government of the United States are virtually designed to rid this nation of its core industrial base.[28]

APPEASEMENT OF JAPAN

Twenty-five years ago, when Japan began to consolidate its grip on the U.S. auto market, wages in Japan were still only one-fifth those of U.S. autoworkers. But when the UAW went on strike in 1970, for a three-year, 35 percent pay increase, the Nixon administration sided with the union, exempting strike dues from income taxes and giving food stamps to the families of striking workers. The Nixon administration thus subsidized a shutdown of the U.S. auto industry at the very moment U.S. trade officials were in Tokyo promising Japan even freer access to the U.S. market.

Another blow fell when a U.S. court ordered GM's dealer network — its crown jewel, with twelve thousand outlets and half a million employees — opened up to foreign-built cars. To create this network, to make GM dealers part of a corporate family, GM had invested billions of dollars over fifty years in start-up capital; inventory financing; training for service, sales, and other personnel; and twenty-five thousand field personnel. Now the federal government was ordering GM to open up this long-nurtured establishment to Japanese firms that were plotting, with Tokyo's guidance, to overrun GM's markets. Writes Stelzer: "The government edict was tantamount to telling a home owner that he must allow a stranger to occupy his home, eat from his table and alienate the affections of his wife."[29]

The Japanese were no such fools. When President Bush, on his fateful January 1992 mission, asked Japan to reciprocate and open up its dealerships to American cars, the CEO of Nissan said in effect, Let the Americans start their own dealerships; we don't owe them anything. Bush and the auto executives he took to Tokyo came home running on empty.

On his Japan trip, the president became ill, and his speech at the Japanese Welcoming Committee Luncheon was delivered by Treasury Secretary Nicholas Brady. In the speech, Bush, his eye more on his adversary in New Hampshire than on America's adversary in Japan, declared, "This century has taught us . . . that isolationism and protectionism lead to war and deprivation."[30]

This is ahistorical nonsense. In repeatedly blaming isolationists for a world war they desperately wanted to stay out of, Bush does an injustice to his fellow Americans. It was not American isolationists but Japanese militarists who launched that sneak attack on Pearl Harbor. As for protectionism, it was the precise policy by which Mr. Bush's hosts in Tokyo had raised Japan from the ashes of World War II and looted America to become the second industrial nation on earth.

The Japanese "miracle" was not produced by free trade; it is a product of economic nationalism. Indeed, the purpose of the Bush visit was to beg Japan to open markets long shut to America. But why should the Japanese give up a trade policy that is working well for them, to adopt one that is failing for us? Only traditional good manners must have prevented the Japanese from laughing out loud at Nick Brady. As author David Halberstam writes:

> By the mid-eighties, its staggering victory in automobiles assured, [Japan] was the most insular of international giants. Trade with Japan was so one-sided as to smack of reverse colonialism: The Western nations shipped raw materials to the Japanese, who turned them into finished goods that they sold back to the West.[31]

Japanese imports not only crippled America's new-car industry, they ruined our used-car industry. Some 70 percent of Americans who turned in a Chevy, Ford, or Olds used to buy a new Chevy, Ford, or Olds. With the cheaper imports now carrying warranties, chains of loyalty that went back generations snapped.

In 1975 Japan had 9 percent of the U.S. auto market; Ford, GM, and Chrysler, 80 percent. Today, Japan has 30 percent of the U.S. market, and the GM-Ford-Chrysler share has shrunk to 64 percent.[32] Singing hallelujahs to the free-trade god, we let protectionist Japan cart off a third of our greatest market. Historians of American

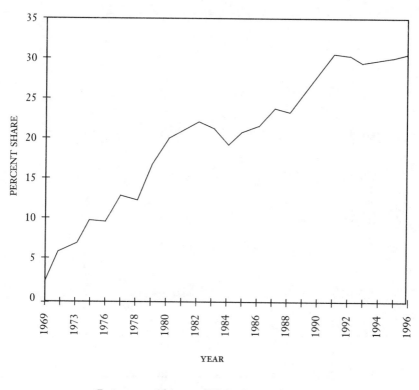

Japanese Share of U.S. Car Sales

Source: American Automobile Manufacturers Association; Ward's Automotive Reports

decline will shake their heads as they relate to one another how this happened.

In the 1980s Japan — to get around Ronald Reagan's import quotas — finally built a few assembly plants here, but the high-value manufacture of Japanese auto parts is still done, by and large, outside the United States.

Unfortunately, this sad story of a magnanimous, foolish America giving away her inheritance to greedy rivals is going to get sadder. The nations of Asia and Latin America have seen how Japan became

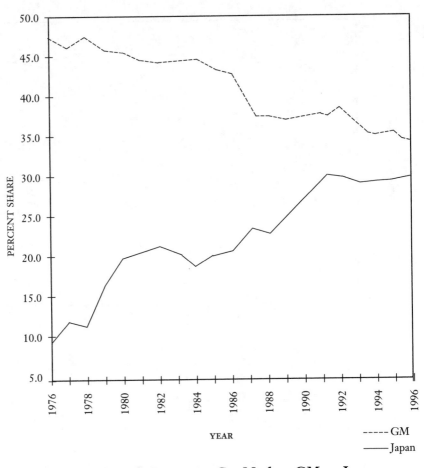

Shares of the U.S. Passenger Car Market: GM vs. Japan

Source: American Automobile Manufacturers Association; Ward's Automotive Reports

a great manufacturing nation; they are intent on copying Japan, preparing their own twenty-first-century invasions of the U.S. market. Massive overcapacity is being deliberately built into national automobile industries. As London's *Economist* reports, auto companies in Asia and Latin America are adding to the world's production far more cars than the entire world market can absorb:

South Korea alone is building an industry with capacity about five times greater than the demand for cars in its domestic market. The South Koreans do not intend to confine their competition to the developing world.[33]

To the free-trade fanatics at *The Economist*, "there is nothing to lament in all this. On the contrary, when too many cars pursue too few customers, consumers are sure to benefit."[34] But the United States is not a consumer cooperative. We are a country, a people, and a mighty auto industry is a vital strategic and industrial asset. Only a senile republic would let a little clique in South Korea overrun the U.S. auto industry. And the only impediment to totally recapturing our auto market for America's workers is this hedonistic free-trade ideology we preach from a global pulpit as foreign nations pick our pockets.

America's situation is not irreversible. As Japan's capturing 30 percent of our auto market was due to the folly of our mindlessly pursuing free trade, recapturing our auto market can be effected, in less than a decade, by a new policy of economic nationalism. The United States should set as a national goal that virtually all cars sold in the USA — Chevys, Fords, Chryslers, Toyotas, Hondas, BMWs, Volvos, Datsuns — be MADE IN THE USA. Nor is it difficult to devise trade and tax policies to guarantee this. Only that foolish consistency that is the hobgoblin of little minds holds us back. If Americans revisit their history (as we shall in Part Two), we can rediscover the principles and ideas that made us the first and greatest technological and manufacturing power in history — and that can take us to new heights in the new century.

FRITZ, BOB, AND PHIL

During the South Carolina primary of 1996, Senator Robert J. Dole and his new ally Phil Gramm appeared at the BMW plant in Spartanburg to denounce protectionism and hail the plant as one of America's great benefits from free trade. As South Carolina's own senator Ernest "Fritz" Hollings instructed, the gentlemen were "misinformed":

> The opposite is the case. Under President Reagan, a modest application of protectionism was employed. With the threat of trade sanctions, voluntary restraint agreements, in steel, cars, televisions and roller bearings were obtained. Ergo, we now have in South Carolina Nucor steel, BMW cars, Hitachi televisions and Koyo roller bearings. Some time ago, Eastman Kodak brought a case against Fuji for dumping photographic paper in the United States — at 360 percent below cost! As a result we will soon dedicate a $200 million Fuji facility in Greenwood, S.C. Protection not only saves jobs, it creates new ones.[35]

Why did BMW come to America? Out of fear of import quotas and because the fall of the dollar against the German mark made production here less costly. BMW also came because South Carolina offered millions of dollars in roads, rail links, plant-site concessions, and tax holidays. But Columbia paid too high a price. With a modest tariff on imported cars, South Carolina could have saved its money, and BMW would have come running hat in hand.

Chapter 5

MASTERS OF THE UNIVERSE

THE NEW TRANSNATIONAL ELITE

I think the nation-state is finished.[1]

— Robert Bartley,
WALL STREET JOURNAL

*Gone is the tight connection between the
company, its community, even its country.
Vanishing too are the paternalistic corporate
heads who used to feel a sense of responsibility for their local community. Emerging in
their place is the new global manager.*[2]

— Robert B. Reich, 1991

In the late nineteenth century a dynamic American capitalism
spawned a new elite, the captains of industry, or "robber barons" and
"malefactors of great wealth," depending on one's point of view. Yet,
for all their eccentricities and faults, John D. Rockefeller and Cornelius Vanderbilt and their peers saw themselves as American patriots, master builders of the greatest nation on earth, with duties to
that nation and, for the best of them, to their workers. In his early
years, Henry Ford seemed to exemplify the breed. In 1914 he startled critics when he doubled the wages of his married workers. A
worker, Ford explained, "is not just an individual. . . . He is a house-
holder. . . . The man does the work in the shop, but his wife does the
work in the home. The shop must pay them both." The alternative
was the "hideous prospect of little children and their mothers being
forced out to work."[3]

With the coming of the Global Economy, the idea that the head of a family must be paid a "living wage," so that his wife and children would not be driven into the labor market, seems quaint. As our century comes to a close, the participation of wives, even mothers with children under the age of six, in the labor force is at the highest level in history. Some consider that a triumph of equality. Ford saw the world differently, and he saw himself as pater familias of Ford Motor Company, a patriarch to whose employees he had social and moral obligations. Men and women of wealth who possess that sense of obligation — similar to what a good commander feels toward his soldiers — are a dying breed. But a few are still among us. Roger Milliken and Aaron Feuerstein are two.

"Conservatives of the Heart"

More than a decade ago, the head of the textile giant Milliken Industries, a legendary benefactor of conservative causes, came to the White House. At seventy, Roger Milliken still ran the family business, which ranks among the most successful privately owned companies in America. Milliken had come to persuade the White House not to veto a bill to give his industry relief from a flood of imports that were killing the jobs of his workers.

My answer was direct. He was, I told Roger Milliken, in the office of the stoutest free trader in the West Wing, with the lone exception of "that fellow down the hall." The Oval Office was fifty feet away. Ronald Reagan was not going to sign the textile bill. Milliken left disappointed; I supervised the writing of the veto message.

Milliken had been waging a long losing battle to save the industry to which he had devoted his life and halt the deindustrialization of his country. His people depended on him; they were losing their jobs in the scores of thousands every year, and Milliken felt a duty to lead the fight for them.

*　*　*

Ten years later Roger Milliken flew me from his headquarters in South Carolina to La Grange, Georgia, to inspect the ruins of a 650,000-square-foot carpet dyeing and finishing plant that employed 680 workers. On January 31, 1995, the plant had been gutted by fire; it looked like something out of Berlin 1945. Destruction was total. But when we arrived, the people of La Grange gave the famous industrialist a rousing reception.

The day of the fire, Milliken had directed his executives to fly in with a message for anyone who thought that his company would take the insurance money and run to Mexico: Roger Milliken was not walking away from La Grange, a company town where one in five workers is employed at one of seven Milliken plants. In half a year, Milliken told the people of La Grange, they would have up and operating on the site "a world-class textile plant with the most modern machines, systems and technology available in the world."[4]

In designing the new plant, Milliken solicited ideas from employees. Some were put to work constructing a scale model of the burned-out plant, from which to try out ideas on how to configure the new plant. Displaced workers went to the top of the list for hire at other plants across the South. One week after the fire, the La Grange High School band was at the airport. The first group of Milliken workers was flying by chartered jet to a plant in England to fill the orders La Grange could no longer meet. Jean Railey watched her son-in-law depart. "Everything went like clockwork," Railey said, "but I don't think I know anybody who doubted for a minute that it would be that way." Within weeks of the fire, nearly all the La Grange workers had jobs. A reporter described what he had seen as a "powerful, if anachronistic, image of small-town Southern paternalism — a company taking care of its company town."[5]

Reconstructing a carpet plant like the one in La Grange would normally require two years. But Milliken brought in three thousand construction workers and craftsmen and put them on round-the-clock shifts. The people of La Grange opened their homes to the workers. One twenty-nine-year-old welder, Thomas Dorsey from Leesville, Louisiana, said he wished "the job would never end."[6] On

August 14, 1995, Milliken spoke outside the newest, most modern carpet factory in the world. He had kept faith with his people, and a great company had done right by its workers.

In the week of the Georgia primary, I toured the new plant. What I said there of Roger Milliken is true of too few of today's capitalists: here, I said, is a businessman who believes that "when he succeeds, all his workers succeed. And when times are tough, everybody shares in the sacrifice. That is what the ideal of free enterprise is all about."[7]

Ten months after the La Grange fire, on December 1, 1995, another fire broke out a thousand miles to the north, in Lawrence, Massachusetts, destroying a plant of Malden Mills. Three thousand workers assumed it was the end of the line, the beginning of months of scratching for new jobs while collecting unemployment. They, too, were wrong.

Like Milliken, seventy-year-old Aaron Feuerstein looked on his workers as his extended family. He announced that he would keep all three thousand on the payroll of his family-owned business for a month, as he began to rebuild the factory. He then paid his workers a second month, then a third.[8] "When he did it the first time, I was surprised. The second time was a shock. The third . . . well, it was unrealistic to think he would do it again," said Bill Cotter, a nineteen-year veteran at the factory. Said Bill's wife, Nancy, "It was the third time that brought tears to everyone's eyes." "Another person would have taken the insurance money and walked away," said one employee.[9]

By the end of the third month, many of Feuerstein's workers had been able to find other jobs. His decency and humanity had tided them over. But it had cost him and his family millions of dollars. Why did he do it? Said Aaron Feuerstein:

> I have a responsibility to the workers, both blue-collar and white-collar. I have an equal responsibility to the community. It would have been unconscionable to put 3,000 people on the streets and deliver a death blow

to the cities of Lawrence and Methuen. Maybe on paper our company is worth less to Wall Street, but I can tell you it's worth more. We're doing fine.[10]

In an interview with *Parade*, Feuerstein quoted the first-century Jewish scholar Hillel: "In a situation where there is no righteous person, try to be a righteous person."[11] By mid-summer 1996, 85 percent of the workers at his gutted plant were busy at the newly rebuilt one. The rest were still being helped by their old boss.

Roger Milliken and Aaron Feuerstein belong to a tradition that is passing away, a tradition of men of authority who act on the biblical dictum that of those to whom much is given, much is asked. Milliken and Feuerstein are "conservatives of the heart."

"FORGET THE SALUTE TO THE FLAG"

As America's Industrial Revolution spawned a new elite, so, too, has the Global Economy. In mind-set and outlook, however, this new elite is a breed apart, another species altogether. Unencumbered by any national allegiance, it roams a Darwinian world of the borderless economy, where sentiment is folly and the fittest alone survive. In the eyes of this rootless transnational elite, men and women are not family, friends, neighbors, fellow citizens, but "consumers" and "factors of production."

Social critic David Morris, who considers global free trade "the Great Destroyer" — as did Karl Marx, who welcomed it — writes that:

the emphasis on globalism rearranges our loyalties and loosens our neighborly ties. "The new order eschews loyalty to workers, products, corporate structure, businesses, factories, communities, even the nation," the *New York Times* announces. Martin S. Davis, chair of Gulf and

Western, declares, "All such allegiances are viewed as expendable under the new rules. You cannot be emotionally bound to any particular asset."

We are now all assets.[12]

Efficiency is the highest value in the Global Economy, and patriotism — country coming before commerce — yields to utilitarianism. Between our new global elite and the Millikens and Feuersteins is a epoch. Former Labor Secretary Robert B. Reich relates a telling anecdote:

Charles (Mike) Harper, head of ConAgra, the giant food-processing and commodity-trading company, which is crucial to the economy of Omaha, Nebraska, recently threatened to move the company unless the state changed its tax code. The bonds of loyalty could slip over the weekend, Harper warned: "Some Friday night, we might turn out the lights — click, click, click — back up the trucks, and be gone by Monday morning."[13]

Inspect the executive ranks of America's Fortune 500 companies, Ford Motor, Alcoa, and IBM. Less and less are they American. More and more of their profits come from outside the United States, and their CEOs point with pride to their lengthening rosters of foreign managers.[14]

Unlike their preglobal predecessors, global managers feel little allegiance to us. In the global enterprise, the bonds between company and country — between them and us — are rapidly eroding. . . . We are witnessing the creation of a purer form of capitalism, practiced globally by managers who are more distant, more economically driven — in essence more coldly rational in their decisions, having shed the old affiliations with people and place.[15]

These global executives see themselves as citizens of the world, not as citizens of the United States. When Gilbert Williamson, president of NCR, was asked about the problem of U.S. workers being unable to compete in the Global Economy, he brushed off the question:

> I was asked the other day about U.S. competitiveness, and I replied that I don't think about it at all. We at NCR think of ourselves as a globally competitive company that happens to be headquartered in the United States.[16]

That is the authentic voice of the transnational elite. In quoting Williamson, the *Washington Post's* Hobart Rowen went on to say approvingly, "The modern corporation looks first to satisfying customers and to rolling up profits — forget the salute to the flag."[17] Forgotten, too, is the American worker. The immense fortunes of these elites are "tied to enterprises that operate across national boundaries," wrote social critic Christopher Lasch. Thus, they are

> more concerned with the smooth functioning of the system as a whole than with any of its parts. Their loyalties — if the term is not itself anachronistic in this context — are international rather than regional, national, or local. . . . The privileged classes in Los Angeles feel more kinship with their counterparts in Japan, Singapore, and Korea than with most of their own countrymen.[18]

Men and women employed by these "privileged classes," however, retain an antiquated belief that it is an honor to be an American. "Every meeting we have in the union, we open it with the pledge of allegiance," says machinists union president George Kourpias. "Maybe the companies should start doing that at their board meetings."[19] But as Rowen reminds us, in the modern corporation they "forget the salute to the flag."[20]

Many transnationals still carry fine old American names, but their workforces are less and less American. In 1985 GE employed 243,000 Americans; ten years later it was 150,000. GM has shrunk its U.S. workforce to 314,000. IBM has lopped off more than half of its U.S. workers, 132,000 in the past decade. Writes journalist William Greider:

By 1995, Big Blue had become a truly global firm — with more employees abroad than at home (116,000 to 111,000). Even Intel, a thriving semiconductor maker, shrank U.S. employment last year from 22,000 to 17,000. Motorola has grown, but its work force is now only 56 percent American. . . . Officials at the Communications Workers of America, which represents AT&T workers, recall that Ma Bell once made all its home telephones in the U.S. and now makes none here.[21]

As Americans look to exports for future growth, they should realize that the nation's greatest exporting companies — Boeing, GE, GM, AT&T, Motorola — make fewer and fewer of their products in factories inside the United States.

COMPANIES WITHOUT A COUNTRY

The transnational corporation is a mutant of the old multinational. Unlike yesterday's IBM, which was a U.S. corporation with subsidiaries abroad, the new transnational has no country. Writes Greider:

> A transnational company is one that operates in the global marketplace, that does its research wherever there are scientists and technicians, that manufactures where economics dictate (in many countries, that is), and that has a management that doesn't feel any allegiance to the economic or national security interests of the country in which it is incorporated. It obtains its financing from institutions around the world. In short, it regards itself as a free agent in a global economy.[22]

Boeing, the legendary U.S. aircraft company begun in Seattle in 1916, got a new chairman in February 1997. In his baptismal interview with *Financial Times*, Philip Condit said that he wants Boeing to be seen as a "global enterprise" and would be happy if, twenty years hence, no one thought of Boeing as an American company.

Condit's goal, said *Financial Times*, is "to forge links with non-U.S. companies in a drive to rid itself of its image as an American group."[23] Added Condit:

> I believe we are moving toward an era of global markets and global companies. I think it is advantageous that your workforce, your executive corps, reflect that. I would expect the nationalities of our executives to be considerably broader.[24]

Asked about the danger of technology theft in joint projects with foreign companies, Condit replied, "I'm a believer that technology transfers very readily. I think trying to say 'I've got a technological edge and I'm going to hold on to it' is impossible."[25] Would not this stance compromise Boeing's role as a pivotal U.S. defense contractor? Condit brushed aside the concern: "As we move in an international direction, we will have to find ways — the US government will have to find ways — of dealing with that."[26] A part of Boeing's assembly line is already in China; when asked later for his "feelings about human rights violations in China," Condit shot back:

> Oh, yeah, absolutely. And I'm going to put it in context: they are the same ones that I have about human rights violations in the United States. . . . Some of the struggles we've had with civil rights don't look all that shiny. People have been shot. People have been beaten. I happened to be in China during the Rodney King beating.[27]

The old corporate mind-set was nationalist-protectionist. The new one is internationalist–free trade. Indeed, much of what is called trade today is not truly trade at all. The *Financial Times* estimates that of the $6 trillion in world trade in 1995, $2 trillion was between corporations and their own foreign subsidiaries.[28] When U.S. merchandise imports totaled $740 billion in 1995, $350 billion, or 47.4 percent, was actually "related party trade" — i.e., merchandise produced abroad by the foreign workers of corporations that still list the United States as their last known address.[29] Princeton professor Helen V. Milner believes that the new global orientation of big business explains why protectionist policies have fallen out of favor:

> These large multinationals with extensive global trade networks have come to prefer a "free trade system," one without barriers obstructing their trade and production flows. These firms have been antiprotectionist, even in times of economic distress.[30]

When a transnational corporation ships millions of dollars in goods to the United States from overseas plants, it becomes a potential loser from policies designed to preserve and protect production *inside* the United States. Thus, the corporation invariably works to disrupt any common front to defend U.S. markets. "With strong ties to the Japanese industry, RCA had no desire to see quotas placed on Japanese imports," writes Milner.[31] RCA thus opposed the filing of unfair trade complaints by American television manufacturers in the 1970s, breaking industry ranks and weakening the political pressure the industry could muster. No relief arrived, and the U.S. industry went under. RCA had colluded with Japan to prevent any rescue, letting the U.S. television-manufacturing industry die, crying in vain for help.

Both Democratic and Republican administrations have crafted their trade policies in concert with these transnationals. The trade deals are then sold to Congress as having "business support." Americans, however, fail to grasp the radical change in the orientation of these transnationals. Their interests and U.S. national interests are more often in conflict than in harmony.

Transnational firms also control the Advisory Committee for Trade Policy and Negotiations (ACTPN). Established by the Trade Act of 1974, the ACTPN was to provide "outside" advice to the government from groups affected by trade deals. There seems little appreciation of just how far "outside" these corporations now are. Of the thirty-seven members of the ACTPN, advising on the GATT-

WTO agreement, thirty-four represented transnational big business. Only one, Jack Valenti of the Motion Picture Association of America, refused to sign the ACTPN report.

To win congressional support for "free trade" deals, the giant companies that dominate business organizations and fund think tanks and political campaigns forge compromises between the transnational and "national" firms. National companies are promised an opening of foreign markets to replace domestic markets lost to imports. But with the United States now importing a third of all manufactured goods we consume, we are running out of domestic market to trade away. Between 1990 and 1995 the "world" market for American exports increased at a real annual rate of 7.6 percent. *But the U.S. market for foreign imports grew by 9.6 percent a year.* America's best market is here at home, and we are giving it away.

The political clout that the transnationals command can be seen in GOP platforms. In their 1972 platform Republicans noted the rise of these corporations and, reacting on sound conservative instincts, stated boldly:

> We deplore the practice of locating plants in foreign countries solely to take advantage of low wage rates in order to produce goods primarily for sale in the United States. We will take action to discourage such unfair and disruptive practices that result in the loss of American jobs.[32]

By 1976 the "party of business" felt it prudent to drop the 1972 language and not even mention what was afoot. The old adage "trade follows the flag" is passé. Today the Republican Party follows big business, as it lowers the American flag.

Among the arguments made for shifting authority over trade to the executive branch is that Congress, with 535 members, is too beholden to "special interests." Members of Congress, it is said, represent local and state interests. Only the president, chosen by the nation, can see the national interest. Disinterested diplomats, directed by the president, are thus more qualified to negotiate trade treaties for the good of the country.

But this rationale begs the question: since diplomats know little about modern business and industry, upon whom do *they* rely for counsel in deciding what to fight for and what to give away? Who was in Geneva at the elbow of Mickey Kantor, the Hollywood lawyer who led the U.S. delegation at the GATT negotiations? Answer: the ACTPN, the hired hands of the U.S. transnationals. "The executive branch depends almost entirely on business for technical information regarding trade negotiations," writes Jeff Gerten, former undersecretary of commerce. "The role of American firms as de facto agents of foreign policy is expanding."[33]

The final GATT treaty, advertised as a bold step toward global free trade, was thus nothing but a mammoth insiders' deal among the transnational giants of America, Europe, and Japan to carve up the world, just as the imperial powers carved up the continent of Africa in Berlin in 1884.

WHO ARE THEY?

Seeing themselves as the first citizens of a new world, the transnational elites yearn to be free of the nations to which they once gave allegiance. They dream of a day when the nation-state is as obsolete as the feudal castle. "The expansion of our consciousness to the global level offers mankind perhaps the last real chance to build a world order that is less coercive than that offered by the nation-state," writes A. W. Clausen, ex-president of BankAmerica Corporation and the World Bank.[34] Echoing Clausen, William I. Spencer, former president of First National City Corporation, declared, "The political boundaries of nation-states are too narrow and constricted to define the scope and sweep of modern business." We must "defang the nationalist monster," says Peter Drucker.[35]

As the church was the despised enemy of the intellectuals of the eighteenth century who echoed Voltaire's "Ecrasez l'infame!" the nation-state is the impediment to progress for the transnational elite. Carl A. Gerstacker of the Dow Chemical Company once dreamed aloud about a brave new world:

> I have long dreamed of buying an island owned by no nation and of establishing the World Headquarters of the Dow Company on the truly neutral ground of such an island, beholden to no nation or society.[36]

"Beholden to no nation or society" — that is the dream!

They want to be rid of the burden of America! A spokesman for Dow rival Union Carbide seconded Gerstacker: "It is not proper for an international corporation to put the welfare of any country in which it does business above that of any other."[37] Putting America first bespeaks a lack of loyalty to the corporation. No man can serve two masters, and the company comes before the country.

Twenty-five years ago, in *Between Two Ages*, Zbigniew Brzezinski looked to the horizon and saw the Global Economy coming — and its progeny: the Masters of the Universe. "A global human consciousness is for the first time beginning to manifest itself," exulted Brzezinski.[38]

> Today we are again witnessing the emergence of transnational elites . . . composed of international businessmen, scholars, professional men, and public officials. The ties of these new elites cut across national boundaries, their perspectives are not confined by national traditions, and their interests are more functional than national.[39]

Brzezinski joined banker David Rockefeller in creating the Trilateral Commission, a group of the most influential of those transnational elites. But he offered a word of caution. The growing distance from the common man, of these "international professional elites," Dr. Brzezinski warned, risks "a dangerous gap between them and the politically activated masses, whose 'nativism' — exploited by more nationalist political leaders — could work against the 'cosmopolitan' elites."[40]

"ALL COUNTRIES . . . ARE ARTIFICIAL"

In the new world, envisioned long ago by the classical liberals, the smooth functioning of that mightiest of machines, the Global Economy, is the highest good, and its corporate offspring have memorized their new gospel. "For business purposes, the boundaries that separate one country from another are no more real than the equator," said the president of IBM's World Trade Corporation in 1974. "They are merely convenient demarcations of ethnic, linguistic and cultural entities."[41] The WTC slogan: World peace through world trade![42] George W. Ball, once described as "part of a new transnational elite that felt frustrated and unduly restricted by the traditional nation-state system,"[43] vented his exasperation with the claims of nation and country:

> The urgent need of modern man [is] to use the world's resources in the most efficient manner. That can be achieved only when all the factors necessary for the production and use of goods — capital, labor, raw materials and plant facilities — are freely mobilized and deployed according to the most efficient pattern — and that in turn will be possible only when national boundaries no longer play a critical role in defining economic horizons.[44]

Where does one's loyalty lie? That is the issue raised by the onset of the Global Economy and the rise of the transnational elite. To whom, to what, do we owe allegiance and love? Is the day of the nation-state over? Robert Bartley of the *Wall Street Journal* believes so. So does Strobe Talbott, Clinton's roommate at Oxford and architect of his Russian policy:

> All countries are basically social arrangements. . . . No matter how permanent and even sacred they may seem at any one time, in fact they are all artificial and temporary. . . . Within the next hundred years . . . nationhood as we know it will be obsolete; all states will recognize a single, global authority. A phrase briefly fashionable in the mid-20th

century — "citizen of the world" — will have assumed real meaning by the end of the 21st.[45]

To Talbott, the WTO, IMF, and World Bank are "protoministries of trade, finance and development for a united world."[46]

How are traditional Americans, jealous of their liberty and proud of their heritage of independence, to be persuaded to give up their national sovereignty for a seat at the table of Strobe Talbott's new world order? By stealth. In 1974 Richard N. Gardner, later Clinton's ambassador to Spain, echoed Brzezinski's warning not to awaken the sleeping giant of American patriotism but to proceed by subtlety and indirection:

> The "house of world order" will have to be built from the bottom up. . . . An end run about national sovereignty, eroding it piece by piece, will accomplish much more than the old-fashioned frontal assault.[47]

Like a shipwrecked, exhausted Gulliver on the beach of Lilliput, America is to be tied down with threads, strand by strand, until it cannot move when it awakens. "Piece by piece," our sovereignty is being surrendered. By accession to NAFTA, GATT, the UN, the WTO, the World Bank, the IMF, America has ensnared itself in a web that restricts its freedom of action, diminishes its liberty, and siphons off its wealth. Most Americans do not understand this. And even to raise the question is to provoke ridicule as a reactionary caught up in conspiracy theories.

Nevertheless, as Citicorp's Walter Wriston concedes, power is slowly shifting away from nation-states to transnational institutions:

> When a system of national economies linked by government-regulated trade is replaced — at least in part — by an increasingly integrated global economy beyond the reach of national regulation, power changes hands.[48]

"The unraveling of national sovereignty," adds UN Under-Secretary-General Brian Urquhart, "seems to be a feature of the post–Cold War period."[49] Indeed, the Cold War has been super-seded by a new struggle that many patriots do not even know is un-derway. "The real divisions of our time," writes scholar Christian Kopff, "are not between left and right but between nations and the globalist delusion."[50] And a question needs to be directed straight to the Right: whose side are you on? If Clinton and Talbott look to a new world order, and believe free trade is the ship to carry us there, to what port do you believe global free trade is transporting America?

DISSOLVING THE BONDS OF LOYALTY

Were Richard Cobden alive, he would be rhapsodic. For Cobden hated the British empire. In 1835 he railed that it can "never be got-ten rid of except by the indirect process of free trade which will gradually loosen the bonds which unite our colonies to us by a mis-taken notion of self-interest."[51] But an acid that can dissolve the bonds of loyalty to a mother country can also dissolve the bonds of loyalty that bind a great and diverse republic. Look at Canada, Italy, Britain. The centrifugal forces pulling them apart are at work here in the United States.

Do we Americans believe in the vision of Cobden, a world of open borders and untrammeled trade, where nations fade away in the brilliant dawn of a new world order? Or do we hold to the grand old ideas of sovereignty and independence for which our Founding Fathers risked their lives, fortunes, and sacred honor? It's time to choose. Nor can the decision be put off much longer, or it will be made by default. Not to decide is to decide. By Newton's first law, a body in motion continues to move in the same direction until an outside force intervenes to divert or stop it. Unless we intervene to halt this momentum and recapture our country, America will wake up like Gulliver, tied down forever, our destiny no longer ours to decide.

Book Two

WHERE AND HOW
WE LOST THE WAY

Chapter 6

WHAT OUR
FATHERS BELIEVED

O ur dependence on overseas markets to buy American goods, and on foreign countries to sell us theirs, is approaching what it was when we were thirteen colonies.

Trade has exploded as a share of the U.S. economy, from a historic average of 10 percent, to 23 percent today, to an anticipated 36 percent in 2010. Imports in 1997 crossed the $1 trillion mark, and total U.S. trade is now more than $2 trillion a year. The benefits: sleek and slimmed-down U.S. corporations are on top again, the envy of Europe and Japan. As corporate profits surge, the Dow-Jones has a built-in expectation of even greater profits. Stocks are selling at twenty times earnings. America's elite is prospering as never before.

The cost: America is no longer one country. The wages of working Americans stopped rising when the free-trade era began. Real

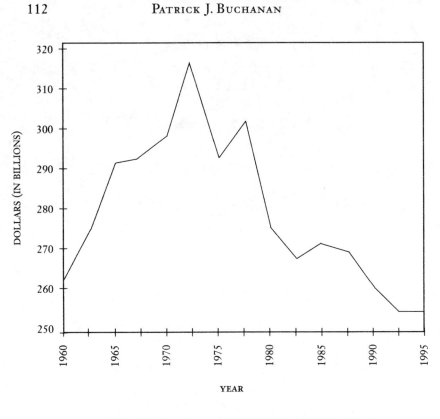

Average Weekly Earnings, 1960–95 (in 1982 Dollars)

Source: U.S. Bureau of Labor Statistics

wages in 1994 were 19 percent below their peak year of 1973. Forced to compete with tens of millions of immigrants, and hundreds of millions of hungry Asian and Latin American workers who make 5–10 percent of U.S. wages, American workers are being undercut all over the world. To transnational corporations, U.S. workers are expensive and troublesome, and the easy way to keep profits rising — and stock prices and executive stock options soaring — is to shut down here and move production outside the United States.

The social costs? As workers' wages stagnated and fell, wives and mothers entered the job market in record numbers to maintain the family standard of living. *In 1960 fewer than one-fifth of women with children under the age of six were in the labor force; today almost two-*

thirds are. No other modern nation has so many of its married women in the labor force. While this keeps median family income (which fell 5.8 percent between 1990 and 1995) from collapsing, the price is paid in falling birthrates and rising delinquency, in teenage drug abuse, alcohol abuse, promiscuity, illegitimacy, and abortions — and in the high divorce rate among working parents. The American family is paying a hellish price for the good things down at the mall.

As the commands of commerce take precedence over the claims of families and the call of patriotism, national unity takes a backseat to ethnic solidarity. In Britain this is manifest in the resurgence of Welsh and Scottish nationalism; in Canada, in the drive for an independent Quebec; in Italy, in the secessionist Northern League. The deconstruction of the United States can be seen in resegregated student dorms, ethnic gangs, a revival of ethnic and racial politics, secessionist movements in the Southwest, all the way over to the white militias and the Southern League.

Another cost of the Global Economy is the corruption of politics — from BCCI to Lippogate to the buying and selling of trade and foreign policy by hirelings of Mexico, Japan, Taiwan. "Influence in Washington is just like in Indonesia. It's for sale," smirked the *Japan Economic Journal* in 1981.[1] In the mid-1990s, Asian moneymen brazenly attempted to buy the Democratic National Committee and get a hook in the president with huge gifts to his legal-defense fund. High among America's imports from the Global Economy: the sleaziest of foreign practices.

The most perilous aspect, however, is the loss of U.S. sovereignty and the potential loss of nationhood itself. Look at Europe. Nations there are meekly transferring control of their defense and foreign policy, of trade and immigration policy, to a superstate called the European Union; they are even giving up control of their currencies, which means control of their destinies. And what is happening to France, Britain, Germany, Italy, will happen here if we do not wake up. Once a nation has put its foot onto the slippery slope of global free trade, the process is inexorable, the end inevitable: death of the nation-state.

*   *   *

Our embrace of the Global Economy is dividing us into two unequal Americas; the elites beckoning us there betray everything the Founding Fathers stood for, fought for, died for. Do the American people understand that

- the independence for which the patriot fathers fought was economic as well as political?
- Washington, Hamilton, and Madison, architects of the nation, abhorred "free trade" and built the tariff wall behind which America secured her economic independence?
- Jefferson ended his days as fierce an economic nationalist as Andrew Jackson, the other father of the Democratic Party?
- Abraham Lincoln was America's Great Protectionist?
- the Global Economy is the brainchild of utopian European intellectuals, none of whom ever built a great nation?
- the Republican eras of economic nationalism — 1865–1913 and the Roaring Twenties — were times of U.S. growth and prosperity unmatched before or since?
- free-trade policy is the legacy not of conservatives but of one-worlders and liberals like Woodrow Wilson?
- the charge that Smoot-Hawley was a cause of the Great Depression, Hitler, and World War II is a myth perpetuated by free-trade zealots, some of whom wish to see the old American republic disappear into a new world order?

If we are to take back our country, we must understand where and how it was taken from us. We must know America's true history. We are today building a Global Economy and a new world order based on the blueprints of intellectuals and zealots whom our greatest men ridiculed for 150 years. To see how we are betraying that heritage and squandering that patrimony, we need to know what that heritage and patrimony are. So, let us go back and retrace the footprints of those greatest Americans.

Chapter 7

THE RISE OF AMERICAN NATIONALISM

"BUY FROM US — OR GO NAKED!"

> *The war of the American Revolution chiefly grew out of the efforts of Great Britain to cripple and destroy our Colonial industries to the benefit of the British trader, and . . . the Independence conquered, was an Industrial as well as Political Independence.*[1]
>
> — Senator John Logan,
> THE GREAT CONSPIRACY, 1886

Returning home from the French and Indian War, the newly married George Washington took over the Custis family plantation. Each dawn he was up on horseback, supervising Mount Vernon. Everything depended on the success of a single crop:

> Tobacco! That was always the end product. It was cut when ripe, hung in special barns, and when just dry enough put in hogsheads weighing from 660 to 1100 pounds. And then off to England to restore his balance with Cary & Co., and to pay for new purchases.[2]

From his first days Washington was writing in protest to Robert Cary & Co. that his tobacco was being sold for less than his neighbors'. The response usually contained a sharp demand that Washington pay down his debt. An accounting from Cary in 1763 was "transmitted . . . with the additional aggravation of a hint at the largeness" of what was owed.[3] "I shall endeavor to discharge it as fast as I can conveniently," the humiliated veteran of Fort Necessity and Fort Duquesne wrote back.[4]

Cary, however, had little to complain of. It was making a double profit: one from selling Washington's tobacco, another from acting as purchasing agent for Mount Vernon. Washington, who could oversee neither transaction, was wholly dependent on Cary to do him justice, as Cary collected interest on the mounting debt.

In the mid-1760s an exasperated Washington stopped growing tobacco for England and began to grow wheat for Americans. His new business proved a startling success. In 1769 his wheat crop was six times what it had been in 1764. He built a schooner and put more seines into the Potomac, pulling out schools of shad and herring, added to his number of weavers, and built a commercial mill that European visitors marveled at for the quality of its flour. The Custis plantation was thriving. Washington was showing his countrymen the way to independence.

But there remained a grating dependency on English goods. When the successful planter decided to purchase "a superfine blue broadcloth coat with silver trimmings," "a fine scarlet waistcoat full laced," and "one pair crimson velvet breeches," they could be bought only in England. Washington sent his measurements. What came back fit so wretchedly that Washington asked in despair whether the tailor could not have gone out into the streets of London and gotten a six-foot man with long limbs, and measured him.[5]

A lover of military history, Washington ordered for his mantelpiece busts of Alexander the Great, Julius Caesar, Charles XII of Sweden, and the King of Prussia, "not to exceed 15 inches high," and smaller busts of the Duke of Marlborough and Prince Eugene. Back came a bust of Aeneas carrying his father out of Troy, and others of Bacchus and Flora.[6]

The final straw came with Washington's proudest purchase.

Wishing to present himself on Virginia's roads as the success he had become, he ordered a coach "in the newest taste . . . made of the best seasoned wood . . . by a celebrated workman." The coach was to be green, "unless any other color [is] more in vogue." To hasten its arrival, he sent cash. Cary shipped a "new handsome chariot made of the best materials, handsomely carved." Its interior was lined with green morocco, trimmed with lace, and its windows sported mahogany venetian blinds. It was magnificent.

> As it came off the boat, the chariot gleamed, a vision of transatlantic elegance elevating provincial America. However, the English builder had not bothered to use for export seasoned wood. Before the chariot had been in use two months, some panels had slipped out of their mouldings and others had split from end to end.
>
> If only Washington had ordered his chariot from Philadelphia, where an American maker would not have despised and cheated his American market![7]

This dependence on Britain galled other Americans of independent spirit, too. Jefferson later wrote that English merchants conspired to get Americans into debt by initially paying good prices and offering easy credit; then, when the planter was hooked, they cut his prices. Virginia planters, said Jefferson, had become a "species of property annexed to certain mercantile houses in London."[8] Washington and other Virginians such as Richard Henry Lee began to look to manufacturing as the key to unlock the prison door of their dependency. As historian John C. Miller writes:

> Many Americans recognized that if the colonies were to wage successful economic war with the mother country, it was necessary that they manufacture for themselves the necessities they had formerly imported from Great Britain. As the Tories unkindly pointed out, Americans had the alternative in 1768 of buying from Great Britain or going naked. . . . Colonial manufacturing came to be widely regarded as "the only way to unrivet the chains, and burst asunder the bands of Iron that are fastened on us."[9]

"Let us be ashamed to be dependent on other Countries for our Manufactures," exclaimed a New Yorker. "Let it be our glory to make use only of such Articles as are manufactured in this Country."[10] These were brave sentiments; but such thinking came perilously close to treason. For Washington and his rebellious friends were tampering with the economic order of the empire.

Since Jamestown, the colonies had been ruled under the mercantilist system; for a century, their commerce had been controlled by the Acts of Trade and Navigation. Out of America came raw materials; back went the finished goods of British industry. Trade was done in British ships. Colonial trade with the West Indies, France, and Spain was strictly regulated. In 1766 the *London Magazine* quoted a proud Englishman: "The American is apparelled from head to foot in our manufactures . . . he scarcely drinks, sits, moves, labours or recreates himself without contributing to the emolument of the mother country."[11] Colonies were not even allowed to print their own Bibles; they had to be imported from London, Dublin, and Edinburgh, the centers of printing in the British Isles.[12] Behind the mercantilist system lay a conviction common to all British statesmen:

The British Colonies are to be regarded in no other light, but as subservient to the commerce of their mother country; the colonists are merely factors for the purpose of trade, and in all considerations concerning the Colonies, this must be always the leading idea.[13]

The Seeds of Rebellion

After victory in the Seven Years War delivered France's North American empire to the king, Britain bestrode "the narrow world like a Colossus." In the courts of Europe, British diplomats walked ahead of the humiliated French, to whom all had deferred in the time of the Sun King. And the English carried themselves so. Of his contemporaries, Horace Walpole wrote that they were "born with

Roman insolence" and acted with "more haughtiness than an Asiatic monarch." [14]

Not unreasonably, Britain decided that the cost of defending and administering the vast North American empire should be shared by the colonies. For Parliament was convinced that they benefited most from the imperial ties, which was not as it was meant to be. Indeed, an investigation by the Lords of the Treasury into why the Molasses Act of 1733 had failed to raise the anticipated revenue had concluded, on October 4, 1763:

> We observe with concern that through neglect, connivance, and fraud, not only the revenue is impaired, but the commerce of the colonies is diverted from its natural course and the salutary provisions of many wise laws to secure it to the mother country are in great measure defeated. [15]

The colonies, their lordships concluded, were swindling the mother country! Parliament's response: the American Revenue Act of 1764, known as the Sugar Act, which put duties on molasses, sugar, wine, silk, and linen and required the colonies to buy rum from Great Britain. (Rum, John Adams would write, "was an essential ingredient in American independence.") [16] The Sugar Act was the work of one Charles Jenkinson, whose intent went far beyond raising revenue.

> The increase in our Colonies is certainly what we wish, but they must increase in a manner as will keep them useful to the Mother Country. . . . With this view all the provisions of [the act] are formed, and as far as it is necessary for this purpose to restrain the commerce of our Colonies, it is an evil to which I think they ought to submit for the good of the whole. [17]

The Sugar Act was followed by the Currency Act, denying the colonies the right to issue paper money, and the Stamp Act of 1765, requiring stamps on all newspapers, pamphlets, legal papers, bills of lading, mortgages, skins, parchments, college diplomas, almanacs, calendars, playing cards, tavern licenses, and advertisements. Lawyers, printers, editors, merchants, and clergymen were hardest hit. New York Governor Cadwallader Colden thought this tax a grave mistake. "Associations of lawyers are the most dangerous of any next to the military," the governor warned.[18] He was right.

Parliament had misjudged the mood in the colonies; the Stamp Act caused an uproar. "Taxation without representation is tyranny!" went the cry through Colonial taverns and towns. A Boston mob sacked the home of Lieutenant Governor Thomas Hutchinson and scattered manuscripts and books on American history that he had been collecting for thirty years. Colonial pacts were formed to cut back on purchasing British goods. Orders were canceled. British ports gradually shut down; the unemployed walked the streets. British merchants began to call for a repeal. In March of 1766 the House of Commons, following the wish of Prime Minister William Pitt ("America must be embraced with the arms of affection") and the will of George III, repealed the Stamp Act.

Celebrations broke out. Pitt and the king were heroes. In New York's Battery Park, statues were erected to both. Americans felt that they had powerful friends in the government, men like Pitt, the Great Commoner, soon to be Earl of Chatham. They were right — up to a point. On "No taxation without representation!" Pitt stood with the Americans: "We may bind their trade, confine their manu- factures, and exercise every power whatsoever, except that of taking their money out of their pockets without their consent," he declared in the House of Commons.[19] But on where manufacturing must be done, Pitt stood behind the mercantilist system. "If the Americans should manufacture a lock of wool or a horse shoe," he said, "[he] would fill their ports with ships and their towns with troops."[20]

Little noticed on the day the Stamp Act was repealed was that Parliament, enraged by the colonists' assertion that they could not be taxed without their consent, passed the Declaratory Act, which stated, in explicit terms, that the colonies were

> subordinate unto, and dependent upon the imperial crown . . . of Great
> Britain; and that the King's majesty . . . in parliament assembled, had,

hath, and of right ought to have, full power and authority to make laws and statutes . . . to bind the colonies and people of America . . . in all cases whatsoever.[21]

Here were sown the seeds of rebellion.

"The Worst Man That Lives"

In 1767 Charles Townshend was Chancellor of the Exchequer. Though detested by the king, he had been brought into the cabinet by Pitt. "Mr. Charles Townshend's conduct," wrote George III, "is what I should not have thought any other man capable of, but himself very much so, for I look on him as the worst man that lives. . . . I would as soon employ a common thief."[22]

Taunted that he would never dare tax the Americans, Townshend declared, "I will, I will!"[23] He decided to make up for a shortfall in revenue by imposing new duties on America's imported glass, paint, lead, paper, and tea. On June 15, 1767, the Townshend Acts passed. Americans responded with calls not to import any of the goods covered by the new duties. Parliament retaliated by extending the Treason Act of Henry VIII to North America — any man charged would be returned to England for trial — and voted to send two regiments to Boston. In the capital of the greatest empire on earth, exasperation with its obstreperous colonies was rising. Asked his thoughts on the cousins across the sea, Samuel Johnson responded, "Sir, they are a race of convicts, and ought to be thankful for anything we allow them short of hanging."[24]

The Townshend Acts contradicted Pitt's policy of not directly taxing the Americans without their consent. Why had Pitt failed to stop them? Because Pitt was gone. On taking power in 1766, he had come down with the gout; worse, the Earl of Chatham, the one statesman who might have averted the American Revolution, was going insane. Now, with the work done for which his name would be remembered, Townshend passed from this earthly scene at the age of forty-two. "Our comet is set," wrote Walpole:

> All those parts and fire are extinguished; those volatile salts are evaporated; that first eloquence of the world is dumb! That duplicity is fixed, that cowardice terminated heroically. He joked on death as naturally as he used to do on the living.[25]

Townshend had struck the spark that ignited the revolution that changed the world. Ironically, when imposing those duties, he had as tutor to his stepson a Scottish moral philosopher who, said a biographer, "fed Charles Townshend with the material for his luckless budget of 1767."

The tutor's name was Adam Smith.

"SUBMIT OR TRIUMPH"

When the British regiments landed, Bostonians refused to quarter the "lobsterbacks." On March 5, 1770, following a snowball fight, a mob attacked the troops and badly beat a soldier with sticks and stones. He was rescued by a platoon, one of whom opened fire, triggering a volley that killed five Americans. The Boston Massacre had been witnessed by John Adams, who believed the assault had been provoked, and who bravely undertook the legal defense of the British soldiers.

Meanwhile, America's "nonimportation" decisions were destroying Britain's colonial trade. Only a fraction of anticipated revenue was being realized. In April of 1770, Lord North had the acts repealed, except for the duty on tea. George III was determined to impress on the colonies that they were subject to all laws of Parliament and crown: "I am clear that there must always be one tax to keep the right, and as such I approve the Tea Duty."[26]

Their victory sealed, the colonists split into two camps. Most Americans wanted to end the nonimportation agreements. They were not rebels; they did not seek a conflict with the king and feared that radicals like the Sons of Liberty and Sam Adams, "the orchestra leader of revolution," wanted to get on with the confrontation.[27] Parliament soon played directly into the hands of Sam Adams. To save the failing British East India Company, it passed the Tea Act, giving the company a monopoly on the sale of tea to the colonies, cutting out our honest American merchants and smugglers alike. The enraged colonists retaliated by refusing to allow the tea to be off-loaded in American ports.

On December 16, 1773, 150 men dressed as Mohawks boarded three British ships in Boston Harbor and, as thousands watched, dumped the cargo of tea overboard. John Adams instantly recognized the importance of the act of defiance: "This Destruction of the Tea is so bold, so daring, so firm, intrepid & inflexible, and it must have so important Consequences, and so lasting, that I cannot but consider it as an epocha in History."[28]

For once, George III agreed. When word reached England of the Boston Tea Party, he wrote to Lord North: "The dye is now cast. . . . The Colonies must either submit or triumph."[29]

Parliament's answer: the Intolerable Acts, as they were called in the colonies. The port of Boston was closed until full restitution was made. Massachusetts was stripped of the right to elect its leaders. General Thomas Gage was made governor to put the rebels in their place, and more regiments were sent to Boston. Parliament was rapidly turning Loyalists into rebels. Gage discovered that the colonists were uniting behind the Bostonians. On May 27, 1774, at the Raleigh Tavern in Williamsburg, the Virginia Assembly called for a Colonial congress, which met in September in Philadelphia. Patrick Henry roused the delegates by declaring, "The distinctions between Virginians, Pennsylvanians, New Yorkers, New Englanders are no more. I am not a Virginian, but an *American*."[30]

Parliament met the colonial defiance by augmenting Gage's force to ten thousand troops and imposing the Restraining Acts, which restricted America's trade to only Britain, Ireland, and the British West Indies and forbade the colonies from trading with one another. The crisis was out of control. On March 22, 1775, Edmund Burke rose in Parliament to decry the folly of Lord North and plead that the colonists be accorded all the rights of Englishmen. He was too late. On April 18, 1775, Gage ordered eight hundred men on a night march eighteen miles to Concord to destroy the munitions that his spies had told him were there. Alerted by William Dawes, seventy Minutemen were waiting at Lexington under Captain John Parker.

So began the Revolution. Men who had counted themselves loyal British subjects began taking up arms against a "tyrant" they had toasted seven years before. And nothing did more to ignite the rebellion than the cloying British control of America's internal commerce, constant British interference with American trade, and the mother country's insistence that her colonies existed for her benefit and were subject to her maternal dictation.

The war that began with the "shot heard round the world" thus was fought for economic freedom as well as for political independence. And the lessons of those years were burned into the minds of the patriot fathers: the empire had used its control of manufacturing to keep the colonies in submission. As we could not rely on British goodwill for our liberty, so too could we never again rely on British trade for our prosperity or on British industry for the needs of nationhood. The umbilical cord to the mother country had to be cut.

Washington's Grand Strategy

When Washington came home from Yorktown, he was more than a Virginian; he was an American who had turned his back forever on Europe. Never again could the liberated colonies rely on British goods carried in British ships. Never again could king and Parliament hold the power to strangle America with customs duties, embargoes, or blockades. Washington intended to replace bonds of trade across the ocean with bonds of commerce over the Alleghenies into the West.

Unlike most of his great American contemporaries, Washington was a man of the West. "No other President . . . before Andrew

Jackson was so largely a product of the west and the frontier. . . . Washington had served in the wilderness as a surveyor, a messenger traversing unknown trails, an explorer, and an Indian fighter."[31] Washington saw America's future in the West. But looking west, he saw America's expansion blocked. There were no roads for Western farmers and frontiersmen to transport their goods over the mountains; they had to move them by water. But Spain controlled the Mississippi, outlet to the sea for Kentucky, Tennessee, western Virginia, and western Pennsylvania; and Spain had closed New Orleans to American commerce. To the northwest Britain had refused to honor the terms of the peace and would not surrender the forts controlling the Great Lakes. Britain had also closed the outlet to the Atlantic through the Saint Lawrence.

> The crisis, Washington believed, would be grave if either European nation, "instead of throwing stumbling blocks in their [the western settlers'] way as they now do, should hold out lures for their trade and alliance." Then the new west, far from strengthening the American Utopia, might become a very dangerous neighbor.[32]

"The Western settlers . . . stand as it were as upon a pivot; the touch of a feather would turn them any way," Washington concluded after a trip over the mountains.[33] Rather than challenge Spanish power, he wanted to win the West by the art of peace, "clearing rivers, building bridges, and establishing conveniences for traveling,"[34] to tie the West to the coast with bonds of commerce, before Britain or Spain awoke to its opportunity.

Washington came up with a stupendous idea. Having crossed the Blue Ridge and the Alleghenies many times, he knew that the headwaters of the Potomac were close to the rivers that flowed into the Ohio. He wanted to join these rivers with a canal so goods from the Northwest could be floated down the Potomac to Alexandria and then put onto ocean-going ships. The hometown he had laid out as a surveyor would become America's greatest port. Washington was passionate on the subject. Visitors who came to Mount Vernon to dine on stories of Trenton and Yorktown came away saying that all the general talked about was his Potomac Canal. At his table, the spirits flowed freely and the great man was seen to rise many times, glass in hand, to toast loudly, "Success to the navigation of the Potomac!"[35]

Britain Declares a Trade War

As the western crisis preoccupied Washington, another was brewing overseas from a familiar source. While the son of William Pitt had urged reconciliation, Lord Sheffield pressed Britain to retake control of trade with the former colonies, without the burden of ruling them. In his *Observations on the Commerce of the American States,* Sheffield argued that

> Parliament should endeavor to divert the whole Anglo-American trade to British bottoms. America cannot retaliate. It will not be an easy matter to bring the American States to act as a nation. They are not to be feared as such by us. . . . We might as reasonably dread the effects of a combination among the German as among the American States.[36]

Sheffield prevailed. By a series of Orders in Council in 1783, American ships were excluded from ports in Canada and the West Indies and were to be treated in British ports like the ships of a European power. His purpose, said Sheffield, was the "strangling in the birth" of American shipping. Americans, however, were already doing that to one another.

Chaos in Commerce

Since Yorktown, the former colonies had been governed under the Articles of Confederation and Perpetual Union. All power over trade was retained by the states. Memories of the Townshend Acts, the Tea Act, the Intolerable Acts, were too vivid for the states to relinquish control. The sole exception: Congress was charged with "regulating the trade and managing all affairs with the Indians, not members of the states." But with their competing tariffs, trade restrictions, and transit fees for passage through their territories, the states had created commercial anarchy.

> Interstate brawls caused . . . grave disquiet. . . . The New York Assembly in 1787 increased customs duties on foreign merchandise and assessed heavy entrance and clearance fees on all vessels coming from or bound to New Jersey and Connecticut. New Jersey retaliated by taxing the lighthouse on Sandy Hook. . . . Virginia and Maryland, long at loggerheads because Maryland's charter gave her jurisdiction over the Potomac up to the Virginia shore, managed to make a peaceable settlement at a joint conference in Alexandria. Pennsylvania and Delaware were also concerned because some of their commerce had to pass through Virginia's territorial waters.[37]

With the country drifting toward an internecine economic war, American nationalists began to envision a unified economic and trading system, with a strong central government to oversee it. The Virginia assembly, "in a nationalist mood, invited all the states to send delegates to a convention at Annapolis, 'to take into consideration the trade of the United States.' "[38] The Annapolis Convention of 1786 would be the forerunner to the Philadelphia convention of 1787.

When he traveled to Philadelphia to take up the presidency of the Federal Constitutional Convention, Washington was firmly in the nationalist camp. His allies were the brilliant young man he had come to look upon almost as a son, Alexander Hamilton, and the fellow Virginian who would author the Constitution, James Madison. But not all the Founding Fathers shared the nationalism of Hamilton and his patron. Benjamin Franklin and Thomas Jefferson were free traders. Commerce, said Dr. Franklin, should be "as free between all the Nations of the World, as it is between the several Countys of England. . . . No Nation was ever ruined by Trade."[39]

Jefferson's views at the time, however, were of little help in devising a policy to deal with the crippling chaos in America's domestic commerce and foreign trade. In 1785, he had written that

> were I to indulge in my own theory, I should wish them [the Americans] to practice neither commerce nor navigation, but to stand, with respect to Europe precisely on the footing of China. We should thus avoid wars, and all our citizens would be husbandmen.[40]

Repelled by the idea of America becoming a manufacturing nation, Jefferson believed farming, husbandry, and planting superior to all other ways of life. In a celebrated passage he had declared:

> Those who labor in the earth are the chosen people of God, if ever he had a chosen people, whose breasts he has made his peculiar deposit for substantial and genuine virtue. It is the focus in which he keeps alive that sacred fire, which otherwise might escape from the face of the earth. Corruption of morals in the mass of cultivators is a phaenomenon of which no age nor nation has furnished an example. . . . While we have land to labour then, let us never wish to see our citizens occupied at a workbench, or twirling a distaff. . . . For the general operations of manufacture, let our work-shops remain in Europe. . . . The mobs of great cities add just so much to the support of pure government, as sores do to the strength of the human body.[41]

Only it was not Thomas Jefferson who was "laboring in the earth" of Virginia; it was the men and women whose ancestors had been brought over from Africa.

Congress Wins Control of Trade

As the delegates had been sent to Philadelphia to rewrite the Articles of Confederation, not to write a new constitution, what happened has been described as a coup d'état. Only the towering prestige of Franklin and Washington enabled the conspirators to succeed.

When the great work was done and the Constitution was sent to the states for ratification, all power to regulate trade had been stripped from the states and given to Congress — an extraordinary transfer of power when one reflects that the Revolution, still fresh in the mind of every patriot, had been ignited by British interference with America's trade. With just two sentences, the Founding Fathers had created something new in history, the world's largest free-trade zone, a common market of hundreds of thousands of square miles — for the benefit of Americans alone:

> No Tax or Duty shall be laid on Articles exported from any State.
>
> No State shall, without the Consent of the Congress, lay any Imposts or Duties on Imports or Exports.[42]

Mandating that Congress "shall regulate" foreign trade, the framers imposed the national obligation to protect this internal free market from predators; it was to be the privileged sanctuary of the American people. At Philadelphia, however, the states paid a historic price. As Washington wrote in his letter of transmittal to the Congress:

> It is obviously impracticable in the federal government of these states, to secure all rights of independent sovereignty to each, and yet provide for the interest and safety of all: Individuals entering into society, must give up a share of liberty to preserve the rest.[43]

SLAVERY — AND FREE TRADE

There is another reason why Washington shared Hamilton's nationalist vision: slavery. Hamilton was an outspoken foe of slavery, and Washington detested it, though he was a slave owner himself. All his life his conscience troubled him, and he sought ways to improve the lives of those in his custody. On taking command of the revolutionary forces, he was astonished to find free blacks in the New England army and soon ordered Rhode Island forces desegregated. Anticipating Confederate generals like Patrick Cleburne, Washington "reached the point of urging that, even in the Deep South, slaves be enlisted with the promise of freedom at the war's end."[44] Alone among Virginia's Founding Fathers, he decreed that on his and Martha's death, his slaves be set free.

Washington also knew that the agrarian republic of Jefferson's vision depended on slavery. Were slavery abolished, who would till the fields of Jefferson's Arcadia? But the system forming in the mind of Hamilton had no need for slaves. Hamilton envisioned an America that was not only an agrarian country but was also a mighty industrial nation that could stand alone in the world.

> Washington's repugnance to slavery was a major reason for his backing Hamilton's financial planning against Jeffersonian attacks. . . . The Hamiltonian system had no need for slavery. Washington felt that it was the Virginia institution that would have in the end to give way. "I clearly foresee," he told an English caller, "that nothing but the rooting out of slavery can perpetuate the existence of our union by consolidating it in a common bond of principle." To Randolph, he revealed a conclusion that tore at his most deeply seated habits and emotions. He stated that should the Union separate between North and South, "he had made up his mind to move and be of the northern."[45]

Washington and Hamilton, both soldiers, understood that to defend America's independence, we would have need of those "workshops" that Jefferson abhorred. How else could America guarantee the necessities of nationhood? Where else would the republic acquire the ships and guns to hold off the predator empires of Europe? Hamilton knew that disunity and weakness in the face of a Great Britain determined to reimpose its will had almost brought us to ruin. Having won its liberty dearly, America needed the means to defend itself in a world where empires looked with jealousy and hatred on the infant republic. To Hamilton, that meant a strong central government and a manufacturing base capable of sustaining the nation and supporting the army and navy needed to secure American independence in a hostile world.

TOWARD NATIONAL SELF-SUFFICIENCY

The first American nationalists had triumphed in Philadelphia. After the necessary states ratified the Constitution, Washington rode to New York to become president. Hamilton was sworn in as secretary of the treasury. And Madison, Speaker of the House, began to shepherd through the new Congress its first legislation, the Tariff Act of 1789. Said the Speaker:

> Sir, a national revenue must be obtained; but the system must be such a one, that, while it secures the object of revenue, it shall not be oppressive to our constituents: Happy it is for us, that such a system is within our power; for I apprehend that both these objects may be obtained from an impost on articles imported into the United States.[46]

On the thirteenth anniversary of the Declaration of Independence, the Tariff Act of 1789 became the second bill signed by Washington. Its stated purpose: "the encouragement and protection of manufactures." This was America's declaration of economic independence. Most imported goods were subject to a 5 percent ad valorem duty, i.e., they were taxed at 5 percent of their value. Some imported items carried specific taxes, like wine, ten cents a gallon, and boots, fifty cents a pair.[47]

"A free people . . . should promote such manufactories as tend to render them independent on others for essential, particularly military supplies," Washington declared in his first address to Congress.[48]

Two weeks after Washington signed the Tariff Act, Congress enacted the Tonnage Act, taxing all foreign shipping. The U.S. merchant marine was born. So, the nation's course was set for six generations.

Under mercantilism, the colonies had been subservient to the mother country. Under the American system, territories over the mountains were to be brought into the Union "on an equal footing with the original states" as soon as their populations justified doing so. Under mercantilism, the mother country had kept her colonies dependent upon her for manufactured goods. Under the American system, the states were to grow to depend on one another. Under mercantilism, the mother country had imposed duties on America's imports and taken the money back to England. Under the American system, the United States imposed tariffs on British imports, and American capital remained here, to develop the United States.

Architect of the Nation

A teenager when the Revolution broke out, Alexander Hamilton had risen to become aide-de-camp to Washington, a general, and an author of the *Federalist Papers*. When Robert Morris, the "financier of the Revolution," declined Washington's offer to become secretary of the treasury, he recommended Hamilton. It was a providential proposal.

Born to an unknown father and an immigrant with no ties to any one state, this veteran of Valley Forge and Yorktown was a born nationalist. Envied for his brilliance, disliked for his brashness, disparaged for his origins (Adams called him the "bastard brat of a Scotch pedlar"), Hamilton gave his love, loyalty, and eventually his life to his country.[49]

On December 5, 1791, Treasury Secretary Hamilton delivered his famous *Report on Manufactures*. The goal of U.S. trade policy was national self-sufficiency. America had to stand on its own. Calling for subsidies to build a web of turnpikes, roads, and canals and for tariffs to shelter the home market, Hamilton's report would become our blueprint of economic independence. In it he spoke of those necessities of nationhood for which Americans could not depend on foreign trade:

> The wealth . . . independence and security of a Country, appear to be materially connected with the prosperity of manufactures. Every nation . . . ought to endeavour to possess within itself all the essentials of national supply. These comprise the means of *Subsistence habitation clothing* and *defence*.[50]

Of that report, future senator Arthur Vandenberg would write in his 1921 tribute, *The Greatest American*, that it "remains to this day the most lucid and convincing and complete defense of a protective tariff system which has ever been given to the American people."[51]

This was the Washington-Hamilton plan to "create a more perfect union": tie the seacoast to the West with bonds of commerce. Use tariffs to favor U.S. manufacturers and raise the revenue to pay off the war debt. Establish public credit. Institute a policy of "internal improvements" — roads, canals, bridges, turnpikes — to bind the states together into a nation.

Protectionism, then, is not some alien dogma. It is America's own invention, the defense perimeter of the world's greatest free-trade zone, an integral element of the American free-market system, and an indispensable contributor to national prosperity. Protectionism was MADE IN THE USA. As we shall see, it is free trade that is the foreign import.

"Too Long Subject to British Prejudice"

On April 30, 1789, John Adams escorted Washington out onto the second-story portico of Federal Hall at Broad and Wall Streets in New York. A thunderous roar rose from a crowd that stretched up both avenues as far as the eye could see. "Never has [a] sovereign reigned more completely in the hearts of his subjects than did Washington in those of his fellow-citizens," the French minister marveled. "He has the soul, look and figure of a hero united in him."[52]

Washington put his right hand on the chest of his brown broadcloth suit and bowed. A moment later, he put the same hand on a leather-bound Bible and took the oath as president of the United States. At the crowning moment of American independence, George Washington finally had a suit that fit! It had been tailored at Mount Vernon of cloth that Washington had taken special care to order from a mill in Hartford. "This apparel," writes Douglas Southall Freeman, "was to advertise American industry; it was, also, in a homely way to proclaim American liberty since the device on the buttons was that of a wing-spread eagle."[53] In January of 1789 Washington had written to Lafayette:

> I have been writing to our friend Genl. Knox this day, to procure me homespun broad cloth, of the Hartford fabric, to make a suit of cloaths for myself. I hope it will not be a great while, before it will be unfashionable for a gentleman to appear in any other dress. Indeed we have already been too long subject to British prejudices. I use no porter or cheese in my family, but such as is made in America.[54]

In seeking timely delivery of the cloth, one of the commissaries of Washington's army, Colonel Jeremiah Wadsworth, wrote that it was being purchased in the "hope it will be worn by one whose example will be worth more than any other encouragement that can be given to our infant Manufactures."[55] Washington would set the style and fashion for all Americans, that of buying American. It was what the old hero had in mind.

The gesture succeeded splendidly. The following morning the *New York Journal* reported: "The President . . . appeared dressed in a complete suit of homespun clothes, but the cloth was of so fine a fabric and so handsomely finished that it was universally mistaken for a foreign manufactured cloth."[56] The Dutch representative wrote his government: "His Excellency was dressed in plain brown cloths which had been presented to him by the mill at Hartford, Connecticut."[57] On the day he became the first president of the United States, Washington was showing his fellow Americans how to put America first.

Chapter 8

JEFFERSON TO JACKSON

*Our commerce on the ocean . . . must be paid
for by frequent war.*[1]

— Thomas Jefferson
LETTER TO JOHN JAY, 1785

*Protection . . . of our own labor against the
cheaper, ill-paid, half-fed, and pauper labor
of Europe, is, in my opinion, a duty which
the country owes to its own citizens.*[2]

— Daniel Webster

Cheered by the success of the Tariff Act of 1789, Washington and Hamilton raised tariffs again in 1790. Revenue poured in. The war debt was being discharged, the credit of the republic was getting established. America had begun her long drive to self-sufficiency. By 1803, when Napoleon offered to sell Louisiana for $15 million, President Jefferson had $5 million in the Treasury left over from the $12.4 million in tariff revenue of the previous year. He seized the offer. That Bonaparte had no right to sell Louisiana, and Jefferson no authority to buy it, seemed not to matter to either. Said Napoleon, This accession of territory affirms forever the power of the United States; I have given England a rival that "sooner or later will humble her pride."[3] Two weeks after closing the sale, Napoleon launched a war against England that would last until the eagle was chained to the rock of Saint Helena in the Atlantic.

JEFFERSON'S UNILATERAL DISARMAMENT

During the Napoleonic Wars, the United States' problem was a familiar one to twentieth-century Americans. The nation had declared its neutrality but did not maintain the naval power to guarantee its neutral rights. Despite the splendid showing of American warships in the Revolution, the "pure Republicans" of Jefferson's party, such as John Randolph, believed a navy to be the natural enemy of liberty; Jefferson himself believed in a policy not far distant from unilateral disarmament. On his taking office,

> the army was reduced by a "chaste reformation," as Jefferson called it, from about 3500 to 2500 men. . . . During the election and before, the Republican [Jeffersonian] press had viciously attacked the navy as a sink of waste and corruption, an English imitation, and the like. Jefferson, who knew nothing about ships, shared these feelings to some extent. An act of the last Federalist Congress allowed the President to reduce the respectable navy that had been built up . . . to thirteen frigates; and Jefferson not only did that, selling the rest of the navy for merchantmen, but stopped all new construction, discharged all naval contractors, and had a majority of the frigates that were retained hauled out to save the expense of pay and rations. Naturally, they went to pieces; wooden ships could not be "put up in mothballs" like modern steel warships.[4]

"I believe that gunboats are the only *water* defense which can be useful to us," Jefferson had written, "and protect us from the ruinous folly of a navy."[5] Federalists hooted at his naïveté and his lilliputian fleet. In a world at war, the brilliant intellectual who was America's president had chosen to defend her peace and honor by leaving her naked to attack while trading vigorously with both belligerents.

"I Had Only to Open My Hand"

With the U.S. Navy rotting in dry dock, American merchants began shipping with abandon to England and to Bonaparte's empire. The British merchants whose markets we were merrily pirating were enraged. Even more so were British patriots whose countrymen were dying. In England, Americans were looked on as the avaricious collaborators of a criminal regime.

Desperate for seamen to replace crews lost in battle or to desertion, His Majesty's navy began boarding U.S. merchant ships and seizing "British subjects" for impressment into service. Eight to ten thousand Americans were eventually kidnapped in this way. The Republic fumed, but the practice continued. On June 22, 1807, the British went too far. The fifty-gun *Leopard* maneuvered alongside the U.S. frigate *Chesapeake* off Hampton Roads, and its captain demanded to send a party aboard to search for British nationals. The American captain refused. *Leopard* opened fire, pouring broadside after broadside into the unprepared *Chesapeake*, killing three Americans and wounding eighteen before the U.S. ship struck its colors. The British boarded; four sailors were taken off. When the crippled, battered frigate limped back into port, there was a clamor for war.[6] "Never since the battle of Lexington," Jefferson wrote, "have I seen this country in such a state of exasperation as at present, and even that did not produce such unanimity. I had only to open my hand and let havoc loose."[7]

Reluctant to go to war against the world's mightiest naval power, Jefferson persuaded Congress to pass the Embargo Act of 1807. No U.S. ship could carry cargo to Europe. To punish Britain and France, America had declared a blockade on herself. Jefferson called his policy "peaceable coercion"; as he explained in a letter to George Logan,

> our commerce is so valuable to them that they will be glad to purchase it when the only price we ask is to do us justice. I believe we have in our

own hands the means of peaceable coercion; and that the moment they see our government so united as that they can make use of it, they will for their own interest be disposed to do us justice.[8]

"Peaceable coercion" proved a colossal bust. The British continued to kidnap American sailors while the Embargo Act ravaged the U.S. export trade, which fell from $48 million in 1807 to $9 million in 1808. Tariff revenue fell by more than half.[9] New England merchants began talking secession, and smuggling from U.S. ports and through Canada soared. So rampant was the defiance of Jefferson's embargo that

> when Napoleon seized Spain, in 1808, and put his brother Joseph on its throne, he also seized 250 American vessels and their cargoes in Spanish ports. When the U.S. ambassador demanded an explanation, Napoleon calmly replied . . . that he was only helping to enforce the Embargo Act.[10]

Before he left office in 1809, Jefferson's Embargo Act was repealed and replaced by the Nonintercourse Act, which prohibited U.S. ships from trade only with Britain and France. Jefferson's embargo, however, had produced an immensely beneficial result. It drove capital out of shipping and into manufacturing, spurring U.S. industrial development, especially in New England. Cut off from Europe, Americans turned inward and began to use their native ingenuity and natural resources. Unwittingly, Jefferson had taken America far toward realizing the Washington-Hamilton vision of a self-sufficient republic.

Under James Madison, U.S.-British relations worsened. The British despised "Little Jemmy," five feet two inches tall in his stocking feet, and believed (with justification) that he had swindled their Spanish ally out of West Florida. From Canada the British began to arm the Indians committing atrocities against pioneers in the Ohio Valley. American rage grew. With the arrival of the "coonskin Congressmen" from the West in 1811 and the election of Henry Clay as

Speaker of the House, the "war hawks" got their wish. In June 1812 the United States declared war on Great Britain; a principal cause of this war, too, had been interference with U.S. trade.

The War of 1812 was, as the Duke of Wellington said of Waterloo, a "damn near-run thing" for the United States. Royal warships swept our commerce from the seas; a British army invaded Washington and burned the Capitol and White House. Parliament planned to cut the United States in half at the Mississippi and effect the secession of New England, a hotbed of antiwar and Federalist sentiment. Napoleon's sudden return from Elba, however, concentrated British minds wonderfully — and elsewhere — and elicited a just peace to the United States. Then Andrew Jackson's stunning victory over a veteran British army at New Orleans restored American honor. As Bismarck would observe, Divine Providence seemed to be looking out with special care for idiots, drunks, and the United States of America.

THE FREE TRADERS SEE THE LIGHT

These perilous years changed forever the minds of two presidents about free trade. Jefferson had been a romantic. In 1774 he had called "free trade with all parts of the world" a "natural right." To John Adams he had written, "I think all the *world would gain* by *setting commerce* at perfect *liberty.*"[11] Adams agreed. Even with America under British blockade in 1777, he had written a friend: "I am against all shackles upon Trade. Let the Spirit of the People have its own way."[12]

Neither Jefferson nor Adams believed this any longer. Dependence on trade had left the nation dangerously vulnerable to great naval powers and their blockades and had been high among the reasons the United States was forced to fight. Adams and Jefferson, revolutionaries in 1776, rivals a generation later, were now venerable statesmen and wiser men. In an 1815 letter to French economist Jean-Baptiste Say, Jefferson argued passionately for protectionism — to guarantee America's independence:

> The prohibiting duties we lay on all articles of foreign manufacture which prudence requires us to establish at home, with the patriotic determination of every good citizen to use no foreign article which can be made within ourselves, without regard to difference of price, secures us against a relapse into foreign dependency.[13]

Now the echo of his old rival Hamilton, Jefferson was enraged by those dredging up his thirty-year-old quotations. In a blazing January 9, 1816, letter to Benjamin Austin, Jefferson conceded that he had once supported free trade. But "how are circumstances changed!" Citing abuses by Britain and France, the Sage of Monticello thundered:

> He . . . who is now against domestic manufacture, must be for reducing us either to dependence on that foreign nation, or to be clothed in skins, and to live like wild beasts in dens and caverns. I am not one of these; *experience has now taught me that manufactures are now as necessary to our independence as to our comfort;* and if those who quote me as of a different opinion, will keep pace with me in purchasing nothing foreign where an equivalent of domestic fabric can be obtained, without regard to difference of price, it will not be our fault if we do not soon have a supply at home equal to our demand, and wrest that weapon of distress from the hand which has wielded it.[14] (Emphasis added.)

When critics cited his former notions about an agrarian republic that left manufacturing to Europe, Jefferson denounced them for using his *Notes on the State of Virginia* "as a stalking horse, to cover their disloyal propensities to keep us in eternal vassalage to a foreign and unfriendly people."[15] He had come to believe that free trade and a reliance on Europe for manufactured goods could no longer be reconciled with American patriotism.

Thomas Jefferson had become an economic nationalist.

THE TARIFF ACT OF 1816

With Europe embroiled in the Napoleonic Wars, America was free to extend its reach across the mountains, to thicken the bonds of unity, and to grow in industrial might. During Jefferson's embargo and Madison's war, U.S. trade with Europe had shrunk to one-tenth of what it had been in 1807. Forced to fall back on its own ingenuity, industry, and resources, America had become a self-reliant nation.[16]

Between 1809 and 1815, the number of cotton spindles in the United States rose from 31,000 to 500,000. Production of woolen goods rose from $4 million to $20 million. In 1807 four new factories were established in all of New York, New Jersey, and New England; in 1815, 128 were started.[17] The Embargo Act of 1807 and the War of 1812 proved to be among the most fortuitous events in American economic history.

To British manufacturers, however, a newly industrialized America was a mortal threat. Not only did they face the permanent loss of their American market, they would now have to compete with U.S. goods in other markets. To crush the American challenge, British manufacturers, merchants, and politicians plotted to flood America with goods and drown the infant industries. The future Lord Brougham was quite candid about the ends of British policy:

> It was well worth while to incur a loss upon the first exportation, in order by the glut, to stifle in the cradle, those rising manufactures in the United States, which the war had forced into existence, contrary to the natural course of things.[18]

The British, writes trade historian William J. Gill, "openly dumped their goods on the American market at a loss in order to capture our commerce, much as the Japanese, Koreans, and even the Europeans and English are doing today."[19]

Rabbeno in his *America Commercial Policy* wrote that "The English man-ufacturers . . . rushed as if to the attack of a fortress." And like the walls of Jericho, and all the great ports of the United States in recent times, the walls came tumbling down. Imports, valued at less than $13 million in 1814, soared to $147 million two years later.[20]

John Adams was stunned by the activity in Boston Harbor. As he lamented in an 1819 letter to William E. Richmond, he felt that the Republic had failed to learn the lesson he himself had learned:

I am old enough to remember the war of 1745, and its end; the war of 1755, and its close; the war of 1775, and its termination; the war of 1812, and its pacification. Every one of these wars has been followed by a general distress; embarrassment on commerce, destruction of manu-factures, fall of the price of produce and of lands, similar to those we feel at the present day, and all produced by the same causes. I have wondered that so much experience has not taught us more caution. The British merchants and manufacturers, immediately after the peace, disgorged upon us all their stores of merchandise and manufactures, not only without profit, but at certain loss for a time, with the express purpose of annihilating all our manufacturers, and ruining all our manufactories.[21]

But Madison, who had also had a youthful flirtation with free trade, knew how to deal with the British invasion. As Speaker of the House, he had steered to passage the Tariff Act of 1789, and he had seen how tariffs had started the Republic on the road to economic independence. To halt British dumping, Madison adopted the Fed-eralist policy of economic nationalism, with a 25 percent tariff on cotton and woolen goods, and a 30 percent tariff on iron products. The Tariff Act of 1816 was America's first purely protectionist tar-iff. Led by Henry Clay, the House voted to approve, 88–54. Ironi-cally, "no man labored harder and did more effective service in securing its passage" than the South Carolinian who had come to Congress with Clay as a twenty-nine-year-old war hawk, John C. Calhoun. Our liberty and the union, declared Calhoun, depend on the principle of protectionism. "Neither agriculture, manufactures, nor commerce, taken separately, is the cause of wealth; it flows from the three combined and cannot exist without each."[22] Under Calhoun's leadership, the South provided twenty-three "yes" votes for the Tariff of 1816.

This final act of statesmanship by the father of the U.S. Constitution stopped the British invasion cold. How effective was Madison's Tariff of 1816? How beneficial was it for America to be cut off from Europe by Jefferson's embargo and Madison's war? Consider how the production of cotton cloth grew and contracted in those crucial years:

Year	Yards of Cloth Produced (in Thousands)
1805	46
1807	84
1810	648
1815	2,358
1816	840
1820	13,874
1830	141,616
1840	323,000
1860	857,225

Production rose almost 800 percent in the three years after the Embargo Act of 1807 and nearly quadrupled again in the next five. But note how Great Britain almost killed the U.S. industry after peace was signed in December of 1814, by flooding the American market. The need for, and effect of, Madison's tariff is seen here dramatically. American production — cut two-thirds by British dumping in 1816 — grew an astonishing 1,650 percent within four years of Madison's tariff becoming law.[23]

Clay and Calhoun were now the powers on Capitol Hill; and they labored together with a common vision. As historians Samuel Eliot Morison and Henry Steele Commager write:

Henry Clay and John C. Calhoun were the nationalist leaders in Congress at this period. Both feared the growing particularism of the sections. Like Hamilton, they could imagine no stronger binding force than self-interest; and their policy was but a broader version of his reports on public credit and manufactures. Their formula, which Clay christened the "American System," was protection and internal improvements: a protective tariff for the manufacturers, a home market and better transportation for the farmers. "We are greatly and rapidly — I was about to say fearfully — growing," said Calhoun in 1817. "This is our pride and our danger; our weakness and our strength. . . . Let us, then, bind the Republic together with a perfect system of roads and canals." Protection "would make the parts adhere more closely. . . . It would form a new and most powerful cement."[24]

But the congressional giants now had a new rival. The hero of New Orleans had come to understand that the preservation of liberty required more than brave soldiers and brilliant captains. Urging a protective tariff to secure the nation's defense and independence, Andrew Jackson declared that

> the experience of the late war ought to teach us a lesson; and one never to be forgotten. If our liberty and republican form of government, procured for us by our revolutionary fathers, are worth the blood and treasure at which they were obtained, it surely is our duty to protect and defend them.[25]

THE SOUTH DRIFTS APART

The "Era of Good Feelings" did not survive the presidency of James Monroe. By 1824 the tariff question was back and boiling, no longer the common ground it had been in 1816 but a cause of deepening sectional conflict that would push the nation as close to breakup as it would come before 1860. Clay, now America's champion of economic nationalism, declared:

Poverty befalls any nation that neglects and abandons the care of its own industry, leaving it exposed to the action of foreign powers — there is a remedy and that consists in — adopting a Genuine American System accomplished by the establishment of a tariff — with the view of promoting American industry — the cause is the cause of the country, and it must and it will prevail.[26]

By now, however, the South had concluded that Clay's "Genuine American System" was the Genuine Northern System. Tariffs protected Northern manufacturers, who produced most of the nation's goods, and the U.S. government used the tariff revenue to build the turnpikes and canals that carried Northern products south and west. The South manufactured next to nothing. It grew cotton, tobacco, and rice that were sold to Europe to buy British manufactures. Rising tariffs raised the price of those manufactures. The South had begun to see itself in relation to the North as the colonies had in relation to Great Britain, as dependencies whose interests were ignored at the seat of power. Historian Burton J. Hendrick writes that

> the truth is that the South was still economically part of the British empire, not of the United States. The way in which the North was using its power to pass tariff acts that forced Southern planters to purchase manufactures from the Yankees, to whom they sold practically nothing, instead of acquiring goods at much lower prices from the English, to whom they sold the whole output of their plantations, seemed to Southerners little less than tyranny.[27]

Calhoun had by now departed the nationalist camp. Historians disagree as to when he left. He had once been a fervent nationalist, describing the War of 1812 as a "second war for independence" and "disunion" as a "new and terrible danger [that] . . . comprehends almost the sum of our political dangers."[28] Hamilton's son James quotes Calhoun as confiding the following to him as late as 1824:

> Sir, I have a clear conviction, after much reflection and an entire knowledge and familiarity with the history of our country and the working of

our government, that his [Hamilton's] policy as developed by the measures of Washington's administration, is the only true policy for the country.[29]

But Calhoun's public stand had radically changed. Clay might yet speak of a high tariff as the "cause of the country [that] . . . must and shall prevail"; Calhoun spoke now for the South. Detractors contend that with the rise of Jackson, Calhoun knew that his presidential ambitions were dead and turned his bitterness and frustration on America, "seeking to rend limb by limb the Union which had denied him its greatest honor."[30]

This is too partisan and savage. Southern grievances over the tariff were valid, and Calhoun had a duty to speak for his people. The tragedy of these years was that men ceased to see themselves as Americans and more and more saw themselves as belonging to distinct and separate civilizations. Not unlike our own time, beneath a superficial prosperity, bonds of nationhood and brotherhood were disintegrating.

Many Southerners also remained faithful to the agrarian tradition of the young Jefferson. They recoiled at industrializing America. Echoing poet William Blake ("And was Jerusalem builded here / Among those dark satanic mills?"), John Randolph pronounced manufacturing an unfit calling for America, suited only for such as the British Isles:

> It is in such a climate only that the human animal can bear, without extirpation, the corrupted air, the noisome exhalations, the incessant labor of these accursed manufactories. Yes, sir, accursed, for I say it is an accursed thing. We should have the yellow fever from June to January, and January to June. The climate of this country alone, were there no other natural obstacles to it, says aloud — You shall not manufacture.[31]

Randolph is the beau ideal of numerous conservatives. Yet, in his rhetoric one hears echoes of environmentalism, even of the Green Parties of Europe. His is one conservative tradition, but there was another — to be found in the passionate patriotism of Andrew Jackson, a nationalist who believed with Washington that the Republic's survival called for economic independence. And it was to Old Hickory, now emerging as a candidate for president, that the nation was listening, not to Randolph. Declared Jackson,

> we have been too long subject to the policy of the British merchants. We need to become more *Americanized*, and instead of feeding the paupers and laborers of Europe . . . feed our own, or in a short time . . . we shall all be rendered paupers ourselves. It is my opinion . . . that a careful and judicious tariff is much wanted.[32]

The nationalists prevailed, and the tariff bill of 1824 became law. In the bitterly contested election that year, Jackson won a plurality of popular and electoral votes but was denied the presidency when Henry Clay threw his support in the House to John Quincy Adams.

Jackson was again a candidate in 1828, and tariffs were again about to be raised. Calhoun now made one of the great blunders of a career that contained too many. He sought to make the new tariff bill intolerable to Northern manufacturers by raising tariffs on their raw materials, expecting them to reject the entire measure. The Northerners swallowed it whole. "Its enemies spiced it with whatever they thought would render it distasteful," said Daniel Webster, "its friends took it, drugged as it was."[33]

The Tariff Act of 1828 covered 92 percent of U.S. imports, with an average tariff of 62 percent! America had seen nothing like it. To its enemies it was the "Tariff of Abominations." To South Carolina it was a declaration of economic war. Said one South Carolina pamphleteer, "It is time to calculate the value of the Union."[34]

NULLIFICATION

Though defeated, Calhoun was not finished. In an essay he secretly penned in 1828, the "South Carolina Exposition," he breathed new life into an old doctrine, the doctrine of "nullification" — the assertion of a state's right to declare null and void an act of Congress that imperiled that state's vital interests. Calhoun's case was compelling. The thirteen states, he wrote, not the people, ratified the Constitution, creating the United States. Can a creation be greater than its creators? And if the states were sovereign in 1789, were they not sovereign in 1828? Sovereign states have a moral right to reject acts that threaten their survival!

In asserting a state's right to nullify federal law, Calhoun had invoked the Kentucky and Virginia Resolves. And who were their authors? None other than Thomas Jefferson and James Madison, who had written them to challenge the alien and sedition laws that Federalist judges were using to lock up Jeffersonian journalists critical of President John Adams. Writes Madison biographer Robert Ruthland:

> For years Jefferson's tracks were so well covered it was not public knowledge that he goaded Madison into writing the Virginia Resolutions of 1798 and wrote the Kentucky version himself. In these resolutions, the two Republican chieftains convinced followers that an unconstitutional law could be upset by the collective action of the states. The notion that a state legislature could declare an act of Congress unconstitutional was original but loaded with political gunpowder.[35]

It was this gunpowder that Calhoun was now packing into the cannons of nullification in South Carolina.

Jeffersonians for years had been reading the resolves at rallies as the "true principles of the Democratic Party." Now they were being deployed by Calhoun against a tariff that had to be collected by President Andrew Jackson. Madison was furious to find himself charged with paternity of this "preposterous and anarchical pretension" for which "there is not a shadow of countenance in the Constitution."[36] But one historian would not let the Sage of Montpelier off so easily: "The father of the Constitution was also one of the men who sowed the seeds of secession and civil war."[37]

"OUR UNION — IT MUST BE PRESERVED!"

Calhoun, however, counseled South Carolinians not to invoke nullification except as a last resort. The state's hopes for tariff relief were high. Calhoun had just been elected vice president under Jackson, himself a native son.

But tariff reform did not come. Though Jackson hated Clay for casting his lot with Adams in the election of 1824, he agreed with Clay that a protective tariff was critical. "A careful Tariff is much wanted to pay our national debt, and afford us the means of that defense within ourselves on which the safety and liberty of the country depend," he had concluded, with the War of 1812 fresh in his mind.[38] And so the issue simmered.

On April 13, 1830, at the annual dinner in celebration of the birth of Jefferson, it came to a climax. Smoldering through dozens of Southern toasts hailing the Kentucky and Virginia Resolves, equating nullification with Jeffersonian orthodoxy, the president rose, fixed his glare directly on his vice president, raised his glass, and declared, "Our Federal Union — it must be preserved!"[39] Calhoun was stunned. "His hand trembling so that a little of the yellow wine trickled down the side of the tumbler," Calhoun rose and drank.[40] Minutes passed. Other toasts were made. Then Calhoun rose, turned to the president, raised his glass, and declared, "The Union — next to our liberty, the most dear!"[41] The battle was joined.

At this explosive moment Jackson was sent a letter concerning his vice president. Calhoun had insisted that he was Jackson's strongest defender in the Cabinet in 1818, when others were demanding Jackson's scalp, after Old Hickory had rampaged through Spanish East Florida and executed two British agents, Alexander Arbuthnot and Robert Ambrister. The letter alleged that Calhoun, as secretary of war, had been Jackson's secret enemy and had pushed for his arrest and trial. Jackson was sickened by the letter: "It smelled so much of deception that my hair stood on end for an hour."[42] Jackson sent the letter with a note to his vice president, demanding an explanation. Calhoun's answer failed to satisfy. "This is full evidence of the duplicity and insincerity of the man," said Jackson.[43] Vice President Calhoun now found himself with a mortal enemy in the president of the United States.

So long as South Carolina did not act to nullify the tariff law, no action was required of Jackson. Meanwhile, the Treasury was filling up with customs duties, the national debt was being paid off, a surplus was about to appear. Tariff opponents had a fresh argument: all this revenue was not needed. But Clay's 1832 tariff bill, while eliminating duties on goods and raw materials America did not produce, kept tariffs high on imports that competed with U.S. manufactures.

In South Carolina patience ran out. On November 24, 1832, a convention called by the state legislature passed the Ordinance of Nullification, declaring the tariff laws of 1828 and 1832 to be "unauthorized by the Constitution . . . null, void, and no law, nor binding upon this State, its officers, or citizens."[44] The state ordered federal agents to cease collecting customs duties after February 1. Should the U.S. government use force, the convention declared, South Carolina would immediately secede. Calhoun rode north to resign the vice presidency.

It was one of the most dramatic moments in American history.

Jackson answered South Carolina's declaration with one of his own:

> I consider, then, the power to annul a law of the United States, assumed by one State, incompatible with the existence of the Union, contradicted expressly by the letter of the Constitution, unauthorized by its spirit, inconsistent with every principle on which it was founded, and destructive of the great object for which it was formed.[45]

Beware of your leaders! Jackson warned the South Carolinians: "Their object is *disunion;* be not deceived by names. *Disunion* by armed force is *Treason*."[46] A right to secede, said Jackson, did not exist: "To say that any State may at pleasure secede from the Union is to say that the United States is not a nation."[47] Jackson made a final appeal to the "fellow citizens of my native State" to cease their acts of disunion, or face the "dreadful consequences."[48] On Christmas Day, he wrote to (now) Vice President–elect Martin Van Buren that he would issue a proclamation to capture the

> leaders for rebellion and treason . . . regardless of the force that surrounds them, deliver them into the hands of the judicial authority of the United States and let it decide whether they have committed rebellion or treason against the U. States.[49]

The president ordered Forts Moultrie and Sumter reinforced and sent Coast Guard cutters south to collect the duties. South Carolina put out a call for volunteers.

Old Hickory Threatens a Hanging

Andrew Jackson was deadly serious. Earlier he had given a South Carolina congressman a warning to take home: "Tell [the Nullifiers] from me that they can talk and write resolutions and print threats to their hearts' content. But if one drop of blood be shed there in defiance of the laws of the United States, I will hang the first man of them I can get my hands on to the first tree I can find!"[50] Missouri's Thomas Hart Benton overheard South Carolina's Robert Hayne express doubt that the president would go that far. Senator Benton pulled his old colleague aside, saying,

> "Well, before he invaded Florida on his own hook, few people could have believed that he would hang Arbuthnot and shoot Ambrister — also on his own authority — could they? I tell you, Hayne, when Jackson begins to talk about hanging, they can begin to look out for ropes![51]

Benton knew his man. In Nashville years earlier, Old Hickory had come after Benton with a horsewhip, shouting, "Now, defend yourself, you damned rascal!" Benton's brother had shot Jackson twice, nearly killing him. Yet, within weeks Jackson was back leading his troops in battle against marauding Creek Indians.[52]

At this moment of confrontation and deadlock, Clay, who would come to be known as the Great Compromiser, stepped in and urged the chairman of the Committee on Ways and Means to write a new bill lowering tariff rates. "I want harmony," said Clay. "I wish to see the restoration of those ties which have carried us triumphantly through two wars. I delight not in this perpetual turmoil. Let us have peace, and become once more united as a band of brothers."[53] South Carolina responded by suspending nullification of the tariff acts until the new bill became law.

On March 2, 1833, Jackson signed two bills. The first lowered tariff rates over a ten-year period until they reached 20 percent ad valorem. Anything above 20 percent was thought to be protectionist. The second, the Force Act, gave the president authority to use the army and navy to collect the customs duties. "Old Hickory winced as he signed the tariff bill."[54]

The South Carolinians then met to repeal the nullification of the tariffs but voted to nullify the Force Act, which was now not needed.

The threat of secession and war had brushed by the nation and passed on. Both sides declared victory, with Jackson telling friends of his bitter disappointment that the confrontation had ended before he had a chance to deal with the traitors: "I thought I would have to hang some of them and I would have done it."[55] Kentucky congressman Robert Letcher returned from a White House visit to report that the president had been more specific, saying, "If one more step was taken he would try Calhoun for treason and, if convicted, hang him as high as Haman."[56] Awakened in the dead of night to be told of Jackson's ruminations on his hanging, Calhoun listened intently, "drinking in every word . . . pale as death and . . . trembling like an aspen leaf."[57]

America was ceasing to be Henry Clay's "band of brothers."

* * *

Half a century after the battle over the Tariff of Abominations, Senator John Logan wrote in *The Great Conspiracy* of what he always believed was a monstrous plot to use free trade to destroy the Union:

> After-events proved conclusively that the enactment of this Compromise Tariff was a terrible blunder, if not a crime. Jackson had fully intended to hang Calhoun and his nullifying coadjutors if they persisted in their Treason. He knew that they had only seized upon the Tariff laws as a pretext with which to justify Disunion, and prophecied that "the next will be the Slavery or Negro question." Jackson's forecast was correct. Free Trade, Slavery and Secession were from that time forward sworn allies; and the ruin wrought to our industries by the disasters of 1840, plainly traceable to that Compromise Tariff measure of 1833, was only to be supplemented by much greater ruin and disasters caused by the Free Trade Tariff of 1846 — and to be followed by the armed Rebellion of the Free Trade and Pro-Slavery States of the South in 1861, in a mad attempt to destroy the Union.[58]

To Logan, free trade was the devil's plan to murder the Union; and free trade and slavery were twins. Such was the passion and intensity with which men viewed a tariff issue that had brought the Republic to the precipice of dissolution and war. Nor would it die. For America's great economic nationalist, Henry Clay, who produced the Compromise Tariff of 1833, had found an admirer who thought him the greatest man of the age.

The disciple's name was Abraham Lincoln.

Looking back on this era, we can see lessons for our own time. Washington and Hamilton after the Revolution, and Madison after the War of 1812, confronted similar challenges and responded in similar ways. Discerning British mercantilist plots to crush America's infant industries, recapture control of her trade, and reestablish a dependency on the mother country, they imposed tariffs — temporary sacrifices on the part of consumers, for the long-term independence of the nation. This was enlightened nationalism.

Such enlightened nationalism is desperately needed today.

For just as Japan became a manufacturing power by denying us fair access to its home market, while invading and capturing a huge slice of our market, China and the nations of Asia and Latin America are planning similar assaults, as we shall see.

By the end of the Jacksonian era, however, new attitudes were arising. The "America first" spirit of Washington and Madison — and the spirit of compromise of Clay, who would yield on his beloved tariff rather than see the nation come apart — was fading away. Both the industrial North and agrarian free-trade South were beginning to put regional interests ahead of the national interest. If there is a lesson central to this book, it is this: The economy is *not* the country; and the country comes first. When this principle has been forgotten, America has torn itself apart, as it seems about to do today, in the name of a free-trade ideology that has the leadership of both parties in its grip.

Chapter 9

THE GREAT PROTECTIONIST

"An Old Henry Clay Tariff Whig"

Abandonment of the protective policy by the American Government must result in the increase of both useless labour, and idleness; and so, in pro[por]tion must produce want and ruin among our people.[1]

— Abraham Lincoln, 1847

There are two potential causes of revolution in the United States: slavery and the high protective tariff.[2]

— Frédéric Bastiat, 1851

In 1845 there came the presidency of James K. Polk. The dark horse of the Baltimore convention had won the endorsement of Andrew Jackson and his party on one issue: immediate annexation of Texas. This most underrated of presidents believed America's destiny was to become a continent-wide nation stretching to the Pacific. In one term, Polk brought it about, enlarging the country by as much territory as had Jefferson when he purchased Louisiana. "Jimmy" Polk took the Southwest and California as war booty from Mexico, compromised with Britain on the boundary of the Oregon Territory, and, his mission complete, went home and was dead in 100 days. "Young Hickory" was the personification of Manifest Destiny, and no public figure was more hostile than a rising young Whig lawyer in Illinois.

"Give Us a Protective Tariff"

Abe Lincoln had been denied his party's nomination for Congress in 1844, but his campaigning was the highlight of the Whig effort in Illinois. Lincoln, as scholar Gabor S. Boritt explains, concentrated his fire on a single issue: the tariff.

> He had been a high tariffite from the beginning, but only the 1842 repeal of the Compromise Tariff of 1833 opened a practical way for renewed discussion. In 1842 he may have composed and certainly signed a petition that contained the gist of his party's view on the matter. . . . His 1843 statements argued that protection was an absolute necessity "to the prosperity of the American people." They also gave evidence that he had studied the tariff problem at some length.[3]

By the spring of 1844, the tariff was the dominant issue in Illinois, and an eyewitness describes how Lincoln "exerted himself powerfully" on behalf of Henry Clay's final try for the White House:

> The contest of that year in Illinois was mainly on the question of the tariff. . . . Mr. Lincoln, in these elaborate speeches, evinced a thorough mastery of the principles of political economy which underlie the tariff question, and presented arguments in favor of the protective policy with a power and conclusiveness rarely equalled, and at the same time in a manner so lucid and familiar and so well interspersed with the happy illustrations and apposite anecdotes as to seduce the delighted attention of his auditory.[4]

Carrying his campaign into Indiana near his childhood home, Lincoln, a kinsman remembered, gave an impassioned plea: "Give us a protective tariff, and we will have the greatest country on earth."[5]

By mid-year Illinois Democrats were being soundly trounced. They were sick of hearing of the tariff issue. But with the nomination of Polk, their fortunes were revived by a blazing new issue: Texas!

In calling for a return to high tariffs, Lincoln had been playing the nationalist card: higher tariffs would force British capitalists to finance the U.S. government. But Lincoln's nationalism was "inward-oriented," not the Manifest Destiny nationalism of the Jacksonians. The Democrats' shift threw him off balance. Lincoln muttered that the Polk platform was "nothing but Texas"; to him, this was a distraction from the real issues.

But with British diplomats maneuvering to prevent annexation and create a permanent Texas republic to block America's westward expansion, Democrats turned the tables and denounced Abe Lincoln as the leader of "a British anti-Texas junto." Lincoln's strongest jingoist argument, that Clay was the father of the American system of protection while Democrats were pushing the British system of free trade, was trumped.

Lincoln countered that the British were pouring money into the country to defeat Whigs who would protect U.S. industry. All fall he hammered the tariff issue; it "may have been a fatal mistake." For Texas and expansion were the issues of the hour, and Democrats were running away with them. On Election Day, a full third of Polk's popular majority came from Illinois. Lincoln ruefully remarked, "We got gloriously whipped."[6]

A Cobdenite in the Cabinet

Some Polk Democrats, like Treasury Secretary Robert J. Walker, disagreed with their old chief at the Hermitage. Walker was not opposed to tariffs, but he did object to *protective tariffs* in which rates were set so high that foreign goods were priced out of the U.S. market. Believing in his own version of the Laffer curve, Walker favored a *revenue tariff.* If tariffs were set too low, the government would receive little revenue. But if tariffs were set too high, the government would also get little revenue because few foreign products would enter the country. Robert Walker sought a golden mean, tariff rates that averaged about 23 percent.

Walker also had an ideological motive in opposing protective tariffs. He shared the belief of England's Richard Cobden that free trade was the panacea that would rescue mankind from the scourge of war. Cobden and John Bright had triumphed in England with the 1846 repeal of the Corn Laws, which heavily taxed imported grain to protect British agriculture.

While a belief in the redemptive power of trade had not captured the party of Jackson, it was putting down roots. As early as 1856, with the nomination of James Buchanan, the Democratic Party would go beyond Polk and Walker to proclaim its new faith: "The time has come for the people of the United States to declare themselves in favor of . . . progressive free trade throughout the world."[7]

Yes to Coffee, No to Cotton

Abe Lincoln believed none of this. He was no romantic but a hardheaded realist and economic nationalist in the tradition of Hamilton and Clay. As far back as 1832, he had laid his cards on the table. My politics, he said, are "short and sweet, like the old woman's dance. I am in favor of a national bank. I am in favor of the internal improvement system and a high protective tariff. These are my sentiments and political principles."[8]

Lincoln had been attracted to the Whig Party by the "Father of the American System." "Henry Clay is my beau ideal of a statesman, the man for whom I fought all my humble life," he confided late in life.[9] Lincoln had cast his first presidential vote in the Clay-Jackson race of 1832 for the gallant "Harry of the West."

Lincoln saw no intrinsic merit in trade. Trade should be maintained, he argued, "where it is *necessary*," discontinued "where it is not." He said yes to imported coffee, which Americans did not produce, no to imported cotton.[10] He also believed that tariffs were necessary to protect the high wages of American workers. If a farmer was able to buy cheaper supplies in Europe than in America, he said, it "would be owing to the fact that the price of labor is only one quarter as high there as here."[11] As Gabor Boritt writes:

> The roots of Lincoln's protectionism were divergent and deep. . . . Whether the Westerner's unionism drew him to economic nationalism or vice versa is a moot question. He gave his allegiance to the federalist faction of the American political spectrum early in his life. And the tariff "more than any other issue," asserted James G. Blaine, represented throughout the nineteenth century the "persistent line of division between . . . the party of State Rights and the party of National Supremacy."[12]

There was another reason Lincoln favored tariffs. To him, there were two sources of revenue: tariffs and income taxes. Whereas an income tax was a mandatory tax that all had to pay, a tariff was a discretionary tax. Those who did not buy foreign goods did not pay. And a tariff was a less costly and intrusive method of raising revenue. As Lincoln put it:

> The tariff is the cheaper System. . . . By the direct-tax system the land must be literally covered with assessors and collectors going forth like swarms of Egyptian locusts. By the tariff system the whole revenue is paid by the consumers of foreign goods, and those chiefly the luxuries, and not the necessaries, of life. By this system the man who contents himself to live upon the product of his own country pays nothing at all.[13]

Here, Lincoln exaggerates. If a tariff is to provide the revenue to run a government, even in the nineteenth century, it must apply to more than "luxuries." But doesn't Lincoln's phrase "the land covered with assessors and collectors going forth like swarms of Egyptian locusts" aptly describe our IRS, America's monument to the income tax?

*   *   *

After the Whigs nominated Lincoln for Congress in 1846, his only recorded campaign speech had the protective tariff as its "principal subject, with which he showed himself to be thoroughly acquainted."[14] As one Illinois newspaper of the time wrote:

> In a most logical, argumentative effort, [Lincoln] demonstrated the necessity of a discriminating tariff, and the excellence of that adopted by the Whig Congress of 1842; and also that the consumer does not usually pay the tariff, but the manufacturer and importer.[15]

After his victory and arrival in Congress, Lincoln went hard after Polk on two fronts: the Mexican War and the tariff. Surviving notes of Lincoln's, which he probably hoped to use in House debate, emphasize a point he would make again and again:

> But if duty amounting to full protection be levied upon an article which can be produced here with as little labour, as elsewhere, as iron, that article will ultimately, and at no distant day, in consequence of such duty, be sold to our people cheaper than before, at least by the amount of the cost of *carrying* it from abroad.[16]

These notes, on eleven foolscap half sheets, survive as Lincoln's most extensive consideration of the tariff issue. To Lincoln, protecting home manufactures, in the long run, produced lower prices. In his time, shipping expenses added 25–50 percent to the price of goods. Lincoln considered such costs "useless labour" if the articles could be manufactured in "as good quality, and sufficient quantity, with as little labour at the place of consumption."[17] Nor was Lincoln averse to populist rhetoric. In a campaign circular from his Whig committee, he is quoted as follows:

> Those whose pride, whose abundance of means, prompt them to spurn the manufactures of our own country, and to strut in British cloaks, and coats, and pantaloons, may have to pay a few cents more on the yard for the cloth that makes them. A terrible evil, truly, to the Illinois farmer,

who never wore, nor ever expects to wear, a single yard of British goods in his whole life.[18]

How high did Lincoln feel tariff rates should be? In Congress he declared his support for the Tariff Act of 1842, which had taken rates up to an average of 34.4 percent, but he opposed the Walker Tariff Act of 1846, which reduced them to 22.5 percent.

Walker and Polk prevailed, and Lincoln and his Whig allies failed to restore the 1842 rates. As Walker had predicted, imports surged at the lower tariff rate. Revenue grew, and budget surpluses appeared. The Whig position was fatally weakened. Why raise tariffs when running a surplus? Yet, Lincoln never recanted. Campaigning in 1848 for Zachary Taylor, he was disappointed that Old Rough and Ready ducked the issue. In 1852 he campaigned for another Mexican War hero, Winfield Scott. The *Peoria Weekly Republican* reported that on the tariff question, Lincoln favored the "American side," demanding to know why

> instead of sending a distance of 4,000 miles for our railroad iron, the immense iron beds of Missouri were not worked, affording a better article than that of English manufacture, and giving employment to American labor.[19]

There was, however, a sharp difference between Lincoln and the old Whigs. To Webster and Clay the tariff had been about independence and the security of the Union. Lincoln argued the tariff case almost exclusively on economic grounds. In those eleven foolscap sheets, not once did Lincoln mention the national interest. He had "developed a great propensity to see matters in terms of economic ingredients or interests. . . . This propensity came to loom large when he turned his attention from economics, first to slavery, and later to making war and peace with the South."[20]

By the 1850s the Whig Party was dying. Lincoln had moved on to the new Republican Party, which was silent on the tariff. Yet, reading more than two decades of Lincoln's arguments for protectionism, one finds in this self-educated man a richer, deeper understanding of the economics of tariffs and trade than may be found in almost any political leader today.

Pennsylvania: A Key to the White House

In 1856 John C. Frémont, an abolitionist and the first Republican to run for the presidency, lost to Buchanan in a narrow election. Sagacious Republicans realized that they must cut back on the abolitionist rhetoric and broaden their appeal. Editor Horace Greeley suggested how to do so in 1859:

> Now about the Presidency: I want to succeed this time, yet I *know* the country is not Anti-Slavery. It will only swallow a little Anti-Slavery in a great deal of sweetening. An Anti-Slavery man *per se* cannot be elected; but a Tariff, River and Harbor, Pacific Railroad, Free Homestead man *may* succeed *although* he is Anti-Slavery.[21]

Greeley was advocating a Hamiltonian policy: raise tariff rates to promote manufacturing, keep wages high, and pay for the roads, bridges, canals, and railroads that knit the nation together. Joseph Medill, editor of the *Chicago Tribune*, had found just the man to pull together the disparate elements of that coalition. In 1859 he hailed the failed Senate candidate Abe Lincoln as an "old Clay Whig [who] is right on the tariff and he is exactly right on all other issues. Is there any man who could suit Pennsylvania better?"[22] Medill's last point was crucial. Pennsylvania had the largest bloc of electoral votes after New York; its loss had cost Frémont the White House.

What was the key to Pennsylvania? In 1858 Republicans had discovered it. As Lincoln was losing to Stephen A. Douglas on the slavery issue, the People's Party of Pennsylvania inflicted a stunning defeat on the Democrats by advocating a high tariff to protect Pennsylvania's coal mines and steel mills. Republicans suddenly recalled that their 1856 platform had no protectionist plank.

As Medill was writing his editorial launching him, Lincoln was carefully answering a letter from Edward Wallace, a Pennsylvania physician and relative by marriage interested in endorsing him for vice president. Wallace wanted to sound him out on the tariff. Lincoln's reply told Wallace exactly what he wanted to hear:

> My dear Sir: . . . I was an Old Henry Clay tariff whig. In old times I made more speeches on that subject, than on any other.
>
> I have not since changed my views. I believe yet, if we could have a moderate carefully adjusted protective tariff, so far acquiesced in, as not to be a perpetual subject of political strife, squabbles, charges, and uncertainties, it would be better for us.[23]

But Lincoln, his ambition "a little engine that knew no rest," was as savvy as Richard Nixon.[24] He knew that what the Pennsylvanians desired, many Democrats who had crossed over to the new party despised. Lincoln thus closed his letter carefully:

> We, the old whigs, have been entirely beaten out on the tariff question; and we shall not be able to re-establish the policy until the absence of it, shall have demonstrated the necessity for it, in the minds of men heretofore opposed to it. With this view, I should prefer, to not now, write a public letter on the subject. I therefo[re] wish this to be considered confidential.[25]

Between the lines Lincoln was saying, Politically, this is not the time to push the tariff. We must wait for an economic crisis. But I am with you. Put out the word in Pennsylvania that protectionism has a friend in Old Abe — but keep this letter confidential!

Meanwhile, in Washington Republicans were pounding the issue. The Panic of 1857 had followed by a few months a reduction in the Walker Act tariffs. Republicans had opposed these reductions, if only feebly. But when the depression hit, the party went all-out, blaming the Democratic tariff cuts. The "Ajax of Protection," political economist Henry C. Carey, flooded the press with articles.[26] In

August of 1859 Congressman Justin Morrill of Vermont boxed in free-trade Democrats by introducing a bill to reraise the tariff rates to "force the Democratic controlled Senate to accept or defeat it."[27] On May 10, 1860, the Morrill Tariff Act passed the House, and the voting breakdown exposed the depth of national division. Only fourteen "nay" votes came from free states; only eight "yea" votes from slave states. The nation was as bitterly divided over tariffs as over slavery.

The day Morrill's bill passed the House, the Illinois Republican Convention nominated Abraham Lincoln for president. He was soon back in touch with his friend in Pennsylvania:

> In the days of Henry Clay, I was a Henry-Clay-tariff-man, and my views have undergone no material change upon that subject. I now think the Tariff question ought not to be agitated in the Chicago convention, but that all should be satisfied on that point, with a presidential candidate, whose antecedents give assurance that he would neither seek to force a tariff-law by Executive influence; nor yet to arrest a reasonable one by a veto, or otherwise. Just such a candidate I desire shall be put in nomination.[28]

Lincoln's message: If you want a protective tariff, nominate a high-tariff man at the Chicago convention without stirring up the free traders. And I have in mind a fellow who fits the bill perfectly.

The Twelfth Plank Carries Pennsylvania

At that June 1860 convention, the party's wise men knew that anti-slavery was not enough to defeat the Democrats. As the Harrisburg correspondent of Greeley's *New York Herald* wrote: "The opposition [anti-Democratic] politicians here say you may cry [Negro, Negro] as much as you please, only give us a chance to carry Pennsylvania by crying tariff. Without this state you cannot elect your President."[29]

But the platform writers had a dilemma. While they wanted to accommodate the Pennsylvania protectionists, many Democrats who had come over to the party were free traders. Was it possible to hold them, and still deliver for Pennsylvania? The tariff plank finally adopted, the famous twelfth plank, was as vague as they could make it while still alluding to raising tariff rates:

> While providing revenue for the support of the general government by duties upon imports, sound policy requires such an adjustment of these imports as to encourage the development of the industrial interests of the country.[30]

The writers had finessed the issue beautifully. These moderate, even anodyne, words ignited a convention explosion.

> "The Pennsylvania and New Jersey delegations were terrific in their applause over the tariff resolution," wrote one observer, "and their hilarity was contagious, finally pervading the whole vast auditorium." Another eyewitness confided to his diary: "The scene this evening upon the reading of the 'Protection to Home Industries' plank was beyond precedent. One thousand tongues yelled, ten thousand hats, caps and handkerchiefs waving with the wildest fervor. Frantic jubilation."[31]

Lincoln carried the Pennsylvania delegation and walked off with the nomination. Michael McMorton, the publisher of Philadelphia's bible of protectionism, the *North American*, wrote: "Mr. Lincoln was, throughout, well known for his firm and unwavering fidelity to Henry Clay, and the great policy of protection to American industry."[32] All fall Medill hammered home the theme in his *Chicago Tribune*: Lincoln is "safe on protection, homesteads, rivers and harbors, and the Pacific railroad."[33]

BATTLEGROUND STATE

As the campaign began, all eyes turned to Pennsylvania. For the Quaker State was an "October state," its governor chosen a month before the presidential election. Both parties went all-out. Between September 1 and October 11, the *North American* carried sixteen editorials on the tariff issue. The slavery issue would get only six the entire fall.

From Springfield Lincoln fired off letter after letter to editors in Pennsylvania, urging them to look at his old pro-tariff speeches but to keep the letters confidential. "In 1844 I was on the Clay electoral ticket in this State [i.e., Illinois], and, to the best of my ability, sustained, together, the tariff of 1842 and the tariff plank of the Clay platform," he wrote on October 2, 1860.[34] To Simon Cameron he sent the notes of his 1847 House debates, cautioning, "Nothing about these must get into the news-papers."[35]

Republican orators and their Pennsylvania gubernatorial candidate, Andrew Curtin, made the tariff the altarpiece of the campaign. It was working. Panicked Democrats implored their presidential nominee Stephen Douglas: "The Republicans, in their speeches, say nothing of the [Negro] question, but all is made to turn on the Tariff."[36] His hopes for the presidency slipping away, Douglas came to Harrisburg in September, abandoned his low-tariff position, and came out for protectionism. The deathbed conversion did not work. Republicans denounced the Little Giant as a big fraud, and Curtin triumphed in October. On the eve of the November election, the final Republican manifesto carried this appeal: "Every voter in Pennsylvania who desires to-day to emphasize his vote in favor of protection to American industry and to the best interest of this State, should give it to Abraham Lincoln."[37]

In November Lincoln carried Pennsylvania and the nation — without a single Southern electoral vote. The crucial element of the victory, the one that started him on the road to immortality?

In achieving success for Lincoln in Pennsylvania and New Jersey, the . . . promise of a protective tariff and the Democratic rupture were the decisive factors. Pennsylvania's twenty-seven electoral votes, given to any other candidate, would have reduced Lincoln's majority to three. The additional loss of New Jersey's four electoral votes would have thrown the election into Congress with unpredictable results.[38]

Protectionism had made Lincoln president. Both James G. Blaine and William McKinley believed that the twelfth plank at Chicago had been the key to Pennsylvania and victory. Without that protectionist plank, there might have been no President Abraham Lincoln.[39]

Secession and the Tariff

Lincoln left Springfield early in 1861. Arriving in Pittsburgh in mid-February, he began his speech by reading the twelfth plank and recalling the old arguments of the young congressman of the Polk era:

I have long thought that to produce any necessary article at home, which can be made of as good quality, and with as little labor at home as abroad, would be better made at home, at least by the difference of the carrying from abroad. In such a case, the carrying is demonstrably a dead loss of labor. . . . Labor being the true standard of value, is it not plain, that if equal labor gets a bar of railroad iron out of a mine in England, and another out of a mine in Pennsylvania each can be laid down in a track at home, cheaper than they could exchange countries, at least by the cost of carriage.

The condition of the Treasury at this time would seem to render an early revision of the tariff indispensable.[40]

The Pittsburgh speech was the last one Lincoln would ever deliver on the tariff. He concluded by saying that he would study the matter thoroughly when he got to Washington, looking to all the varied interest of our common country, so that when the time for action arrives adequate protection can be extended to the coal and iron of Pennsylvania, the corn of Illinois, and the reapers of Chicago . . . that all sections may share in the common benefits of a just and equitable tariff.[41]

A rousing ovation followed. Why was Lincoln's language a study in moderation? With Republicans coming to power in Washington, Southern states were seceding. Writes Boritt: "There was no need for piling Yankee insult upon Southern injury by an articulate support of protectionism. Lincoln, therefore, was undeviatingly circumspect in his speech."[42]

Before Lincoln had slipped into Washington by night, the first of the Morrill tariffs had passed Congress, on February 20, 1861 — nine months after it had first passed the House. Many Democrats who had fought the tariff were gone — back home to Deep South states already in secession. Buchanan signed the Morrill Tariff Act on March 2, two days before Lincoln took his oath of office. To Henry Carey it was the "most important measure ever adopted by Congress."[43] On August 5, 1861, Congress would pass another tariff hike, which Lincoln would sign. The issue had helped him win the presidency, and the "old Henry Clay tariff Whig" was being true to his convictions and commitments. On July 14, 1862, another tariff bill was passed by Congress and approved by Lincoln. Customs duties, which had averaged 18 percent in 1860, were raised to an average of 37 percent. The free list established in Morrill's 1861 tariff was cut nearly in half. Upward and upward tariff rates went. In June 1864 duties were raised to 47 percent.[44] These measures would have far-reaching consequences.

Above all, the habits engendered during this period of comprehensive protection to almost everything led to a crystallization of the sentiment in favor of national economic exclusion and isolation. For many decades American commercial policy was molded by the feelings and habits generated during Lincoln's wartime administration.[45]

The Great Emancipator was the Great Protectionist. During the war Congress raised import duties ten times, and ten times Lincoln affixed his name to the bill. Thus began six decades of protectionism, a Lincoln-Republican tradition that would endure until Eisenhower. What was in back of this economic nationalism? Again, Lincoln scholar Gabor Boritt:

> There were three major fountainheads of pressure that led to ever higher tariff levels. The first of these was internal taxation, which fostered the demand for "countervailing" duties on foreign goods. "If we bleed the manufacturers," declared Justin Morrill, "we must see to it that the proper tonic is administered at the same time." Another source was plain old protectionist Whiggery, that descendant of Hamiltonian economics that was to become an unshakable tenet of latter day Republicanism. Finally, the new financial arrangement of the country was preeminently in harmony with the growing nationalism in the North.[46]

Lincoln never spoke again of the importance of tariffs, and Carey was bitterly disappointed that he never used the power of his rhetoric to argue the case for protection. All the president talked of now was the war that consumed him. In February 1865 Carey vented his bitterness:

> Protection made Mr. Lincoln president. Protection has given him all the success he has achieved, yet has he never, so far as I can recollect, bestowed upon her a single word of thanks. When he and she part company, he will go to the wall.[47]

There was reason for this neglect. With the First Battle of Bull Run, Lincoln knew his place in history depended not on the tariff issue but on the outcome of the great war.

Did Tariffs Cause the War?

South Carolina, Georgia, Florida, Alabama, Mississippi, Louisiana, and Texas did not wait to see how Lincoln would govern. All seceded before his inauguration. All knew what was coming. Even before Lincoln took the oath, the first of the Morrill tariffs had been signed by Buchanan.

Consider the situation of the South: Dixie purchased two-thirds of the nation's imports, and tariff revenue was the prime source of U.S. tax revenue. Thus, the South was already carrying a disproportionate share of the national tax burden. By raising tariffs, Congress, in Southern eyes, was looting the South. Southern imports would cost more, while the new tariff revenue would be sent north to be spent by Republicans who despised the South. The South's alternative: buy Northern manufactures instead of British ones. Either way, more of the South's wealth was headed north. Dixie was unwilling to quietly observe customs officers haul their fattened satchels of duty revenue out of Southern ports, to be spent by a president who had not won a single Southern state.

> The Morrill Tariff . . . was Lincoln's big victory. His supporters were jubilant. He had fulfilled his campaign and IOUs to the Northern industrialists. By this act he had closed the door for any reconciliation with the South. In his inaugural address he had also committed himself to collect customs in the South even if there were a secession. With slavery, he was conciliatory; with the import taxes he was threatening. Fort Sumter was at the entrance to the Charleston Harbor, filled with federal troops to support U.S. Customs officers. It wasn't too difficult for angry South Carolinians to fire the first shot.[48]

Believing itself an exploited region in a country where newly empowered Republicans despised it, the Deep South decided to leave. But the North could not let it go. For the free-trade Confederacy had written into its constitution a permanent prohibition against protective tariffs: "nor shall any duties or taxes on importation from foreign nations be laid to promote or foster any branch of industry."[49] To Northern manufacturers this spelled ruin. Imports would be massively diverted from Baltimore, New York, and Boston, where they faced the Morrill Tariff, to Charleston, Savannah, and New Orleans, where they would enter duty-free. Western states would turn to Southern free ports as places of entry for their goods from Europe. So would many Northerners. The *Boston Transcript* argued that a free-trade Confederacy would be so mortal a threat to the industrial North that secession must be reversed, whatever the cost.

> The difference is so great between the tariff of the Union and that of the Confederated States, that the entire Northwest must find it to their advantage to purchase their imported goods at New Orleans rather than New York. In addition to this, the manufacturing interests of the country will suffer from the increased importations resulting from low duties. The [government] would be false to all its obligations, if this state of things were not provided against.[50]

Tax historian Charles Adams describes the situation the North would have confronted:

> This would compel the North to set up a chain of custom stations and border patrols from the Atlantic Ocean to the Missouri River, and then some. Northerners would clamor to buy duty-free goods from the South. This would spell disaster for Northern industrialists. Secession offered the South not only freedom from Northern tax bondage but also an opportunity to turn from the oppressed into the oppressor. The Yankees were going to squirm now![51]

Nor was Lincoln unaware of the dread prospect. In his inaugural address, he had been conciliatory toward the South on slavery, offering a constitutional amendment to make slavery untouchable in the fifteen states where it existed, even offering a new federal law to mandate the return of fugitive slaves. He had pledged to the South "no bloodshed or violence" — with one glaring exception:

The power confided in me, will be used to hold, occupy, and possess the property, and places belonging to the government, and *to collect the duties and imposts; but beyond what may be necessary for these objects, there will be no invasion* — no using of force against, or among the people anywhere.[52] (Emphasis added.)

The message to the Confederacy: you may keep your slaves, but you cannot keep your duty-free ports! British intellectuals like John Stuart Mill might blithely declare, "Slavery [was] the one cause of the Civil War," but others in Great Britain put the cause elsewhere.[53]

In the British House of Commons in 1862, William Forster said he believed it was generally recognized that slavery was the cause of the U.S. Civil War. He was answered from the House with cries, "No, no!" and "The tariff!" It is quite probable the British commercial interests, which dominated the House of Commons, were more in tune with the economics of the Civil War than were the intellectuals and writers.[54]

The tariff was "a prime cause of the Civil War," writes John Steele Gordon, scholar of American economic history.[55] Yet, Lincoln never mentioned the tariff again. And given his devotion to the Union, the cause to which he subordinated all others, it seems that for him, as for Jackson, the tariff was but the means to a greater end: the Union. One critic was not far off when he wrote that Lincoln "made a god out of the Union."[56] And he served that god as faithfully as any Old Testament prophet, and was martyred for that faith.

Chapter 10

FREE MARKETS VS. FREE TRADE

*The question of free trade is, next to the
Reformation, next to the question of free
religion, the most momentous that has ever
been submitted to human decision.*[1]

— Nassau William Senior, 1828

There is truth in the bold assertion of Nassau Senior. Until 1861 only slavery so convulsed and divided the nation as did the question of tariffs and trade. Why is this question so "momentous"? Because free trade is about more than who gets what. It is about who we are, what kind of country we shall be, whether the United States will endure as an independent republic or be melded into the Global Economy of a new world order in which the nation-state is a relic of a dead past.

Many today will laugh at such an assertion; but the men of yesterday understood it; and this generation will soon awaken to that truth. And to understand the stakes, we need to explore the philosophical, political, and religious roots of this great quarrel.

"Global free trade," the regime imposed on us today, is neither the American system of the Founding Fathers nor the free-market system of Adam Smith. It is rooted in an ideology that did not begin to mature until twenty-five years after Smith's death. Born of rebellion against church and crown, free-trade ideology is a first cousin to Marxism, i.e., a secularist faith embraced by intellectuals in rejection of the world they lived in, the world of empires and nation-states.

With communism dead, the economic conflict of our time is between the free-market vision of the American nationalists and Adam Smith and the free-trade doctrine advanced by Jeremy Bentham, David Hume, David Ricardo, James Mill, John Stuart Mill, Richard Cobden, Jean-Baptiste Say, Frédéric Bastiat, and the other scribblers — none of whom was an American, almost all of whom were possessed of a deep animus toward church, state, and empire. And this struggle will determine the fate of the nation-state and the future of the world.

ADAM SMITH LEADS ALL THE REST

As early as the time of the ancient Greeks and Persians, philosophers clashed over the wisdom and morality of trade. The early Christian fathers were skeptics. "Let Christians amend themselves; let them not trade," Saint Augustine admonished.[2] The Bishop of Hippo was echoed by the Angelic Doctor, Saint Thomas Aquinas, in his treatise *On the Governance of Rulers:*

> If the citizens themselves devote their lives to matters of trade, the way will be open to many vices. . . . It is better, therefore, that the supplies of food be furnished to the city from its own fields than that it be wholly dependent on trade. . . . The pursuit of trade is, also, entirely opposed to military activity. For tradesmen, whilst they seek their leisure, do no hard work, and whilst they enjoy all pleasures, grow soft in spirit and their bodies are weakened and rendered unsuited to military labours. . . . Consequently, the perfect city will make a moderate use of merchants.[3]

In 1776 Adam Smith published *An Inquiry into the Nature and Causes of the Wealth of Nations*. In this most famous of economic treatises, the justification of a free-market economy was first set forth. Ever since, Smith has been conscripted as lead witness in the prosecution's case against protectionism. But contrary to conventional wisdom, Adam Smith was no open-borders, free-trade *über alles* libertarian.

The system described in *The Wealth of Nations* is a *national* free-market system. Nations, said Smith, should sell abroad what was not needed for home consumption and buy abroad what could not be produced at home. Smith supported the Acts of Trade and Navigation under which British trade had to be carried in British ships manned by British seamen, calling the laws the "wisest of all the commercial regulations of England." Said Smith, A nation's "defence is of much more importance than opulence."[4]

Reclusive intellectual, friend of Voltaire and Turgot, Smith was tutor to the stepson of Chancellor of the Exchequer Charles Townshend when he imposed the customs duties that ignited the American Revolution.[5]

SMITH'S "EXCEPTIONS" TO FREE TRADE

That Smith put national interests first is evident in the "exceptions" he listed to a British policy of free trade. There are occasions, he wrote, when it must be "advantageous to lay some burden upon foreign [imports], for the encouragement of domestic industry."[6]

> The first is, when some particular sort of industry is necessary for the defence of the country. The defence of Great Britain, for example, depends very much upon the number of its sailors and shipping. The act of navigation, therefore, very properly endeavours to give the sailors and shipping of Great Britain the monopoly of the trade of their own country, in some cases, by absolute prohibitions, and in others by heavy burdens upon the shipping of foreign countries.[7]

Smith felt that Great Britain must maintain her monopoly of trade, even if it meant keeping foreign ships out of British ports. Smith's conviction, shared by British statesmen, guaranteed trouble. For independent colonists would surely one day seek to control their own trade; then, the clash must come.

> The second case, in which it will generally be advantageous to lay some burden upon foreign [imports] for the encouragement of domestic industry, is, when some tax is imposed at home upon the produce of the latter. In this case, it seems reasonable that an equal tax [i.e., tariff] should be imposed upon the like produce of the former.[8]

Smith's free-market system is thus perfectly consistent with Lincoln's Morrill Tariff, which rose to 47 percent in 1864. Imposing tariffs on imports, to offset taxes on domestic manufacturers, was the argument Justin Morrill used to raise Civil War tariffs to Alpine heights. As the Union imposed heavier and heavier direct taxes on U.S. manufacturers, forcing prices up, their products could be undercut by imports. Tariffs had to be raised to maintain the parity that existed before Fort Sumter. For example, if the Union levied a 20 percent direct tax on U.S. builders of steel rails, forcing a markup in price, an offsetting tariff had to be placed on imported British rails. Otherwise, U.S. factories would lose their home market, and Mr. Lincoln his anticipated revenue.

Smith listed two other occasions when the national interest might require tariffs:

> As there are two cases in which it will generally be advantageous to lay some burdens upon foreign, for the encouragement of domestic industry; so there are two others in which it may sometimes be a matter of deliberation. . . .
>
> Some foreign nation [may restrain] by high duties or prohibitions the importation of some of our manufactures into their country. Revenge in this case naturally dictates retaliation, and that we should impose the like duties and prohibitions upon the importation of some or all of their manufactures into ours . . .

There may [also] be good policy in retaliations of this kind, when there is a probability that they will procure the repeal of the high duties or prohibitions complained of. The recovery of a great foreign market will generally more than compensate the transitory inconveniency of paying dearer during a short time for some sorts of goods.[9]

Tariffs as "revenge" on nations that closed markets to British goods and for the "recovery of a great foreign market" is economic nationalism. Using Smith's rule of reciprocity, the United States would today be imposing on China tariffs equal to the taxes and tariffs China imposes on U.S. imports. Smith also believed that tariffs should be reduced gradually, to prevent a surge of imports that might throw thousands out of work:

Humanity may . . . require that the freedom of trade should be restored only by slow gradations, and with a good deal of reserve and circumspection. Were those high duties and prohibitions taken away all at once, cheaper foreign goods of the same kind might be poured so fast into the home market, as to deprive all at once many thousands of our people of their ordinary employment and means of subsistence.[10]

When free-trade purists summon Adam Smith as lead witness, they ignore his famous "exceptions." But had we read Smith rightly, the United States would have saved its TV-manufacturing industry. Instead, we turned a deaf ear to pleas for temporary protection when Japan began the massive dumping of high-quality Japanese TV sets at prices below the cost of production. American-made televisions were driven off department-store shelves, and the U.S. industry drowned in a tidal wave of Sonys. Tens of thousands of high-paying jobs were lost, as were all the future benefits of television manufacture. In a premeditated strike, Japan destroyed America's industry; and in the name of free trade, our government passively observed the industrial equivalent of Pearl Harbor. Smith would never have tolerated such a blow to British national interests.

*   *   *

Adam Smith, then, was no libertarian purist. He would keep foreign ships out of British ports to maintain naval supremacy. He favored tariffs as "revenge" on nations discriminating against British goods, as levers to wrench open foreign markets, and as weapons to recapture lost markets. He believed in tariffs on imported manufactures to offset direct taxes on the home industry. Adam Smith believed in "Britain first." From 1778 until his death, he served as a commissioner of customs, strictly enforcing Britain's protectionist policy against America's trade. "To expect . . . that freedom of trade should ever be entirely restored in Great Britain, is as absurd as to expect that an Oceana or a Utopia should ever be established in it," said Commissioner Smith.[11]

Years after his death some of his self-professed heirs claimed to see in Smith's work ideas that would have repelled him. Despising church and crown, these economists, philosophers, and polemicists came to look on nations themselves as artificial and to long for a new world in which the nation-state ceased to exist. To these men, paradise was not beyond the grave. It could be created here on earth, reached by booking voyage on the only vessel that sailed to that promised land: free trade.

Among these was David Hume, a militant atheist and intimate of Smith who despised the British empire. All nations are but "accidents of battles, negotiations and marriages," said Hume.[12] Loving things French, Hume opposed a tax increase to pay for the Seven Years War that had driven the French out of North America and made his country the world's greatest empire. There "was nothing ever equal in absurdity and wickedness as our present patriotism," said Hume.[13] Across the Channel the church-baiting Voltaire echoed Hume, decrying policies that let nations "destroy each other at the extremities of Asia and America." Such policies make us "enemies of the human race." Voltaire embraced free trade as the way to world government. So, too, did German philosopher Immanuel Kant, who saw a world government as mankind's cure for the evils endemic to the nation-state.[14] In 1795 Kant wrote that for states, in their relation to one another, there can be . . . no other way of advancing from that lawless condition which unceasing war implies, than by giving up their savage lawless freedom, just as individual men have done and yield to the coercion of public laws. Thus they can form a state of nations *(civitas gentium)*, one, too, which will be ever increasing and could finally embrace all peoples of the earth.[15]

Defiantly antipatriotic, these alienated men and their philosophical offspring — not Adam Smith — propagated the idea that a new world order was necessary and could be realized through global free trade.

AMERICA GOES HER SEPARATE WAY

Fearing a French invasion in 1798, John Adams called Washington back to lead the defense of his nation. The old hero agreed, asking only that his protégé be commissioned next in command:

> That Hamilton is ambitious I shall readily grant, but it is of that laudable kind which prompts a man to excel in whatever he takes in hand. He is enterprising, quick in his perceptions, and his judgement is intuitively great.[16]

This is a remarkable tribute from the man who was "first in war, first in peace, and first in the hearts of his countrymen" and arguably the greatest man of his age.

A hero of Yorktown, coauthor of the *Federalist Papers*, and, at thirty-four, secretary of the treasury, Hamilton is entitled to a chapter of his own in any history of political economy. He was the first architect of the free-market system under which America rose from a coastal agrarian country into the greatest industrial power on earth; his *Report on Manufactures*, which guided American statesmen for a century, remains a masterpiece of economic nationalism.

Hamilton's great genius lay in his ability to apply the principles of the free market, elaborated by Smith in *The Wealth of Nations*, to an infant republic of thirteen disputatious states.

> Curiously enough, Hamilton, the first protectionist, was . . . a student of *The Wealth of Nations*. Numerous paraphrases of passages in that book may be pointed out in the Report on Manufactures. . . . Indeed, the whole cast of Hamilton's argument seems to have been affected by the study which he had made of *The Wealth of Nations*.[17]

Historians have sought to create a conflict between Hamilton and Smith. It does not exist. Both were patriots concerned with the causes of the wealth of nations, not of the world. Both believed in free markets. Both understood the pivotal role of capital in creating wealth and employing the labor of a nation. And Hamilton had seized upon the truth of Smith's great insight, in his classic treatise, *that commerce inside a home market is twice as productive as foreign trade*. Wrote Smith:

> Though the returns . . . of the foreign trade of consumption should be as quick as those of the home-trade, the capital employed in it will give but one-half the encouragement to the industry or productive labour of the country. . . .
>
> But a capital employed in the home trade, it has already been shown . . . puts into motion a greater quantity of domestic industry, and gives revenue and employment to a greater number of the inhabitants of the country, than equal capital employed in the foreign trade of consumption.[18]

Though capital expended in foreign trade would never give a nation the same benefit as capital used in domestic investment, Smith argued, the natural tendency of investors to employ their capital at home would, *as by an invisible hand*, lead to the desired result. Here, Hamilton parted company with Smith. He was not willing to entrust his nation's destiny to the blind forces of the market. Hamilton thus created a system to steer America's capital toward making the United States a mighty manufacturing power, independent of foreign countries. In creating the American system, Hamilton integrated Smith's ideas with his own and those in the Declaration of Independence and the Constitution.

Hamilton had read history. He knew that the technological superiority of the European powers had enabled them, with tiny numbers, to overwhelm the native peoples of the Western Hemisphere. He had also lived history. He knew his country had almost lost its revolution because it lacked the essentials of nationhood and the implements of war that Great Britain produced in abundance. At Yorktown French warships and muskets had been decisive. Thus, for Hamilton issues of tariffs and trade were not an intellectual exercise; they were matters of national survival.

Hamilton also disagreed with Smith on the latter's belief in the superior productivity of agriculture. Hamilton argued the superior productivity of manufacturing. Smith wanted his nation, the world's most advanced, to export more; Hamilton believed that U.S. vital interests first mandated national self-sufficiency. Before going out into the world, America must become independent; and to be independent, a nation "ought to endeavor to possess within itself all the essentials of national supply . . . subsistence, habitation, clothing, and defence."[19]

The master builder of a country far greater in territory than the mother country and richer in resources than any in Europe save Russia, Hamilton was painting on a colossal canvas. He could dream dreams of self-sufficiency that no Europeans could. Where the small and medium-sized countries of Europe had to trade with one another out of necessity, Hamilton saw that America did not need any other country.

Critics contend that Hamilton sought narrowly to favor U.S. industry at the expense of foreign manufacturers and to protect the war industries that had sprouted in the Revolution. This does Hamilton an injustice. He was no lobbyist; he was a statesman with a vision. Hamilton's

> plea for protection, unlike that of many protectionists after the subsequent wars in which the country has been involved, is not based upon

the need of nurturing "war babies." The feature of "vested interests," indeed plays on the whole no significant role in Hamilton's argument. To be sure, he indicates a "most ardent" wish to "cherish and bring to maturity this precious embryo" of the Hartford woolen factory, and elsewhere shows keen interest in existing enterprises; but [his] whole tone . . . is one of anticipating a glorious future for its own sake, and not one of attempting by government intervention to provide shelter for the accidents of the past.[20]

Hamilton laid the first layer of brick and mortar on America's tariff wall. Half a century before Europe's political economists broached the idea of "infant industries," Hamilton had created a system to nurture and protect them. A theoretical and practical genius, he rejected the "static analysis of immediate advantage in favor of a dynamic analysis of future development."[21] He was less interested in today's bargain than in tomorrow's America. The Hamiltonian system rested on several pillars: the centrality of manufacturing to national power and long-term prosperity. Tariffs to protect industry. A strong central government — financed by excise taxes and customs duties — capable of defending the nation. Federal assumption of war debts to establish the public credit. "Internal improvements" — dredging rivers, canals, post roads, turnpikes — to develop the skeletal infrastructure of the nation and to tie Americans together by *domestic* trade.

Washington and Hamilton were America's first great economic nationalists. To them it was inseparable from patriotism. And in the manner of his death, Hamilton demonstrated the depth of his patriotism. While he and Jefferson had been the most bitter of rivals in Washington's cabinet ("If there is one man I ought to hate it is Jefferson"), in the election of 1800 Hamilton had thrown his support to his enemy rather than let the country fall into the hands of Aaron Burr. With the electoral vote tied, and the House deadlocked for thirty-five votes over who would become our third president, Hamilton persuaded several Federalists to back Jefferson and abandon Burr, of whom Hamilton said, "This man has no principle, public or private. . . . I could scarcely name a discreet man of either party in our state, who does not think Mr. Burr the most unfit man in the U.S. for the office of president."[22] The "public good," said Hamilton, "must be paramount to every private consideration."[23]

His moral courage cost him his life. In 1804, in a duel with Vice President Burr on the New Jersey shore of the Hudson, Hamilton refused to fire to wound or kill his enemy. Burr, who had issued the challenge, had no such qualms. Hamilton was mortally wounded. His death robbed America of a great statesman and a bold and innovative thinker who helped make it the most prosperous, productive, and free nation in history. He was a man of words who was also a man of action. No economist who follows him can make such a claim. Wrote Arthur Vandenberg in 1921, "The Greatest American gave himself to the Greatest Nation in the cycles of Time. . . . We need his immutable loyalty to the Constitution, his unswerving faith in the Republic, his unhyphenated attachment to 'America First.' "[24] Even in our own time, Hamilton's ideas continue to inspire. As one historian wrote in 1950:

> As soon as they achieved self government, Canada, Australia, and New Zealand followed the example of the United States in adopting protective tariffs to foster their infant industries. Today, wherever the question of economic development is raised . . . the arguments of Alexander Hamilton and the United States are invoked.[25]

RICARDO AND COMPARATIVE ADVANTAGE

Not until a quarter of a century after the death of Adam Smith would the ideology of global free trade be grafted onto the free-market system of Hamilton and Smith.

David Ricardo is credited with discovering the law of comparative advantage: all nations will prosper most if each produces what it makes cheapest and best, and trades for what it does not. Ricardo's friend James Mill summed up the theory as follows:

When a country can either import a commodity or produce it at home, it compares the cost of producing at home with the cost of producing from abroad; if the latter cost is less than the first, it imports. The cost at which a country can import from abroad depends, not upon the cost at which the foreign country produces the commodity, but upon what the commodity costs which it sends in exchange, compared with the cost which it must be at to produce the commodity in question, if it did not import it.[26]

(This passage is what passes for clarity in economics.)

What Ricardo and Mill are saying is this: if Great Britain is more efficient than Portugal at making cloth *and* at making wine, but Portugal's most efficient industry is wine, Britain should focus on its most efficient industry, producing cloth, shut down its wineries, and buy its wine from Portugal. Each nation should produce what it produces best and trade for what other nations produce best. Thus is the production of both cloth and wine maximized. "It is this principle," Ricardo wrote in 1817, "which determines that wine shall be made in France and Portugal, that corn shall be grown in America and Poland, and that hardware and other goods shall be manufactured in England."[27] This principle is the justification for free trade and creation of a world economy.

Ricardo's theory, however, has foundered on the reef of nationalism. Less-developed nations — America in the nineteenth century, China today — have refused to cede permanent leadership in advanced technologies to rival powers. And investors and workers in advanced countries eventually rebel at being sacrificed to an abstraction — just as they are rebelling today.

With the arrival on the scene of John Stuart Mill, son of James Mill, and his 1848 *Principles of Political Economy*, the theory of comparative advantage became defined dogma. Tutored in Greek at three, in Latin and mathematics at eight, in logic at twelve and political economy at thirteen, John Stuart Mill, to the intelligentsia of his time, was "a saint without God." His following in Crimean War–era Britain, with its "Charge of the Light Brigade" patriotism, was less enthusiastic. For J. S. Mill was a socialist with a deep radical streak. He believed that the traditional British family was "a school of despotism,"[28] embraced his father's view that "the creed of Christianity" was the *ne plus ultra* of wickedness," and declared in 1852 that he would prefer "Communism, with all its chances" to British society in the Victorian Age.[29]

Unlike his father and the early classical liberals, Mill was not a free-trade purist. Indeed, he was the first European intellectual to make a powerful case for protecting infant industries, though this had been the practice in the United States since 1789. These industries, a nation's hothouse flowers, argued Mill, needed time in the nursery and shelter from an unexpected hailstorm of imports, to take root and grow until they could survive in the elements and compete in the world. As trade historian Douglas Irwin writes, "Mill's standing and reputation among economists gave intellectual credibility to the infant industry argument for the first time."[30]

Mill also acknowledged that there were losers from free trade and proposed a "compensation principle." Beneficiaries of free trade should "compensate" victims. In the case of the repeal of Britain's Corn Laws, losers would be landowners who saw property values collapse as foreign grain flooded Britain's home market.

FREE TRADE BECOMES RELIGIOUS DOGMA

Half a century after Smith wrote *The Wealth of Nations*, free trade had begun to capture the hearts and minds of intellectuals and transcend the realm of economics to become a new gospel of salvation. Wrote Mill:

> The economical advantages of commerce are surpassed in importance by those of its effects which are intellectual and moral. It is hardly pos-

sible to overrate the value, in the present low state of human improvement, of placing human beings in contact with persons dissimilar to
themselves.[31]

As early as 1836, classical liberal Henry Fairbairn had looked into
the future and seen free trade coming on the wings of angels:

> Seeing then, that in the natural order of things the triumph of Free
> Trade principles is now inevitable, magnificent indeed are the prospects
> that are opening for mankind. Nations will become united in the golden
> bands of peace; science, liberty and abundance will reign among the in-
> habitants of the earth; nations will no longer be seen to descend and de-
> cline, human life will become prolonged and refined; years will become
> centuries in the development of the blessings of existence; and even now
> the eye can reach to the age when one language, one religion, and one
> nation alone will be existing in the world.[32]

Whose language, whose religion, Fairbairn does not say. Reading
this passage of vaulting human pride, one recalls the story from
Genesis:

> And the whole earth was of one language, and of one speech. . . . And
> they said one to another . . . let us build us a city and a tower, whose top
> may reach unto heaven. . . . And the Lord came down to see the city and
> the tower. . . . And the Lord said, Behold . . . this they begin to do: and
> now nothing will be restrained from them, which they have imagined
> to do. . . .
>   So the Lord scattered them abroad from thence upon the face of all
> the earth. . . . Therefore is the name of it called Babel; because the Lord
> did there confound the language of all the earth.[33]

As Christianity lost its hold on the intelligentsia, free-trade ideology took on the aspect of a messianic faith. Held to the heart, pursued with perseverance, the doctrine must bring us to paradise.
Those who diluted doctrinal purity were not just behind the times,

they were heretics to be burned at the stake. Mill's reasoned argument that protection of infant industries might justify temporary tariffs was now moral high treason.

> I believe that the harm which Mill has done to the world by the passage in his book on *Political Economy* in which he favors the principle of protection in young communities has outweighed all the good which may have been caused by his other writings.[34]

So declared Richard Cobden on his deathbed.
And who was Richard Cobden?

THE GREAT EVANGELIST

Seven decades after Smith published *The Wealth of Nations*, Richard Cobden became to free trade what Saint Paul is to Christianity: its greatest evangelist, a man for whom free trade was the path to salvation.

> Commerce is the grand panacea, which, like a beneficent medical discovery, will serve to inoculate with the healthy and saving taste for civilization all the nations of the world.[35]

As much as any man, this Quaker leader of the Anti–Corn Law League persuaded Britain to lift all barriers to imported grain and to embrace free trade. Cobden never denied that his agenda was about much more than cheap grain for the poor. He was a romantic, a visionary, a master orator. When he rose at Free Trade Hall in Manchester on January 15, 1846, the audience was so great that seats in the hall had to be removed so more could be accommodated:

> I believe that the physical gain will be the smallest gain to humanity from the success of this principle. I look farther; I see in the Free Trade

principle that which shall act on the moral world as the principle of gravitation in the universe — drawing men together, thrusting aside the antagonism of race, and creed, and language, and uniting us in the bonds of eternal peace.[36]

Free trade, like God's grace, had salvific power to persuade men to cast aside hatred and greed and embrace one another in love. Christians might believe in the millennium, the Second Coming of Christ, and his earthly rule of a thousand years. Karl Marx might prophesy the coming of communism, an end to the exploitation of man by man, the withering away of the state, a world of universal brotherhood.

But to Richard Cobden, free trade was the way, the truth, and the light.

A new magazine was begun in 1843 "solely for the purpose of advocating these principles." *The Economist* made an early profession of faith: "We seriously believe that *free trade*, free intercourse, will do more than any other visible agent to extend civilization and morality throughout the world."[37] To the editors and writers at *The Economist*, the voice thundering through Free Trade Hall was preaching the new gospel:

> I have looked even farther. I have speculated, and probably dreamt, in the dim future — say, a thousand years hence . . . on what the effect of the triumph of this principle may be. I believe that the effect will be to change the face of the world, so as to introduce a system of government entirely distinct from that which now prevails. I believe that the desire and the motive for large and mighty empires; for gigantic armies and great navies — for those materials which are used for the destruction of life and the desolation of the rewards of labor — will die away; I believe that such things will cease to be necessary, or to be used when man becomes one family, and freely exchanges the fruits of his labour with his brother man. . . . I believe that the speculative philosopher of a thousand years hence will date the greatest revolution that ever happened in the world's history from the triumph of the principle which we have met here to advocate.[38]

Men emptied of an older faith were enthralled. Across the Channel, French economist Frédéric Bastiat wrote with the same millenarian fervor:

> Let us banish from political economy all expressions borrowed from the military vocabulary: *to fight on equal terms, conquer, crush, choke off, be defeated, invasion, tribute.* What do these terms signify? Squeeze them, and nothing comes out. Or rather, what comes out is absurd errors and harmful preconceptions. Such expressions are inimical to international cooperation, hinder the formation of peaceful, ecumenical and indissoluble union of the peoples of the world, and retard the progress of mankind.[39]

Cobden and Bastiat were one-worlders; they looked to free trade to ring down the curtain on the theatrics of nations and bring about the "ecumenical and indissoluble union of the peoples of the world." Like Hume and Ricardo, Cobden was a "Little Englander," a pacifist who hated the empire and saw free trade and disarmament as inseparable. "It would be well to engraft our free trade agitation upon the peace movement," he declared. "They are one and the same cause."[40] Bastiat urged France to embrace unilateral disarmament, proclaiming in 1849, "I shall not hesitate to vote for disarmament . . . because I do not believe in invasions,"[41] and instructed France on how to deal with the problem of invading armies:

> If the emperor Nicholas should venture to send 200,000 Muscovites, I sincerely believe that the best thing we could do would be to receive them well, to give them a taste of the sweetness of our wines, to show them our stores, our museums, the happiness of our people, the mildness and equality of our penal laws, after which we should say to them: Return as quickly as possible to your steppes and tell your brothers what you have seen.[42]

Economic historian William Hawkins wryly observes: "Bastiat did not bother to mention how he would get the Russians to return to their steppes if they did not wish to go. Nor was this an academic question given France's problems over the next century with 'visiting Germans.' "[43]

Reading Bastiat, one is reminded of Orwell's observation: only an intellectual could have made a statement like that; no ordinary man could be such a fool. But Bastiat was unstoppable: "Free trade means harmony of interests and peace between nations. . . . We place this indirect and social effect a thousand times above the direct or purely economic effect."[44]

Paradoxically, one may hear tough-minded U.S. conservatives today, champions of "peace through strength," cite as mentors utopians and pacifists like Bastiat and Say, who declared, "Far from protecting [the national security], a great military apparatus is what most jeopardizes it." "All nations," added Say, "are friends in the nature of things."[45]

What is the common thread that runs from these classical liberals to modern conservatives? An intense hostility to statism, to the idea of strong national governments. But in the nineteenth century the bloated, intrusive welfare state that conservatives abhor did not exist. National security was the business of cabinets and kings. It was military preparedness, great power diplomacy, and empire building that the classical liberals savaged in language to warm the heart of any New Leftist.[46]

Bastiat's one-worldism is anticonservative, antitraditionalist, and at bottom, heretical. It holds out the promise that if we follow the gospel of free trade, paradise can be created on earth. This one-worldism is also deeply un-American. The "ecumenical and indissoluble union of the peoples of the world" that Bastiat and Cobden dreamed of is the antithesis of what Jefferson declared to be the aim of our Revolution, i.e., the *severing* of the "Political Bands which have connected" us to England and for Americans to "assume among the powers of the Earth the *separate* and equal station to which the Laws of Nature and of Nature's God entitle [us]."[47]

Ultimately, global free trade means global interdependence. But independence is why the Revolution was fought, independence is why the Founders came to Philadelphia, independence is why the American system was invented. Invited on his deathbed to make a toast, John Adams uttered two words: "Independence, forever!" That is the American heritage.

Utopian as the vision of Ricardo, Cobden, Bastiat, and Say was, it caught fire in the minds of men and began to emerge in the rhetoric of statesmen. Free trade, military disarmament, and world government would become points three, four, and fourteen of the Fourteen Points of Woodrow Wilson.

America went her own nationalist way, but in England Cobden and the free traders triumphed. The Corn Laws were repealed. Grain poured in. Britain threw her markets open to the goods of all nations, some of which, like the United States, imposed ever steeper tariffs on British imports. Ignoring Adam Smith's advocation of tariffs as "revenge" on nations that closed their markets to British goods, Britain sailed on through the century, proclaiming the new gospel of unfettered free trade.

Perceived imperial interest caused British statesmen to go along. By free trade, wrote Lord Macaulay in 1842,

> we might supply the whole world with manufactures, and have almost a monopoly of the trade of the world. . . . whatever temporary distress we might feel, we should be cheered by the reflection, that other nations were raising abundant provisions for us on the banks of the Mississippi and the Vistula.[48]

Victorian economist William Stanley Jevons was "even more lyrical in his description of the entire planet as an agricultural hinterland of industrial Britain."[49] Jevons wrote in 1865 that

> the plains of North America and Russia are our corn-fields; Chicago and Odessa our granaries; Canada and the Baltic are our timber forests; Australasia contains our sheep farms, and in Argentina and on the western prairies of North America, are our herds of oxen; Peru sends her sil-

ver, and the gold of South Africa and Australia flows to London; the Hindus and the Chinese grow tea for us, and our coffee, sugar, and spice plantations are all in the Indies. Spain and France are our vineyards, and the Mediterranean our fruit-garden; and our cotton-grounds, which for long have occupied the Southern United States, are now being extended everywhere in the warm regions of the earth.[50]

Only it did not quite work out that way. While free trade brings immediate visible benefits — in Britain's case, cheap imported food to feed the British working class — the debilitating effects are at first hidden. But within decades of the Corn Laws being repealed, Britain was so dependent on imported grain that it could no longer feed itself. With U.S. manufactures pouring in, it began to lose its industrial supremacy. Soon, it would lose the capacity to defend the sea-lanes on which it now depended. When the Great War came, free-trade Britain had to rely on protectionist America to deliver the food and weapons essential to British survival.

Free trade is not free.

A Germanic Echo of Hamiltonian Nationalism

Across the Atlantic, it was not Smith, Ricardo, or Cobden who carried the day. Hamilton had won the argument and constructed the system under which America had prospered for half a century. His heirs were Henry Clay; Mathew Carey, the Irish-American pamphleteer; his son, Henry C. Carey; Hezekiah Niles and his *Niles Weekly Register* — and Friedrich List.

A professor of political economy, List had fled to America in the 1820s to escape imprisonment for having criticized the government of Würtemberg. He took up farming near Harrisburg and edited a German-language newspaper. As he had arrived with letters of introduction from the legendary Lafayette, List was able to develop friendships with Jackson, Clay, and even the aging Madison. In the battle over the 1828 Tariff of Abominations, List volunteered his pen to the Union cause. In a series of letters to C. J. Ingersoll, president of the Pennsylvania Society for the Promotion of Manufactures, published in 1827 as *Outlines of American Political Economy*, List made the intellectual case for the system devised by Hamilton and perfected by Clay.

The Ricardian school had by then conscripted Adam Smith, and List felt the sting of challenging the political correctness of his day:

> The system of Adam Smith has assumed so great an authority, that those who venture to oppose it, or even to question its infallibility, expose themselves to be called idiots. Mr. Say, throughout his whole work, is in the habit of calling all objections to his sublime theory the opinion of the rabble, vulgar views, etc. etc. . . . These infallible theorists assure us, as gravely as modestly, that minds like those of Edward III, Elizabeth, Colbert, Turgot, Frederick II, Joseph II, Pitt, Fox, Napoleon Bonaparte, Washington, Jefferson, Hamilton, a chart of the minds of the most enlightened men of all ages, were not enlightened enough to comprehend the true principles of political economy.[51]

An admirer of America, List became a citizen and returned in 1832 to Germany, appointed by Jackson as consul in Hamburg. The Germans refused him. List eventually took up the consul post in Leipzig, where he began urging the Germans to establish a federal and constitutional nation modeled on the United States. But in 1846, at age fifty-seven, suffering a painful terminal illness, List killed himself.

Five years before his death, List published *The National System of Political Economy*, which for a time would attain a prominence to rival *The Wealth of Nations*. Leaning heavily on Hamiltonian ideas and America's experience, List gave three basic arguments for protectionism.

First, "infant industries" of developing nations *had* to be protected. Why should Britain dominate world manufacturing simply because the British arrived first in the Industrial Age? List saw Britain's advocacy of free trade as naked self-interest. In a famous depiction, he described the doctrine as a "clever device that when anyone has attained the summit of greatness, he kicks away the ladder by which he has climbed up, in order to deprive others of the means of climbing up after him."[52]

Second, though protectionism required short-term costs, such costs should be imposed for long-term gain. Like Hamilton he took the long view. A nation that does not make such sacrifices risks being confined forever to producing raw materials and grain, which could never give it the standard of living that manufacturing could. Also in echo of Hamilton, List argued that manufacturing was superior to agriculture.

To Ricardo's argument that we should abandon the home industry and rely on imports if a foreign nation could manufacture more cheaply, List's reply was withering: "Who would be consoled for the loss of an arm by the knowing that he had nevertheless bought his shirts forty percent cheaper?"[53]

Third, as scholar and free-trade advocate Richard Ebeling writes, List introduced Europe to the concept of "national interest."

> List accused Adam Smith and other free-trade economists of "cosmopolitanism." Men were not a part of a global community, List argued, in which their interests harmonized in a network of international commerce and division of labor. Between man and humanity was the nation. . . . Each nation had its own history, culture, stage of development and position of power relative to other nations in the world. And the economic prosperity of each man was tied up with the success or failure of his own nation's struggle for political and economic influence and control in the global competition between nation-states. . . . For the nation's prosperity and betterment, it was often necessary for the individual to sacrifice his private interest in the arena of trade and profit opportunities for the national interest of the country to which he belonged.[54]

List had hit the Achilles' heel of the Cobdenites. They celebrated the benefit of free trade for mankind, not the nation. But to List, mankind did not command one's allegiance; the world had no hold on the heart — it was nation and country that commanded love and loyalty.

> Between each individual and entire humanity . . . stands *the Nation*, with its special language and literature . . . origin and history . . . manners and customs, laws and institutions . . . with its separate territory; a society, which, united by a thousand ties of mind and of interests, combines itself into one independent whole.[55]

List savaged the "cosmopolitical school," mocking that these men wrote for a world in which nations cooperated, though such a world did not exist. In the real world, said List, Europe's nations were rivals, antagonists with interests in conflict. Each was struggling for a superior place in the sun. Moreover, they were at different stages of development. When List wrote in 1841, neither Germany nor Italy was a unified nation.

Whereas the classical economists argued that the choices of consumers would determine what was best for the country, List dissented furiously:

> The foreign trade of a nation must not be estimated in the way in which individual merchants judge it. . . . The nation is bound to keep steadily in view all these conditions on which its present and future existence, prosperity, and power depend.[56]

The classical liberals had declared, "Consumption is the sole end and purpose of all production." List retorted that only production "renders consumption possible." The "power of producing wealth," he wrote, "is therefore infinitely more important than wealth itself."[57]

> The forces of production are the tree on which wealth grows. . . . The tree which bears the fruit is of itself of greater value than the fruit itself. . . . The prosperity of a nation is not . . . greater in the pro-

portion in which it has amassed more wealth (i.e., values of exchange), but in the proportion in which it has more developed its powers of production.[58]

List would be appalled to watch Americans get rich on the soaring stock prices of companies whose profits were exploding because they had moved factories overseas and exchanged American labor for Asian labor.

List had an advantage over his contemporaries. Unlike the classical liberals who had a theory, List had a working model. His ideas had been tested by Washington, Madison, and Jackson. The great Americans were all economic nationalists; and it was evident to the entire world that the United States was the economic marvel of the age.

List had defined the theory by which the Founding Fathers had been guiding the Republic since the Tariff Act of 1789. But in his 1841 book, List went far beyond the economic nationalism of Hamilton. He began to lay the intellectual foundation for wholesale government intervention and the state socialism of imperial Germany. Bismarck would keep a copy of List's work on his desk and make it the standard text of college students. When he came to power, the Iron Chancellor put many of List's ideas into practice. But Bismarck's interventions in the German economy far exceeded anything free-market Americans like Washington, Hamilton, and Clay would have tolerated in a nation dedicated to freedom.

By now other voices were weighing in on the "momentous" question. In the year John Stuart Mill wrote *Principles of Political Economy*, Karl Marx produced his *Communist Manifesto* and delivered his thoughts on free trade to the Democratic Association of Brussels on January 9, 1848:

The Protective system . . . is conservative, while the Free Trade system works destructively. It breaks up old nationalities and carries antagonism of proletariat and bourgeoisie to the uttermost point. In a word, the Free Trade system hastens the Social Revolution. In this revolutionary sense alone, gentlemen, I am in favor of Free Trade.[59]

Marx was right: the protective system is "conservative." And free trade is raising the levels of antagonism in Europe and the United States — between working families with falling standards of living and national elites reveling in the Global Economy. Cobden agreed with Marx about the destructive effects of free trade. Detesting the empire, he believed free trade would kill it. For under free trade, he said, the British colonies

> will be at liberty to buy wherever they can buy cheapest, and to sell in the dearest market. They must be placed in the same predicament as if they were not part of His Majesty's dominions. When, then, will be the semblance of a plea for putting ourselves to the expense of governing and defending such countries?[60]

The insight of Marx and Cobden about free trade dissolving bonds and pulling apart empires applies as well to huge and diverse nations — like the United States.

Philosophical Roots of Free-Trade Theory

The awesome success of the American system notwithstanding, free traders converted most economists to the pure dogma: no state interference with trade! To Adam Smith, who advocated tariffs as "revenge" on nations that closed their markets, Say bluntly responded: Do not retaliate!

> Undoubtedly, a nation that excludes you from all commercial intercourse with her, does you an injury; — robs you, as far as in her lies, of the benefits of external commerce. . . . But it must not be forgotten that retaliation hurts yourself as well as your rival; that it operates, not de-

fensively against her selfish measures, but offensively against yourself. . . . The only point in question is this, what degree of vengeance you are animated by, and how much will you consent to throw away upon its gratification.[61]

Bastiat agreed: "A protective tariff duty is a tax directed against a foreign product; but we must never forget that it falls back on the home consumer."[62] Today's libertarians have kept the faith. Milton Friedman, the Nobel Prize winner, says America should be delighted with foreign nations that subsidize exports to capture U.S. markets:

Another source of "unfair competition" is said to be subsidies by foreign governments to their producers that enable them to sell in the United States below cost. Suppose a foreign government gives such subsidies, as no doubt some do. Who is hurt and who benefits? To pay for the subsidies the foreign government must tax its citizens. They are the ones who pay for the subsidies. U.S. consumers benefit. They get cheap TV sets or automobiles or whatever it is that is subsidized. Should we complain about such a program of reverse foreign aid?[63]

Following Friedman, America allowed subsidized foreign companies from Sony to Airbus to destroy U.S. manufacturers, from TV and textile producers to builders of airplanes and autos. Yet, even though Japan uses subsidies to take over our industries, and shuts us out of its markets, we must not retaliate. After all, Japan is just sending us "reverse foreign aid," "U.S. consumers benefit," and the consumer is king.

"Engine Charley" Wilson was crucified for saying, "What's good for America is good for General Motors." Dr. Friedman is applauded for declaring, "What's good for consumers is good for America." Henry Clay carried such thinking to its logical end:

If the governing consideration were cheapness, if national independence were to weigh nothing; if honor nothing; why not subsidize foreign powers to defend us; why not hire Swiss or Hessian armies to protect us? Why not get our arms of all kinds, as we do, in part, the blankets and clothing of our soldiers, from abroad?[64]

Nevertheless, as the nineteenth century unfolded, the idea that in free trade men had found the Rosetta stone of world peace put down roots and made converts. Intellectuals were enthralled by the doctrine. As the French liberal economist Frédéric Passy wrote in the 1860s:

> Some day all barriers will fall; some day mankind, constantly united by continuous transactions, will form just one workshop, one market, and one family. . . . And this is . . . the grandeur, the truth, the nobility, I might say, the holiness of the free trade doctrine; by the prosaic but effective pressure of [economic] interest it tends to make justice and harmony prevail in the world.[65]

This utopian virus has been passed down through the genes of generations of economists. In the midst of the horrific war with Hitler's Reich, with all the savagery of which nations are capable on gaudy display, the great Austrian Ludwig von Mises succumbed to this flight of fancy:

> We need to imagine a world in which liberalism is supreme. . . . In this liberal world . . . there are no trade barriers; men can live and work where they want. Frontiers are drawn on the maps but they do not hinder the migrations of men and shipping of commodities. In such a world it makes no difference where the frontiers of a country are drawn. Nobody has a special interest in enlarging the territory of the state in which he lives; nobody suffers loss if a part of this area is separated from the state. . . . There would be no more wars because there would be no incentive for aggression. War would not pay. Armies and navies would be superfluous. Policemen would suffice for the fight against crime. In such a world the state is not a metaphysical entity but simply the producer of security and peace. . . .
>
> The reality in which we have to live differs very much from this per-

fect world of ideal liberalism. But this is due only to the fact that men have rejected liberalism for statism. They have burdened the state, which could be a more or less efficient night-watchman, with a multitude of other duties.[66]

At this passage statesmen can only shake their heads in disbelief. As there is no historic replica of the mythical state of Mises's reveries, of what relevance is this utopian liberalism as a guide to national policy?

When men cease to believe in God, said G. K. Chesterton, they do not then believe in nothing; they believe in anything. Briefly, this is the origin of free-trade theory. From the Greek Epicurus came the principle that in this life that ends with death, the greatest pleasure is the greatest good. The Utilitarian Jeremy Bentham built on Epicurus's insight. "The greatest good for the greatest number" is the only proper business of government. Came then Ricardo with his iron law of comparative cost: worldwide free trade must produce the greatest variety of goods at the cheapest price, thus the greatest happiness for all mankind. Therefore, nations must embrace global free trade if we are to achieve the best of all possible worlds. As Bertrand Russell, godson of J. S. Mill, wrote, the ideas of Epicurus were

brought to England by Bentham and his followers; this was done in conscious opposition to Christianity, which these men regarded as hostilely as Epicurus regarded the religions of his day.[67]

Free-trade ideology is thus a product of a shift in perspective, from a God-centered universe to a man-centered one. It finds its intellectual roots in the minds of men, most of whom were pacifists and atheists and looked to the end of empires and nations in a brave new world in which the buying and selling of earthly goods would bring mankind as close to paradise as these utopians believed was possible. It is remarkable that Godly men and women celebrate such dogmas and such dogmatists!

* * *

As decades passed after repeal of the Corn Laws, the first doubts began to arise in England about the secular faith they had embraced, especially as protectionist America and Germany seemed to be eclipsing the empire. In a reflective essay, John Stuart Mill wrote:

> We give to our rivals a free market of 43,000,000 persons in the United Kingdom to add to their own free market. Thus the United States possess an open market of 82,000,000 persons in the United States, plus an open market of 43,000,000 persons in Great Britain, making, altogether, 125,000,000. Similarly, Germany possesses an open market of 43,000,000 persons in Great Britain. As against this, we possess only such residue of our open market of 43,000,000 as the unrestricted competition of foreign nations leaves unimpaired. . . . We call ourselves Free Traders, but we have never secured Free Trade for ourselves; we have merely succeeded in enlarging the area within which our Protectionist competitors enjoy Free Trade.[68]

The Great Apostate

In the first half of the twentieth century, the world's most influential economist was John Maynard Keynes, who began his career as a free-trade purist. As an undergraduate, Keynes had been secretary of the Cambridge University Free Trade Association. In 1923 he wrote of free trade in lyrics as inspired as those of Cobden and Say:

> We must hold to free trade, in its widest interpretation, as an inflexible dogma, to which no exception is admitted, wherever the decision rests with us. We must hold to this even where we receive no reciprocity or treatment and even in those rare cases where by infringing it we could in fact obtain a direct economic advantage. We should hold to free trade as a principle of international morals, and not merely as a doctrine of economic advantage.[69]

Few passages better reveal how free-trade dogma had moved from the realm of economics to that of a religious faith. Keynes here is a preacher, urging his congregation to stand by church doctrine even if martyrdom calls. His 1923 position is comparable to that of a Christian Scientist who refuses to let his child undergo surgery, even though such refusal may mean the child's death. One may admire such adherence to principle in an individual. In a nation such ideological rigidity can be suicidal.

"If there is one thing that protection can *not* do," Keynes declared, "it is to cure unemployment."

> There are some arguments for protection, based upon its securing possible but improbable advantages, to which there is no simple answer. But the claim to cure unemployment involves the protectionist fallacy in its grossest and crudest form. . . . The proposal to cure the present unemployment by a tariff on manufactured goods . . . is a gigantic fraud.[70]

As the Great Depression struck, deepened, and spread, however, the paragon of free traders, the most renowned economist of his age, began to undergo a conversion. And suddenly Keynes recanted.

In 1930 he informed the government that the best way to increase employment was a tariff to cut imports into the British Isles! The reaction among England's elites was as though Pius XI had suddenly beatified Henry VIII. Late that same year, Keynes described the benefits of a tariff as "simply enormous" and urged a 10 percent tariff on all imports and a 10 percent bounty on exports to protect British industry. Such a tariff, said Keynes, would have the benefit of a 10 percent devaluation of the British pound.

In 1931 publication of Keynes's revised views "caused a sensation." For Keynes was proposing "import duties of 15% on all manufactured and semi-manufactured goods without exception, and of 5% on all foodstuffs and certain raw materials."[71] "In so far as it leads to the substitution of home-produced goods for goods previously imported," Keynes argued, "it will increase employment in this country."[72] Like Jefferson, Keynes had come to see free trade as a betrayal of his country, to embrace economic nationalism, and to scoff at the very arguments he once made. A shocked William Beveridge of the London School of Economics denounced Keynes as an apostate. Keynes fired back:

> Defense of free trade theory is, I submit, the result of pure intellectual error, due to a complete misunderstanding of the theory of equilibrium in international trade — an error which it is worthwhile to extirpate if one can, because it is shared, I fancy, by a multitude of less eminent free traders. Does he [Beveridge] believe that it makes no difference to the amount of employment in this country if I decide to buy a British car instead of an American car?[73]

Britain's leading champion of free trade had became a disciple of Hamilton: "I am no longer a free trader . . . to the extent of believing . . . in abandoning any industry which is unable for the time being to hold its own."[74] In a now-famous article, "National Self-Sufficiency," the most honored economist of his age showed himself a man of moral courage. Keynes renounced free trade. And after a century of experimentation with the theory, his country followed. It takes fortitude for a renowned man to concede that he has been wrong, that his critics were right, and then to adopt a position — protectionism — his contemporaries would decry as retarded if not immoral. As Keynes wrote in his apologia:

> I was brought up, like most Englishmen, to respect free trade not only as an economic doctrine which a rational and instructed person could not doubt but almost as a part of the moral law. I regarded departures from it as being at the same time an imbecility and an outrage. I thought England's unshakeable free trade convictions, maintained for nearly a hundred years, to be both the explanation before man and the justification before heaven of her economic supremacy.
>
> [Today] the orientation of my mind is changed.[75]

Despite Keynes's recantation, he and List remain exceptions to the rule: famous economists are free traders. Yet, until our own time, few leaders embraced the vision. Clay once wryly noted that free trade is "everywhere proclaimed; but nowhere practiced. It is truth in the books of European political economists. It is error in the practical code of every European state."[76] For centuries economists ruefully conceded it. "The Protectionist Creed arises like a weed in every soil," wailed the classical economist Walter Bagehot:[77] "The doctrine of free trade, however widely rejected in the world of politics, holds its own in the sphere of the intellect," observed Frank Taussig, the first chairman of the U.S. Tariff Commission.[78] Wrote Milton Friedman,

> Ever since Adam Smith, there has been virtual unanimity among economists, whatever their ideological position on other issues, that international free trade is in the best interest of the trading countries and the world. Yet, tariffs have been the rule.[79]

What causes those who control the destiny of nations to reject free trade? Why is the faith so often abandoned under duress? Why did Jefferson and Madison, free traders in younger days, become economic nationalists? Why did Keynes, a purist from college days, give up the faith and convert to protectionism? In each case experience tempered ideology and altered belief. For the abstract loveliness of the theory dissipates in the hard reality of dying factories and foreign danger. Moreover, leaders know that every great industrial power has become so via economic nationalism: Britain before 1850; Germany from 1870 to 1914; postwar Japan; China today; and most especially and dramatically, the United States of America from 1865 to 1914 — as we shall now see.

Chapter 11

The Time of the Protectionists

*Free trade results in giving our money, our
manufactures, and our markets to other
nations. . . . [It] will bring widespread discontent. It will revolutionize values. It will
take away more than one half of the earning
capacity of brain and brawn.*[1]

— William McKinley, 1892

From 1861 to 1913 Grover Cleveland was the only Democrat to
be elected president. His two terms (1885–89, 1893–97) spliced
fifty-two years of Republican rule. The other presidents between
Lincoln and Theodore Roosevelt — Andrew Johnson, U. S. Grant,
Rutherford B. Hayes, James Garfield, Chester Arthur, Benjamin
Harrison, and William McKinley — are not generously remembered by history. Their era has been called the Gilded Age, the days
of the "robber barons" — of Jay Gould and Jim Fisk, Andrew
Carnegie and Cornelius Vanderbilt, John D. Rockefeller and J. P.
Morgan, E. H. Harriman and James J. Hill. Theirs, it was said, was
the time of the Great Barbecue, when American workers were exploited by the most rapacious and repulsive of all capitalists, when
government was bought and sold, when the common man was at the
mercy of a plutocracy faithful to its motto: The Public Be Damned!

But that is not the whole story. Indeed, it is not the real story of this era of American dynamism and progress unlike any the world had ever seen. These were the Confident Years, an era of intense American nationalism, when the nation continued to follow the wise counsel of Washington and stayed out of Europe's quarrels. The era came to a thunderclap end in 1898, when William McKinley — goaded by Assistant Secretary of the Navy Theodore Roosevelt, Senator Henry Cabot Lodge, and fire-breathing child-publisher William Randolph ("You furnish the pictures and I'll furnish the war!") Hearst — took America to war with Spain. After Admiral George Dewey's stunning victory at Manila Bay, the United States paused, then brashly crashed the world's most exclusive club: the Western imperialists. McKinley came down after a long night of prayer to tell a startled press that God himself had told him to take the Philippines. For the first time in its history, America assumed rule over an alien people it had no intention of letting become American citizens. Tempted in our Eden, we had eaten the forbidden fruit of imperialism.

To pacify, police, and protect its new empire, America needed a new army and world-class navy, which required even more revenue than a bountiful tariff could provide. But we are getting ahead of ourselves.

MORRILL GUARDS THE GATE

From Appomattox to century's end, the recurring problem with the tariff was one unfamiliar to our generation; the tariff produced too much revenue. Every year from 1866 to 1893, the government ran a surplus.

After Lee's surrender, the army had been mustered out, the navy was sold for scrap — and the government shrank. Yet, the Morrill Tariff remained, producing a rising stream of revenue. In 1883 a Republican Congress created a tariff commission to recommend reforms. While President Arthur stacked it with protectionists, it did its work and urged an average 25 percent reduction in tariff rates. The reform bill, however, had the misfortune to be taken into custody by a Senate-House conference that tore up the commission's work, ignored the bills sent over from both chambers, and wrote a new bill pushing tariffs even higher. Signed by Arthur, the law was of such dubious paternity that it came to be known as the Mongrel Tariff.

Until Grover Cleveland's election in 1884, all tariff battles had been resolved as decisively in favor of Republicans who adhered to the Lincoln tradition of protectionism as had the war in favor of the Union. And the watchdog of the tariff was the now-legendary Justin Morrill.

Morrill had entered Congress in 1855 as a Whig and had affixed his name to the tariff laws of 1861–65, which Henry Carey had called the "most important legislation" ever enacted by Congress. By 1885 the crusty Vermonter was chairman of the Senate Finance Committee. Having arrived in Congress half a decade before Fort Sumter, he would not leave until after Manila Bay. Like Cerebus, Morrill guarded the gates against any weakening of the tariff that protected his beloved country. Justin Morrill believed in "America first." In 1857 he had declared his allegiance: "I am for ruling America for the benefit, *first*, of Americans, and for the 'rest of mankind' afterwards."[2] And in 1860 he had equated free trade with economic treason:

> There is a transcendental philosophy of free trade, with devotees as ardent as any of those who preach the millennium. . . . Free trade abjures patriotism and boasts of cosmopolitism. It regards the labor of our own people with no more favor than that of the barbarian on the Danube or the cooly on the Ganges.[3]

But Morrill's new adversary was formidable. A reform Democrat and governor who had stood up to Tammany Hall, Cleveland had bested the Republicans' "plumed knight," James G. Blaine. The Cleveland-Blaine campaign was the most exciting race since the Civil War. Blaine, who had seized his party's nomination away from President Arthur, was an economic nationalist who looked on tariffs as the pillars of an "industrial policy under which the nation has prospered so marvelously since the close of the war."[4] Hugely popular with the party rank and file, Blaine was detested by reformers, who believed he had prostituted the speakership of the House and was no better than a common grafter. Still, Blaine had the election won until, just days before the balloting, a dim-witted clergyman at a New York rally for Blaine castigated Democrats as the party of "rum, Romanism, and rebellion." Insulted Irish Catholics moved at once into Cleveland's camp, giving him the Empire State by 1,149 votes out of more than a million cast — and the presidency.

Watching the surpluses pile up, from the Lincoln-Morrill tariff rates, Cleveland decided that the U.S. tariff schedules were "vicious, inequitable and illogical" and directed Congress to produce a tariff "for revenue only." Reformers, who had come to believe that protective tariffs protected the profits of the powerful industrialists corrupting U.S. politics, hailed Cleveland's courage. But in raising the issue, Cleveland slipped; he used the word "free," exposing himself to the dreaded charge that he was a secret free trader. Republicans pounced. "There's one more President for us in Protection," crowed Blaine.[5]

Cleveland hastily backpedaled, accusing his opponents of "bandying epithets."[6] But he did not yield. His entire third message to Congress in December of 1887 was a frontal assault on the tariff, at the Republicans' strongest point: protection. The great battles fought in the time of Jackson and Calhoun, of Polk and Lincoln, were resumed.

Congressman William McKinley emerged as the champion of Republican orthodoxy. At the 1888 Republican convention, he savaged Cleveland's proposed tariff cuts as having been advanced "at

210

Grover Cleveland reaches for a third term,
but his "free trade" position is his vulnerability.
Special Collections Department, Alden Library, Ohio University

the joint behest of the whiskey trust and the agents of foreign manufacturers."[7] The charge was grossly unfair, but Republican car-
toonists piled on, mocking Cleveland as a suppliant of John Bull.
Once again, the tariff was a central issue in a presidential election.

Meanwhile, Cleveland was having a hellish time escaping the detested label of free trader. "It is a condition which confronts us, not
a theory,"[8] he angrily protested. But McKinley and Ohio's senator
John Sherman would not let him wriggle off the hook.

Sherman dismissed the President's attempts at redefinition as a "delusion and a snare." If Cleveland and the Democrats had their way, Sherman said, "It is the protective industrial policy built by the Republican
party that would break down."[9]

The *Chicago Tribune* thought McKinley's hard tariff line a blunder that would cost Republicans the election. But late in the campaign, the Republicans got a break to even the score for the "rum, Romanism, and rebellion" gaffe of 1884. The *Los Angeles Times* broke a story that British ambassador Sir Lionel Sackville-West had written — in what he thought was a confidential letter to an English-born naturalized American — that Grover Cleveland was considered a good friend by the mother country.

Sackville-West had been had. His actual correspondent was one George Osgoodby, who had used the phony British-sounding name of Murchison. When the letter exploded in the press, Republicans blistered Cleveland as a toady of free-trade Britain who had sold out for British gold. THE BRITISH LION'S PAW THRUST INTO AMERICAN POLITICS TO HELP CLEVELAND roared the headline of one New York newspaper. BOUNCE HIM echoed the *New York World*.

Muttering bitterly about "the damned Englishman," Cleveland had Sackville-West sacked. The British were enraged at the diplomatic insult, but the Anglophobic Irish-Americans had heard enough. If Cleveland was Mother England's boy, Benjamin Harrison was their man.[10]

Osgoodby's trick worked beautifully. For not only was free trade considered an alien idea, while protectionism was Americanism, free trade was the policy that the detested British were attempting to fasten on the world, it was believed, for their own selfish benefit. Cleveland was now carrying too much weight in his saddlebags. Harrison evicted him from the White House, and the Republicans took over Congress.

Man of the hour: William McKinley.

THE MCKINLEY TARIFF

As biographer Margaret Leech writes, McKinley was a man utterly unlike the academic free-trade enthusiasts of his time:

All the circumstances of McKinley's youth had favored his adherence to the Republican principle of the protective tariff. The very village of his birth had been named for Hezekiah Niles, an early protectionist. The duty on foreign iron had not been an abstract idea to an ironfounder's son, but the source of bread and butter, and memories of want rang in McKinley's phrases when he spoke of the low-tariff years of his boyhood. . . . He carried to Congress an emotional conviction that the solution for all the country's economic ills was to make the already high tariff rates still higher.[11]

The boy was a patriot. Within three months of Fort Sumter, seventeen-year-old Bill McKinley had volunteered and was on his way to the Shenandoah Valley with the Twenty-third Ohio to face the army of Stonewall Jackson. On a bloody Maryland field near Antietam Creek, where more Americans died than had been killed in battle in all of America's previous wars together, the teenager rode a mule into the thick of the fighting, to carry hot meat and coffee to the Union troops. The future president had been witness to the bloodiest day in American history. The memory of the dead and wounded on that Sharpsburg field would never leave him.

In 1864, when he obtained a captaincy, he saw hot fighting in the Valley, and had more than one horse shot [from] under him. He distinguished himself at the Union repulse at Kernstown by a daring gallop under fire to give an unsupported regiment the signal to retreat. [Colonel Rutherford B.] Hayes commented on his gallantry at Winchester. His conduct at Opequan was officially mentioned. After service on the staffs of various generals, McKinley was mustered out in 1865, with the brevet commission of major, signed "A. Lincoln," for gallant and meritorious service in the Shenandoah Valley.[12]

This was the man of whom Theodore Roosevelt said, "[he] has no more backbone than a chocolate eclair!"[13] Roosevelt was not the first to misjudge the modest man from Canton who was never given to egotism or boastfulness.

On returning to Congress, McKinley exploited his new national prestige to declare himself for Speaker of the House. He lost to the greatest parliamentary leader of his day, Thomas B. Reed of Maine, but as consolation prize, he was awarded the chairmanship of Ways and Means. There, he would write the McKinley Tariff of 1890. Had he defeated Reed, McKinley would later say, he would have spent the rest of his life in Congress.

Officially titled "an act to reduce revenue," the McKinley bill proposed to cut $50–$60 million from the Treasury's income by ending tariffs on raw sugar and molasses. Tariffs were maintained, raised, or initiated, however, on every imported manufacture that competed with a U.S.-made product. Its purpose: to cut revenue by raising tariffs on imported manufactures so high that foreigners would give up trying to break into the U.S. market. American workers and manufacturers would be protected; at the same time tariff revenue would fall, and the surpluses would fade away.

Battling alongside McKinley was Morrill. Both believed that the tariff was about more than money. Both spoke of Americans as members of a family with duties to one another. "Free trade in the United States is founded upon a community of equalities and reciprocities," said McKinley. "It is like the . . . obligations of a family."[14] But a foreign manufacturer had

> no right or claim to equality with our own. He is not amenable to our laws. . . . He pays no taxes. He performs no civil duties. . . . He contributes nothing to the support, the progress, and glory of the nation. Free foreign trade . . . results in giving our money, our manufactures, and our markets to other nations, to the injury of our labor, our tradespeople, and our farmers.[15]

McKinley and Morrill were conservatives of the heart. Theirs was a rhetoric of passion and conviction, of concrete and colorful phrases that moved men to action. To them the tariff was about justice and patriotism, about guaranteeing Americans the highest standard of living on earth, and about making America the greatest nation on earth. These were not "progressive Republicans."

Completed in the fall of 1890 and signed by President Harrison, the McKinley Tariff was a "new concept in tariffs":[16]

> No longer would the tariff be an instrument of revenue or even an instrument of protection, but . . . an instrument of exclusion, with rates raised so high that cheap foreign goods made by cheap foreign labor would be barred from the United States for good. McKinley hated the word "cheap." "Cheap is not," he said, "a word of hope; it is not a word of inspiration! It is the badge of poverty; it is the signal of distress."[17]

Not every Republican was a McKinleyite. Blaine, now secretary of state, wrote McKinley that his tariff was a "slap in the face to the South Americans."[18] Testifying against it, Blaine became so agitated that he raised his fist and smashed it on the table, crushing his top hat. But McKinley had not written his tariff bill to prosper South America. He was a nationalist. The world was not his concern; America was. In their respective stands, McKinley and Blaine presaged the conflict between Taft Republicans and Dewey Republicans of the 1940s and 1950s and the deepening divide in the party today.

When McKinley returned home in triumph, he got a rude shock: envious Democrats had gerrymandered him into a district where few of his constituents lived. The chairman of Ways and Means went down to defeat in the year he had written one of America's most famous tariff laws. Yet, in defeat, McKinley became even more formidable. He was now a martyr to partisan politics, and Ohio newspapers began denouncing the injustice of what petty Democrats had done to an Ohio statesman who had achieved so greatly.

In December of 1890 McKinley ran into old friends Thomas H. Carter of Montana and Joe Cannon of Illinois in a Chicago hotel. They, too, had been defeated. McKinley told his friends that, overall, he was "really glad that it had happened that way."

"That is what I am saying to everyone," Cannon nodded, "but, boys, don't let's lie to one another."[19]

Carter dined out on the story for years. But in McKinley's case, he had been telling the truth.

PATRIOTISM, PROTECTION, AND PROSPERITY

In 1891 William McKinley was elected governor of Ohio by a margin of eighty-nine thousand votes, the greatest landslide since the war. But in 1892, the year of the Homestead Strike, the most violent in U.S. history, Cleveland recaptured the White House in a three-way race with Harrison and Populist candidate James B. Weaver of Iowa. McKinley had acted as the bayonet of his party during the campaign, denouncing free trade as a rapacious enemy of the American worker:

> This country will not and can not prosper under any system that does not recognize the difference of conditions in Europe and America. Open competition between high-paid American labor and poorly paid European labor will either drive out of existence American industry or lower American wages.[20]

McKinley believed that protection was the best friend working America ever had; it "has made the lives of the masses of our countrymen sweeter and brighter, and has entered the homes of America carrying comfort and cheer and courage."[21] But when the Panic of 1893 struck, McKinley was fortunate not to be in Washington. For a time, his tariff law was blamed. Luck, however, had always been an ally. Not in four years of fighting in the Valley had he suffered a scratch. Now, Cleveland came to his rescue by replacing the McKinley Tariff with a disastrous Democratic bill.

The Wilson-Gorman Tariff of 1894 was botched from the beginning. Insurgents in the Senate first voted to raise tariff rates. Then they voted to strip Cleveland of "reciprocity" power — the power to impose retaliatory tariffs on countries discriminating against U.S. exports. While average tariff rates were marginally reduced, duties were restored on sugar in the middle of a scandal involving sugar interests. The bill also called for a 2 percent flat tax on incomes above $4,000, hitting 85,000 households out of 12 million.[22] Free traders had found their substitute for the tariff.

Under Lincoln, a wartime tax of 3 percent had been imposed on all incomes between $600 and $10,000, and of 5 percent on those above $10,000, later raised to 10 percent. In 1867 the tax rate was cut to 5 percent on all incomes over $1,000, and the tax was allowed to expire in 1872.[23] But it was the lone Democrat to serve as president in the half century after Fort Sumter who, in letting Wilson-Gorman become law without his signature, gave America its first peacetime income tax.

When the Supreme Court struck down the income tax, Cleveland got the worst of both worlds. He had enraged the capitalists by letting the tax become law, and the populists were enraged when it was overturned.

The Panic of 1893 was the worst depression in U.S. history before the 1930s. In its wake came the Pullman Strike, which paralyzed the nation's railroads. When Cleveland decided to break the strike, Attorney General Richard Olney called out the troops and sent federal marshals to Chicago to run the trains. Eugene V. Debs and his new American Railway Union were routed. Cleveland, mused Henry Adams, is "perhaps the best President the Republican party had put forward since Lincoln."[24]

HOW TARIFFS CHANGED WORLD HISTORY

The McKinley and Wilson-Gorman Acts demonstrate the impact that tariffs can have on the course of history.

As noted, the McKinley Tariff was designed to *reduce* the revenue that was creating an embarrassing stream of budget surpluses. Thus, among its provisions was an end to tariffs on foreign sugar, thereby opening the U.S. market, with a compensating bounty of two cents per pound for U.S.-grown sugar. While lifting the sugar tariff was hailed in the Caribbean, to the Hawaiian Islands the McKinley Act spelled disaster.

Since 1875 the United States had had a reciprocal trade agreement with the kingdom of Hawaii. Hawaiian sugar entered the United States duty-free. To exploit the islands' privileged position, American planters had flocked there. But when McKinley's tariff cuts opened U.S. ports to Caribbean sugar, Hawaii's privileged access came to an end. Hawaiian sugar prices plummeted from $100 a ton to $60, and the islands' economy collapsed.

Already infuriated by the nativism of the new queen, Liliuokalani, a "Hawaii for the Hawaiians!" nationalist, the planters rebelled, seized power, set up a republic, and sought annexation by the United States. If the United States would accept the offer, Hawaiian sugar would become U.S.-grown sugar, and every pound produced would qualify for the two-cent bounty. In 1898, as president, McKinley, whose tariff bill created the crisis that caused the Hawaiian revolution, annexed the islands.

In Cuba, however, the McKinley Tariff was as popular as it was unpopular in Hawaii. Cuban sugar, the island's principal crop, could now enter the United States duty-free. As Hawaii's economy collapsed, Cuba's boomed. But three years after the McKinley Tariff became law, Congress reversed course with the Wilson-Gorman Act, which reimposed sugar tariffs.

Now Cuba's economy collapsed. Cuban revolutionaries seized on the crisis, exploited the discontent of the peasants, and renewed their struggle for independence. This new insurrection, which burst into flame in 1895, led to the Spanish-American War, the liberation of Cuba, and America's annexation of Puerto Rico, Hawaii, Guam, and the Philippines. Had there been no Spanish-American War, the United States would not have annexed the Philippines and so might have avoided its future war with Japan. Thus did a juggling of sugar tariffs between 1890 and 1893 change the course of world history.

INDUSTRIAL POLICY VS. PRAIRIE POPULISM

With the Panic of 1893 spreading, America wanted desperately to be rid of Grover Cleveland, and the popular Ohio governor, campaigning in the 1894 elections on "Protection, Patriotism, and Prosperity," was hailed as the Republican messiah. All this Democratic blather about open world markets, said McKinley, is a "great free-trade shadow-dance."[25]

In November Republicans swept all before them, and the future opened up. Mark Hanna, the Ohio kingmaker with the "cash register conscience," retired from his iron-and-coal business to prepare for a career in politics. His first assignment: make McKinley president. Hanna reportedly raised more than $3 million for McKinley's campaign, with unofficial estimates running to five times that. One commentator wrote, "In 1896 Hanna incorporated McKinley, and every business house in the United States . . . subscribed for McKinley stock."[26]

The extraordinary confidence of the conservatives of that era is captured in the 1895 *History of the Republican Party:* "No political organization that has existed in this Republic ever made such a brilliant record as has been made by the Republican Party"[27] is the opening sentence, and the work bristles with nationalistic defiance:

> Throughout its career the Republican party has had but one purpose, the conserving of American interests, and on that account the party has never been popular in Europe. . . . It is the party of protection. It realizes that our mills and factories cannot pay from fifty to seventy-five per cent more wages than are paid in Europe for the same class of work, unless our products are protected against the products of cheap European labor. It has insisted and still insists, therefore, that American labor shall not be pauperized at the dictation of European greed, and is convinced that when labor is prosperous, all classes are prosperous, it carries the banner of protection defiantly.[28]

The *History* denounces as "demagogic" the progressives' charge that tariffs, far from protecting the wages of workers and the national interest, protected the profits of the wealthy few, and asks a relevant question: if Americans, rather than foreigners, pay the tariff in higher prices, why is it always the foreigners who protest the loudest?

> If the consumer pays the tariff, as the opponents of protection assert, what difference can it make to European manufacturers whether this government imposes a tariff or not. . . . Why the universal rejoicing in Europe when a Democratic congress passes and a Democratic President signs a bill lowering tariffs?[29]

Whenever America has protected a commodity — be it be nails, iron, bunting, pearl buttons — asserts the *History*, the price had fallen.

As nominee in 1896, McKinley ran on this oak-solid Republican platform of high tariffs and money as good as gold. Adoring crowds came to Canton. McKinley addressed them from his front porch. Celebrated in his campaign literature as the "Advance Agent of Prosperity," McKinley told his admirers,

> In the mind of every workingman is the thought that this great American doctrine of protection is associated with wages and work, and linked with home, family, country and prosperity. . . . The people of this country want an industrial policy that is for America and Americans.[30]

McKinley's family life became a feature of Hanna's propaganda. Though most of the women who came to Canton could not vote, many came away charmed. One reporter wrote of McKinley that he exuded a "matinée idol's virility."[31]

McKinley's opponent was the thirty-six-year-old Boy Orator of the Platte, William Jennings Bryan, who had electrified the Democratic convention with his "Cross of Gold" speech. His issue: free coinage of silver. With silver pouring out of America's mines, free coinage meant no deflation of the dollar and plenty of money around for farmers and borrowers to pay off debts without foreclosure or bankruptcy. Rooted in biblical imagery and prairie populism, Bryan's words yet have magical power:

> You come to us and tell us that the great cities are in favor of the gold standard; we reply that the great cities rest upon our broad and fertile prairies. Burn down your cities and leave our farms, and your cities will spring up again as if by magic; but destroy our farms and the grass will grow in the streets of every city in the country. . . .
>
> Having behind us the producing masses of this nation and the world, supported by the commercial interests, the laboring interests, and the toilers everywhere, we will answer their demand for a gold standard by saying to them: You shall not press down upon the brow of labor this crown of thorns, you shall not crucify mankind upon a cross of gold.[32]

"Good money never made times hard!" was the cold retort of hard-money Republicans.[33]

The nation was mesmerized by Bryan's oratory. But as the months wore on and the election drew near, Americans grew uneasy, then fearful. Bryan's speeches had become increasingly radical. An alarmed middle class began moving away. Hanna's millions and a Republican press had done their work. By campaign's end, mocking Republicans were taunting Bryanites with the ditty:

> Free trade and free silver, free whiskey, free lunch,
> Free love and free speech is their cry,
> But when all our products are free as they wish,
> From whom will our customers buy?

On Election Day sound-money Democrats, gagging all the way to the polls over his tariff policies, helped give McKinley the greatest popular mandate since Ulysses S. Grant. Some Bryanites were inconsolable. Cried the poet Vachel Lindsay, "Defeat of my boyhood, defeat of my dream."[34]

The American Nationalists

Even before McKinley took the oath, the House passed the Dingley Act, which raised tariff rates to an average close to the highest in history and restored the concept of reciprocity. To promote exports, the president was authorized to enter agreements with foreign nations for mutual tariff cuts. By laying heavy duties on raw sugar, wool, and hides, the Dingley Act gave the government bargaining chips to trade away to foreign governments in return for opening their home markets to American manufactures.

The drafters and backers of the tariff laws of this era were hard-headed men who always kept in mind the national interest of the United States — men like Philadelphia's William "Pig Iron" Kelley, who preceded McKinley as chairman of Ways and Means. To Kelley, iron and steel were the "muscles of our more modern civilization. . . . A people who cannot supply their own demand for iron and steel, but purchase it from foreigners beyond seas, are not independent . . . they are politically dependent."[35] So long as we rely on England for ships, guns, and shells, said Kelley, America "must endure contumely and outrage with unresisting humility."[36]

Pennsylvania steel manufacturer Joseph Wharton saw his country in a mortal struggle. "Foreign legions," he thundered, are attacking us with "missiles launched from their far-distant mines, mills, and factories. . . . Their attack has often devastated homes . . . and broken up industries as effectually as if the conquest had been effected by warlike weapons." But America had a defense. A "tariff can defeat the foreign plunderer . . . better than a fort."[37]

Free trade, to Wharton, was "a fungus . . . a source of infection which healthy political organs can hardly afford to tolerate."[38] In *National Self-Protection*, Wharton argued that any price hikes due to tariffs are only transitory. Imported steel rails from England had cost $165 in gold per ton in 1864, he wrote; five years later, behind a protective tariff, a U.S. steel rail industry was producing all of America's needs for $80 per ton.[39] An implacable Anglophobe, Wharton "raised a clenched fist against England":

We shall take for ourselves, without asking her leave, the same privilege of consulting our own interests and doing our own thinking. We shall grow in strength and national completeness and independence, despite the groans of the Cobden Club, after England shall have distinctly failed at grasping at universal domination through trade. We decline to be her victim or her imitator.[40]

For progressive Republicans, Wharton had only contempt. "The Republican Party cannot afford to be anything but distinctly Protectionist," he said. "Republicans who are shaky on protection are shaky all over."[41]

THE FRUITS OF PROTECTIONISM

From Lincoln's death to McKinley's, there were four critical elements of the Republican economic agenda: (1) high tariffs to protect the wages of workers and the home market of American manufacturers; (2) a balanced budget, or surplus, every year; (3) federal support for "internal improvements," i.e., turnpikes, canals, and especially railroads; and (4) sound money, "a dollar as good as gold." What did these policies deliver?

By 1880, the United States was second only to Great Britain in its share of world manufacturing output, with 14.7 to 22.9 percent; by 1913, the United States (32 percent) was far ahead of Germany (14.8 percent) and a sinking Britain (13.6 percent). "We lead all nations in agriculture; we lead all nations in mining; we lead all nations in manufacturing," McKinley declared. "These are the trophies we bring after twenty-nine years of a protective tariff."[42]

In the history texts American children study, the era from 1865 to 1900 is a time of greed, corruption, and wretched excess, when a new plutocracy plundered the nation and public policy was bought and sold — to the steel interests, the railroad interests, the timber interests, the oil interests, the sugar interests, the money trusts. Before being curbed by the power of law, it is said, the men of the Gilded Age ran wild. "What do I care for the law?" railroad magnate Cornelius Vanderbilt bellowed. "I got the power, ain' I?"[43] Even from the pulpits some began to preach a new "gospel of wealth." "In the long run," said Bishop Lawrence of Massachusetts, "it is only to the man of morality that wealth comes. . . . Godliness is in league with riches."[44]

To check the power of industrialists, railroaders, and financiers and to protect the rights of workers, labor unions formed. Brave voices were raised against the concentration of wealth that put men above the law. Toward the era's end would come the muckrakers, Lincoln Steffens, Ida Tarbell, Theodore Dreiser, and lesser imitators, to expose the often dreadful conditions in which Americans had to live and work. There was truth in what they wrote. But there is also a truth about this era of nationalism and protectionism that is rarely taught to America's young. During this era

- From 1869 to 1900, the gross national product quadrupled.[45]
- The United States ran budget surpluses every year from 1866 to 1893.
- The national debt was reduced by two-thirds; by 1900 it was less than 7 percent of the GNP.[46]
- Customs duties provided 58 percent of all federal revenue from 1869 to 1900.
- There was no income tax — save Lincoln's wartime tax and Cleveland's brief 2 percent flat tax on the rich, which was declared unconstitutional.
- Between 1870 and 1900, commodity prices fell 58 percent.[47]
- Real wages, despite a doubling of the U.S. population, rose 53 percent.[48]
- Annual growth of the U.S. economy averaged *more than 4 percent a year* from 1870 to 1913.[49]
- From 1870 to 1913, U.S. industrial production rose 4.7 percent a year, compared with 2.1 percent a year in the United Kingdom.[50]

- American exports grew by almost 5 percent a year from 1870 to 1913, while free-trade Britain's grew at less than 3 percent.[51]
- Protectionist America's share of world exports rose from 7.9 percent in 1870 to 12.9 percent in 1913 — while free-trade Britain's fell from 18.9 percent to 13.9 percent.[52]
- Between 1869 and 1910, merchandise imports fell from 8 percent of the GNP to 4 percent.[53]
- The United States began the era with half of Britain's production and ended it with more than double Britain's.

Henry Kissinger describes the astonishing expansion of American industrial power in the Republican-protectionist era, which thrust the United States onto the world stage:

By 1885, the United States had surpassed Great Britain, then considered the world's major industrial power, in manufacturing output. By the turn of the century, it was consuming more energy than Germany, France, Austria-Hungary, Russia, Japan, and Italy combined. Between the Civil War and the turn of the century, American coal production rose by 800 percent, steel rails by 523 percent, railway track mileage by 567 percent, and wheat production by 256 percent.[54]

Behind a tariff wall built by Washington, Hamilton, Clay, Lincoln, and the Republican presidents who followed, the United States had gone from an agrarian coastal republic to become the greatest industrial power the world had ever seen — in a single century. Such was the success of the policy called protectionism that is so disparaged today. Though there were still dreadful slums in the great cities and disparities of wealth between the rich and the common people were huge, America between 1865 and 1900 was pulling families out of poverty into the middle class faster than any society had done in history. Commodore Vanderbilt had his new mansion, J. P. Morgan his new yacht, but workers saw their own lives and the prospects of their children improve dramatically as well. America's population had doubled since the Civil War, to more than 70 million; the nation was tied together by telegraph and railroads open to all; there was no income tax, no standing army, no war, a free and robust press, and free public education for America's children. When in 1888 James Bryce finished his great survey of "The American Commonwealth," he declared that life was better for the common man in America than anywhere else on the face of the earth.[55] Historian Samuel Eliot Morison describes the new world of the generation that reached maturity at the time of the Civil War:

> They had seen the frontier of log cabin and stumpy clearings, sod house and unbroken prairie, replaced by frame houses and great barns, well-tilled farms, and sleek cattle. The railroad, the telegraph, the sewing machine, oil and gas lighting and a hundred new comforts and conveniences had come within reach of all but the poorest during their lifetime. Towns with banks, libraries, high schools, mansions and theaters had sprung up where once as barefoot boys they had hunted the squirrel and wildcat.[56]

The Republican Party championed protectionism, celebrated the rising standard of living it produced, and was repeatedly rewarded at the ballot box. The Democratic nominee in 1900 was again Bryan, who campaigned against imperialism and for liberation of the Philippines. McKinley and his running mate Theodore Roosevelt campaigned on the tariffs that guaranteed "the full dinner pail" for the American family. Many had soured on the nasty guerrilla war against Filipino insurgents, but everyone understood prosperity. The president was reelected in a landslide that eclipsed his victory of 1896.

McKinley's first term had been a triumph. He had fought and won a four-month war against Spain that made America a world power, while reducing the national debt. He had presided over a 75 percent rise in the Dow-Jones industrial average, a near tripling of union membership to 1.1 million, and a reduction in the unemployment rate from 14 percent to 4 percent. In McKinley's first term, the U.S. economy had grown *by an average of 7 percent a year.*[57]

The conservative press fairly gushed over the McKinley record. Said the *Washington Post:* "Prosperity may be set down as the chief cause of the Republican triumph. Never before in our history was it the fortune of any party to go to the country with an appeal for a vote of confidence with such a record of promises fulfilled."[58] The *New York Times* was elated and relieved: "This second assault of Bryan having been repulsed, the future lies fair before us. . . . The currency is safe, the National honor is safe. We can now give ourselves with contented minds and assured confidence to our honorable public and private concerns."[59]

ECLIPSE OF THE EMPIRE

Protectionism is said to lead inevitably to inflation and stagnation, to a nation's losing the dynamic of trade and falling behind its rivals. But from 1865 to 1900 the reverse happened. How do free traders explain this? We had the highest tariffs in history; imports fell by 50 percent as a share of the GNP. Yet, America enjoyed the greatest expansion in history. The U.S. standard of living became the envy of the world. Prices fell. "The period in which America had its highest tariff rates, and the smallest involvement with international trade, was also the one in which the country had its greatest economic success," writes a student of the era.[60]

Because of the flamboyant and flagrant abuses of power by rascals and scoundrels who set the tone and style for the Gilded Age, historians ignore America's accomplishments. But the American experience in the nineteenth century was unique in world history, and economists are coming to recognize it. Paul Bairoch, a professor at the University of Geneva, in a pathbreaking book based on a review of nineteenth-century statistics, has contrasted the real history of the century with the prevailing theories of the liberal economists of the day. His conclusion: "Liberalism in international trade had more negative than positive consequences and . . . protectionist measures had predominantly positive outcomes."[61] Bairoch lists six unassailable "hard facts of nineteenth-century history":

The first hard fact is that . . . the great European depression began during the period 1869–1873, when trade policies in Europe had reached an unprecedented degree of liberalism. . . .

The second hard fact is that not only was there a severe slowing down of economic growth but also, and all the more paradoxical in the period of the greatest liberalism, a decrease in [the rate of growth of] international trade. . . .

The third hard fact is that the United States, which did not take part in the free trade movement (on the contrary, it increased its already strong protectionism), during the period of the great European depression went through a phase of rapid growth. Indeed, this period can be regarded among the most prosperous in the economic history of the United States.

The fourth hard fact is that economic growth started to rise again when Continental Europe resumed and intensified its protectionist policies [after 1879]. . . .

The fifth hard fact is that . . . the major cause of the slowdown in the economy was the decline in rural income due to a fall in agricultural prices caused by the influx of imported cereals. . . .

Last but not least of the six hard facts is that, in the nineteenth century, the liberal trade experience of the Third World was a complete failure.[62]

Victorian radicals called free trade "God's diplomacy." But what did it produce for Great Britain? "Bitter consequences," writes Julian Amery in his biography of Joseph Chamberlain: "Ireland was ruined. . . . British agriculture collapsed; the landed interest withered away; and British industry thus lost a major sector of its home market."[63] Between 1846 and 1910 British imports of wheat grew 1,000 percent. On the eve of World War I, once self-sufficient Britain could grow only enough wheat to feed a fourth of her population.[64] As early as 1879 the editor of the Bristol *Times and Mirror* was in despair over the American challenge:

Where is this American competition to end? The Yankees are threatening to take the leather trade out of our hands now. American locks are superseding those of Staffordshire; American apples are taking the place of those of Somersetshire and Devon in the dye-works. American furniture is to be found in many forms in more houses than the inhabitants themselves are aware of, and many English sideboards next Christmas will probably groan under American barons of beef. You cannot go into an ironmonger's shop without finding his cases full of American notions. . . . Even the English agriculturists themselves are cultivating their fields, reaping and gathering their crops, when they can gather them at all, with implements of American invention and American manufacture.[65]

Chamberlain had been converted to economic nationalism by what he saw happening to his country. A Tariff Reform League was set up, and he took his battle to the nation, arguing that tariffs and an imperial preference system would weld the empire together. But in 1906, about to take over leadership of the Unionist Party in the name of protection, he was felled by a stroke. The cause died. Looking back at what free trade had done to his country, Chamberlain dipped his pen in acid:

Free Trade is the negation of organisation, of settled and consistent policy. It is the triumph of chance, the disordered and selfish competition of immediate individual interests without regard to the permanent welfare of the whole.[66]

More ominous than America's doubling the British rate of growth was Germany's outstripping Britain in every decade. America and Germany were protectionist; yet, both rapidly enlarged their share of the world's export trade at the expense of free-trade Britain. In a speech to the Reichstag, May 2, 1879, Chancellor Bismarck coldly stated his reasons for spurning the free-trade philosophy of the British and for adopting the American system:

The dicta of abstract science do not influence me in the slightest. I base my opinion on the practical experiences of the time in which we are liv-

Uncle Sam leads Prosperous Labor and the Kaiser's Germany
to prosperity with protection,
as Joe Chamberlain urges John Bull to abandon free trade
and follow the world's winners.

Special Collections Department, Alden Library, Ohio University

ing. I see that those countries which possess protection are prospering, and that those countries which possess free trade are decaying.[67]

"The greatest empire the world has ever known lasted a little over a hundred years," writes historian Otto Scott:

Its relatively brief period of glory was ended by two huge, complex errors. The first was to assume that geography and governance was sufficient to make it eternally successful. . . .

The second huge error was to substitute liberal sentimentality for thought; to relax its international guard and its tariffs alike, to rely on the goodwill of strangers, and to spend its riches (in the form of industrial and financial loans) on other nations instead of its own.

The British today live, as has Spain, for so long, amid many mementos of a glorious period, in the status of a regional power somewhere between the second and third level . . . of international importance.[68]

The British substituted "liberal sentimentality for thought." Today, America trods the same path. Was Hegel right when he said that the only thing we learn from history is that we do not learn from history? Will the great republic follow the great empire down the same staircase to the same end? Shorn of empire, dependent on trade, her once-dominant navy now a tiny fraction of America's fleet, Britain today agonizes over whether to surrender its national sovereignty and disappear forever into the European Union. That is what happens to nations that rely upon others for what they should do for themselves. And it will be treason to the great Americans who sacrificed for our own economic independence if we permit the fate of Britain in the twentieth century to become our own in the twenty-first. To avert that end, we must relearn these lessons of our history.

"THE PERIOD OF EXCLUSIVENESS IS PAST"

With the nation more prosperous than it had ever been, on September 5, 1901, the hugely popular president attended the Pan-American Exposition in Buffalo. Before a crowd estimated at fifty thousand, McKinley spoke of America's "almost appalling" prosperity, and outlined his future plans.

Distance, he reminded his hearers, had been effaced by the telegraph and cable, by swift ships and fast trains. . . . "We must not repose in fancied security that we can forever sell everything and buy little or nothing." Reciprocity treaties were in harmony with the spirit of the times;

measures of retaliation were not. In phrase after ringing, emphatic phrase, the President pointed to the trend of the future. "Isolation is no longer possible or desirable. . . . God and man have linked the nations together. No nation can longer be indifferent to any other. . . . The period of exclusiveness is past." [69]

Was the great protectionist reaching out to progressives? No one will ever know. The following day, after a delightful side trip to Niagara Falls, McKinley held a reception at the Exposition's Temple of Music. In line to meet him was Leon Czolgosz, twenty-eight, a self-professed anarchist. With a small revolver wrapped in what appeared to be a surgically dressed hand, Czolgosz approached, brushed aside the president's outstretched hand, and shot him twice. The bullet that entered the president's abdomen proved fatal. Eight days later Theodore Roosevelt, forty-two, was president.

At poker between Uncle Sam and John Bull, protection
is a "pat hand" that beats free trade every time.
Special Collections Department, Alden Library, Ohio University

Chapter 12

THE GREAT
SMOOT-HAWLEY MYTH

*We must recognize free trade as a basic
human right.*[1]

— Richard Armey, 1997

Thank God I am not a free trader.[2]

— Theodore Roosevelt, 1895

"**P**ernicious indulgence in the doctrine of free trade," Roosevelt
had added in his 1895 letter, "seems inevitably to produce fatty de-
generation of the moral fibre."[3] As president, he would echo the
martyred McKinley:

These forty odd years have been the most prosperous years this nation
has ever seen; more prosperous years than any other nation has ever
seen. Every class of our people is benefited by the protective tariff.[4]

The hero of San Juan Hill had no use for academic free traders.
Experience had not shown "that we could afford . . . to follow those
professional counselors who have confined themselves to study in
the closet; for the actual working of the tariff has emphatically contradicted their theories."[5]

But Roosevelt's America had bitten into the apple of imperialism and relished the taste. The "Republic That Never Retreats" had a Pacific empire, and the claims of foreign policy began to take precedence over the interests of American farmers, workers, manufacturers. Cuba, Puerto Rico, and the Philippines were first to be offered almost unrestricted access to U.S. markets, to fix them firmly in the new American "sphere of influence." While Roosevelt approved of reciprocal trade treaties, he reminded Americans in 1904 not to forget whom it was the U.S. economy was to benefit first:

> The one consideration which must never be omitted in a tariff change is the imperative need of preserving the American standard of living for the American workingman. . . . Our laws should in no event afford advantage to foreign industries over American industries.[6]

Through the Roosevelt years, the Dingley Act of 1897 remained the basic tariff law. And when he stood for election in his own right in 1904, Roosevelt stood on McKinley's platform:

> Protection which guards and develops our industries is a cardinal policy of the Republican party. The measure of protection should always at least equal the difference in the cost of production at home and abroad.[7]

Theodore's admiring young cousin would echo him three decades later when, in 1932, Franklin declared himself in favor of a "competitive tariff," which he defined as "one that equalizes the difference in the cost of production" between the United States and low-wage countries.[8]

BATTLE FOR THE SOUL OF THE GOP

In the first decade of the twentieth century, a sea change was taking place in politics. Goaded by a national uproar after the Panic of

1907, progressive Republicans began to echo free-trade Democrats and demand a cut in the tariff rates, which both now saw as benefiting powerful industrialists at the expense of American consumers. The muckrakers had done their work.

In 1909 William Howard Taft was elected to succeed his friend and patron Roosevelt, having pledged himself to tariff reform. On taking office, he called a special session of Congress. Hopes for reform ran high but were dashed when Joe Cannon of Illinois was elected Speaker and named his fellow protectionist Sereno Payne of New York to chair the Committee on Ways and Means. Payne drew up a compromise bill to please both the McKinleyites and the progressives. It cut tariff rates on raw materials but raised them on certain finished goods.

The Senate proceeded to eviscerate Payne's bill. Under the guidance of the chairman of the Senate Committee on Banking and Finance, Nelson Aldrich of Rhode Island, 847 amendments were added. Virtually every one raised a tariff. The Payne-Aldrich bill that came out of Congress only marginally reduced tariff rates from the Alpine heights of the Dingley Act. It was sent to the White House, where it was signed by Taft.

Payne-Aldrich, however, armed the president with a new weapon to fight the international trade wars: the "variable tariff." If a nation discriminated against U.S. exports, Taft had the authority to tack 25 percent onto the average duties on that country's goods entering the United States.

By now, however, a new issue dominated the debate. If the United States intended to cut tariffs, how was the lost revenue to be replaced? Free traders were settled on the substitute: a federal income tax. "The focus of the battle in Congress," writes trade historian William Gill, "became not so much the tariff per se as the income tax which was to replace it."[9]

In the second Cleveland administration, an income tax had been tacked onto the Wilson-Gorman Tariff, only to have the Supreme Court strike it down. Now, led by Tennessee congressman Cordell

Hull, Congress was ready to defy the Court, by passing another income tax. Taft, who loved and revered the Court, and would one day sit as chief justice, was horrified at the prospect of a constitutional confrontation. He urged Congress to let the states decide the issue by passing a constitutional amendment allowing for an income tax. Congress did, by 77–0 in the Senate — many of whose millionaires voted for the amendment confident that the states would kill it — and by 318–14 in the House.[10]

This was a crucial moment in economic history. From Taft's initiative would come the Sixteenth Amendment and a permanent tax on the income of all Americans. This revenue engine would quickly replace tariffs as the prime source of federal income, and the immense stream of cash it would generate would be used to finance world wars and expand federal power into every walk of American life. In one of the ironies of history, the federal income tax was the legacy of a Republican named Taft.

AMERICA'S FIRST LIBERAL HOUR

Taft's presidency was not a happy affair. Republicans lost seats in 1910, and two years later Theodore Roosevelt walked out on the GOP and accepted the nomination of the Progressive ("Bull Moose") Party, putting himself and Taft into a three-way race with New Jersey governor Woodrow Wilson. The Republican split was one of the great disasters to befall economic nationalists in U.S. history. For both Taft and TR were protectionists. As late as 1911 Roosevelt had reasserted his allegiance:

> I can put my position on the tariff in a nutshell. I believe in such measure of protection as will equalize the cost of production here and abroad; that is, will equalize the cost of labor here and abroad. I believe in such supervision of the workings of the law as to make it certain that protection is given to the man we are most anxious to protect — the laboring man.[11]

As for Wilson, his views were pure Cobdenism: "I wish I might hope that our grandchildren could indulge in free trade."[12]

In the election of 1912, the president of the United States ran third. A divided GOP gave Wilson the White House and Democrats both houses of Congress. America's first Liberal Hour began. In 1913

- the Federal Reserve Act was passed, creating a national bank to replace the one it was Andrew Jackson's proud claim to have killed;
- the Sixteenth Amendment was adopted on February 3, 1913, authorizing a federal income tax;
- the Underwood-Simmons Act, containing a national income tax and cutting tariffs to the lowest level since before the Civil War, was signed into law; and
- the Seventeenth Amendment, providing for direct election of senators, was added to the Constitution.

Underwood-Simmons marked the first downward revision in tariff rates in a generation, and the deepest since the Buchanan administration. The average duty was cut from 40 percent to 27 percent. To replace the lost revenue, Congress enacted a graduated income tax. Initially, it applied only to corporations and the small fraction of Americans earning more than $4,000. But a momentous shift had begun. From a nineteenth-century base in public lands, alcohol taxes, and customs duties, the U.S. government was moving to mine the mother lode of American prosperity. While the initial rates ranged from 1 percent to 7 percent, within five years the top rate for individuals would hit 70 percent and the bottom, 6 percent.

Free-trade Democrats like Cordell Hull were now in power. With the classical liberals, Hull and Wilson believed that free trade was about more than economics; it was its own reward. They did not demand reciprocal foreign tariff cuts in return for U.S. rate reductions. They stood in the messianic tradition of the Virginia Democrat John R. Tucker who, twenty-five years earlier, had equated free trade with the Christian gospels and the borderless economy with the kingdom of heaven.

> Free trade . . . will spread the banner of peace over the world and promote the glory of God, in "peace on earth and good will toward men." Free trade, the product of the divine doctrines of Christianity, would be the peacemaker of the world![13]

After he won reelection in 1916 on the slogan "He kept us out of war!" Wilson led America into the great European bloodbath "to make the world safe for democracy." In his peace offer to Germany, Wilson listed global free trade as third among his Fourteen Points: "The removal, so far as possible, of all economic barriers and the establishment of an equality of trade conditions among all nations consenting to the peace."[14]

"Prosper America First"

> *America's present need is not heroics, but*
> *healing; not nostrums, but normalcy;*
> *not revolution, but restoration.*
>
> — Senator Warren G. Harding, 1920

World War I and the Versailles peace it produced proved a calamity for Western civilization, and a disaster for Wilson; it brought America "debt, inflation, prohibition, influenza and ingratitude from Allies whom [America] had strained herself to help."[15] The first income tax of 1913 which had 7 percent as its highest rate by war's end stood at 63 percent. The national debt, $1.2 billion in 1916, had passed $25 billion in 1919.[16]

In 1918 Democrats lost both houses of Congress. Two years later Warren Harding captured the White House in the greatest popular landslide in history — 16.1 million votes to 9.1 million for Governor James M. Cox of Ohio and thirty-eight-year-old Franklin D. Roosevelt. "A return to normalcy" and a new tariff to stanch the flow of imports from a recovering Europe were the GOP issues. On asking Congress for emergency tariff legislation, Harding declared, "I believe in the protection of American industry . . . it is our purpose to prosper America first."[17] The Republicans were back!

Amid the horrors of the western front, free traders had suffered a loss of faith. "When goods are not allowed to cross borders, soldiers will," Bastiat had said. But in August 1914 the nations of Europe had been woven together by trade. Goods were crossing borders in record volume. India alone excepted, the best customer for British exports had been Germany; and, next to America, Germany was Britain's chief source of supply. Germany had been the principal supplier of Russia and Belgium, yet invaded both. The warring parties of Europe had been the trading partners of Europe. But when war came, national interests triumphed over economic interests. The Cobdenites had been wrong. The claim of J. B. Say that, as a consequence of his law of markets, "all nations are friends in the nature of things" rang hollow to the survivors of Passchendaele and the Somme. It was Kipling's words that echoed now:

> Then the Gods of the Market tumbled, and their
> 　　smooth-tongued wizards withdrew
> And the hearts of the meanest were humbled and
> 　　began to believe it was true
> That all is not Gold that Glitters, and Two and
> 　　Two Make Four —
> And the Gods of the Copybook Headings limped
> 　　up to explain it once more.[18]

Always a foe of liberalism, Kipling now had a personal reason to damn its hollow doctrines. His only son had been killed on the western front.

RETURN OF THE PROTECTIONISTS

World War I affected thinking in every capital. Industrial power had proved to be the bedrock of military power, and behind industry there had to be secure supplies of food and raw materials to feed man and machine. Statesmen could no longer leave the fate of their nations to Adam Smith's "invisible hand." A closer reading of Smith would have taught them that. As Jefferson had converted to economic nationalism after America's sobering experience in the War of 1812, countless free traders of the Great War generation now underwent similar conversions.

With free-trade dogma discredited, its acolytes demoralized by the rout of Wilsonism, economic nationalists were pushing against an open door. Harding and Treasury Secretary Andrew Mellon led Congress in slashing Wilson's wartime income tax rate all the way back to 25 percent. To protect industry from an anticipated flood of manufactures from low-wage Europe, Harding signed the Fordney-McCumber Tariff Act, which doubled average tariff rates, to 38 percent, although two-thirds of all imports now entered the United States duty-free.

Having pledged to "prosper America first," Harding and Coolidge were true to their word. America took off in her new Stutz Bearcat on the wildest ride in history: the Roaring Twenties. The results were startling. Unemployment, which stood at 12 percent when Harding took office, was down to 3 percent when Coolidge went home.

> If anything roared in the "Roaring Twenties," it was industry and commerce. America was in the midst of a productivity revolution, turning out more goods with less labor. Manufacturing output rose 64 percent, output per workhour 40 percent. *Between 1922 and 1927 the economy*

grew by 7 percent a year — the largest peace time growth ever.[19] (Emphasis added.)

No president of the twentieth century did better at reducing the "misery index" than the maligned Harding; and when Coolidge said good-bye to Washington in 1929, the U.S. share of world manufacturing had reached a record-shattering 42.2 percent![20] Harding, Coolidge, and Mellon had proved another historic point: lower tax rates need not reduce tax revenue. As the top income tax rate plummeted from 73 percent to 25 percent, income tax revenue grew in five years from $690 million to $711 million.

> Even more curious, the distribution of the tax burden became radically *more* progressive, not less. In 1921 those earning less than $10,000 had paid $155 million in taxes, 21 percent of personal income tax revenues. In 1926 they paid only $33 million, or 5 percent. Mellon himself boasted . . . that a bachelor with $4,000 income in 1920 — enough to make him comfortably middle class — would have paid $120 in tax that year, but in 1928 would owe only $5.63.
>
> At the same time the very rich, those earning over $100,000, saw their portion of income taxes rise from 29 percent to 51 percent, paying $194 million in 1921 and $362 million in 1926.[21]

In the Harding-Coolidge era, a doubling of tariff rates and a halving of tax rates produced a record unequaled even by Ronald Reagan.

THE CRASH OF '29 AND SMOOT-HAWLEY

On October 29, 1929, with Winston Churchill looking down from the gallery, the New York Stock Exchange suffered the greatest single-day disaster in history. All day long stocks plummeted. At the closing bell, the ticker showed that 10 percent of the value of the greatest corporations in the citadel of capitalism had vanished in seven hours. The Roaring Twenties had come to a crashing close. America's Great Depression was on. Within six months 10 percent of U.S. workers were unemployed, factories were shutting down, banks were closing, savings were vanishing. America had entered a decade-long decline.

Eight months after the crash, in June of 1930, Congress passed and Herbert Hoover signed Smoot-Hawley, boosting tariff rates from near 40 percent to 59 percent by 1932. As the United States was running a trade surplus and U.S. manufacturers were protected by the Fordney-McCumber Tariff, why did the Republicans raise tariff rates?

The president was honoring a campaign commitment to protect American farmers from Canadian imports. Farmers had been devastated by a worldwide glut caused by the overseas expansion of food and fiber production after the war. But once the Smoot-Hawley train began to roll through Congress, new tariffs were hoisted aboard for import-sensitive industries. Then there was the usual logrolling. But there was another reason for Smoot-Hawley — the Republican conviction, rooted in party history and philosophy, that protectionism was good for America. California senator Samuel Shortridge spoke in debate for the Grand Old Party of his day:

> What the American people want is a tariff that protects . . . American-raised, American-mined, American-manufactured products and American men and women from competition with like foreign products raised, mined, or manufactured by cheap foreign labor. . . . The free-trade theory has cursed America. The protective theory has blessed America. If the free-trade theory were now put into operation, it would bankrupt America.[22]

To many abroad, America seemed to have leaped into a lifeboat yelling, "Every man for himself!" as Western capitalism was going down. No one at that time, however, made the claim that Smoot-Hawley had caused a market crash that occurred eight months before it was passed or that Smoot-Hawley triggered a depression that was already underway before Hoover signed the bill. The myth-makers would come later.

FDR TAKES BOTH SIDES

As Republicans had done to them after the Panics of 1857 and 1893, Democrats blamed Republican tariff policy for the hard times. But the Democrats had a credibility problem. In their own 1928 plat-form, in a bid for votes in the Northeast, Democrats had endorsed tariffs to maintain "legitimate business and a high standard of wages for American labor." Indeed, the party was specific on how high tar-iff rates should be:

> Actual difference between the cost of production at home and abroad, with adequate safeguard for the wage of the American laborer must be the extreme measure of every tariff rate.[23]

William McKinley could have written that plank. Nevertheless, in Seattle on September 20, the Democratic candidate, Franklin Roosevelt, tore into Hoover over the "Hawley-Smoot, otherwise known as the Grundy, Tariff":

> President Hoover probably should have known that this tariff would raise havoc with any plans that he might have to stimulate foreign mar-kets. But he did not, I am afraid, sufficiently understand how insistent are the demands of certain types of Republicans for special high tariff protection. When that tariff bill was passed, with its outrageous rates, the President yielded to the demands of those leaders and started us down the road to the place where we now find ourselves. It is the road to ruin, if we keep on it.[24]

In Sioux City on September 29, FDR again ripped into "Smoot-Hawley-Grundy," claiming the tariff had destroyed the foreign markets of American farmers and brought retaliation on U.S. exports. He pledged to eliminate the "outrageously excessive [tariff] rates" and initiate a practice of bartering in "our Yankee tradition of good old-fashioned trading."[25]

Who was this "Grundy" FDR was pummeling? A long-time lobbyist for the woolen textile industry and benefactor of Republican causes, Joseph R. Grundy of Pennsylvania had been appointed to the Senate in 1929, and sat proudly amid the stalwarts in the Smoot-Hawley debate. Roosevelt was now hammering Grundy's name into the history books.

Hoover, however, gladly accepted FDR's challenge and seized on the tariff issue. In his August 11 address accepting renomination, he charged that Democrats would "place our farmers and our workers in competition with peasant and sweated-labor products."[26] In Des Moines on October 4, he accused Roosevelt's crowd of planning to "reduce farm tariffs if they come to power."[27] On October 15 in Cleveland, he warned that if the Democratic plans to replace protective tariffs with only revenue tariffs were implemented, U.S. workers would be forced to

> compete with laborers whose wages in their own money is only sufficient to buy from one-eighth to one-third of the amount of bread and butter that you can buy at the present rates of wages, and the present price of commodities bad as they are.[28]

Economic nationalism still resonated in 1932. But this Roosevelt believed with the late Senator Henry Ashurst that the clammy hand of consistency should never rest for long on the shoulder of a statesman. In the tariff confrontation of 1932, it was FDR who blinked and backed down. In Boston on October 31, he became the echo of Justin Morrill: "I favor continued protection for American agriculture as well as American industry."[29]

Since those days, generations have been indoctrinated in the myth that if Smoot-Hawley did not cause the Depression, it surely extended and deepened it. The myth has become part of our popular culture. In the 1986 comedy film *Ferris Bueller's Day Off*, Ben Stein, actor-writer son of Herb Stein, who chaired Nixon's Council of Economic Advisers, played a history teacher instructing indolent high school students:

> In 1930, the Republican-controlled House of Representatives, in an effort to alleviate the effects of the — anyone? anyone? — the Great Depression, passed the — anyone? anyone? — the tariff bill, the Hawley-Smoot Tariff Act which — anyone? raised or lowered? raised tariffs — in an effort to collect more revenue for the federal government. Did it work? Anyone? Anyone know the effects? It did not work, and the United States sank deeper into the Great Depression.[30]

When Vice President Al Gore debated Ross Perot on NAFTA in 1993, his clinching argument was a photograph of Senator Reed Smoot and Representative Willis Hawley, which he handed to Perot, saying, "They raised tariffs and it was one of the principal causes, many economists say, the principal cause, of the Great Depression in this country and around the world."[31] The *Wall Street Journal* leaped for joy: "The famous tariff lives on in the annals of invincible ignorance" and "represented a brand of dumb and reactionary Republicanism that consigned the party to also-ran oblivion from 1932 through Robert Taft."[32] *Business Week* excoriated Smoot-Hawley for "triggering the Great Depression and paving the way for World War II."[33] Quite a load for one modest tariff bill to carry.

Consider the bill of particulars in the indictment.

Smoot-Hawley imposed the highest tariff rates in U.S. history; triggered the stock market crash; provoked massive retaliation against U.S. exports, thereby drying up world trade; lengthened and deepened the Depression; brought a sad ruinous end to the careers of Smoot and Hawley — a charge made even by Ronald Reagan — and was a principal cause of the rise of Hitler and World War II.

Historian Alfred E. Eckes, Jr., chairman of the International Trade Commission in the Reagan era, studied the evidence and presented it in his 1995 book *Opening America's Market: U.S. Foreign*

Trade Policy Since 1776. Not one of the charges against Smoot-Hawley stands up.[34]

Smoot-Hawley: Myth and Reality

While Smoot-Hawley did raise the average tariff rate to 53 percent in 1930 and to 59 percent in 1932, the Tariff of Abominations of 1828 produced a rate of 62 percent in 1830. *But Smoot-Hawley applied to only one-third of all U.S. imports.* Compare that with the Tariff of Abominations, which applied to 92 percent of imports, the Morrill tariff (96 percent), the McKinley Tariff (48 percent), and the Dingley Tariff (55 percent). *The list of duty-free imports under Smoot-Hawley was the longest in history.*

Considering Smoot-Hawley duties as a percentage of *all* imports, it ranks, in impact on trade, below every single post–Civil War tariff except the Underwood Tariff of 1913.

Moreover, Congress never imposed a 59 percent rate. The rate hit 59 percent in 1932 only because the prices of so many goods collapsed. (If a $2 tariff is imposed on a $10 toy, and the toy price falls to $3, that $2 tariff has risen from 20 percent to 66.6 percent.) Had 1929 price levels endured, the Smoot-Hawley tariff rate would have been 41 percent, not high by historical standards.

What of the second charge — that the anticipation of Smoot-Hawley caused the stock market crash eight months before the act became law? Yet, in the spring of 1930 — *after* Smoot-Hawley had broken through its opposition on the Hill and was headed to certain passage — the stock market was headed due north. Eckes shows the market often rising as Smoot-Hawley's prospects improve, and falling when Smoot-Hawley appears on the ropes, i.e., no correlation.

* * *

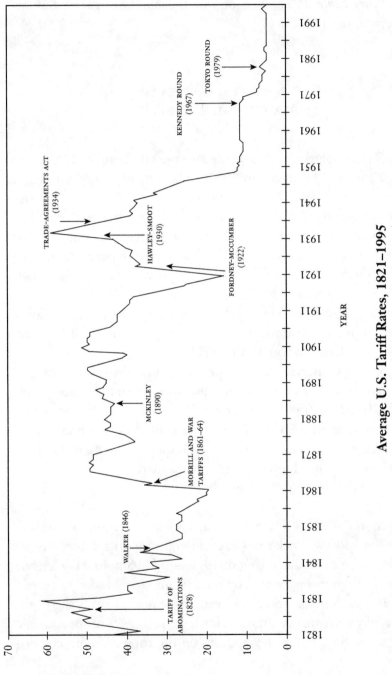

**Average U.S. Tariff Rates, 1821–1995
(Ratio of duties calculated to dutiable imports)**

Source: *Historical Statistics of the United States* and *Statistical Abstract of the United States, 1996*

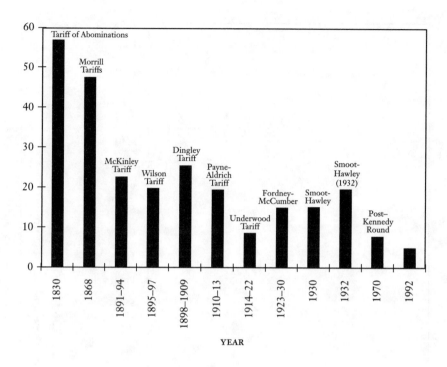

Weight of Tariffs, 1828–1992
(Ratio of all duties calculated to free and dutiable imports)

Source: *Historical Statistics of the United States* and *Statistical Abstract of the United States, 1996*

Moreover, how much adverse effect could Smoot-Hawley have had on the U.S. economy as a whole, *when total imports in 1930 added up to only 4 percent of the GNP and Smoot-Hawley applied to only a third of that, or to 1.3 percent of the GNP?* Is it conceivable that an increase in tariffs on 1.3 percent of the GNP triggered the collapse of five thousand banks, wiped out five-sixths of the stock market, caused a drop of 46 percent in the GNP, and sent unemployment soaring to 25 percent? One economist who studied the consequences of Smoot-Hawley writes that

from 1929 to 1933, America's GNP fell from $104 billion to $56 billion, a loss of $48 billion. However, net exports fell by only $700 million, and domestic spending declined by $47.3 billion. In other words, net ex-

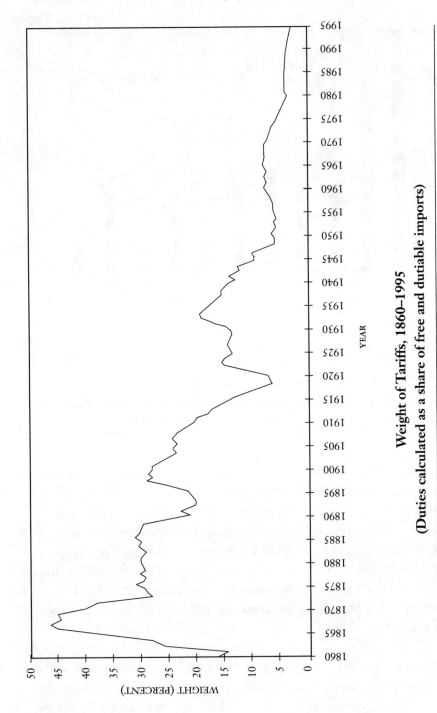

Weight of Tariffs, 1860–1995
(Duties calculated as a share of free and dutiable imports)

YEAR

WEIGHT (PERCENT)

Source: *Historical Statistics of the United States* and *Statistical Abstract of the United States, 1996*

ports decreased by 1.5 percent of the fall in GNP, as domestic demand fell by the remaining 98.5 percent! It is patently absurd to fuss over that 1.5 percent fall and overlook the other 98.5 percent.[35]

The reason the Great Depression endured can be found in a single statistic. With the crash, the stampede for cash to meet margin calls, the run on the banks, their collapse, and the wipeout of savings, *one-third of America's money supply vanished.* And the Federal Reserve did nothing to stop the hemorrhaging or to replace the lost lifeblood of the American economy. Thus, the economy went into shock and almost expired.[36]

Hoover's contribution to the Depression was not Smoot-Hawley. It was the crippling 1932 hike in the income tax, raising the top rate from 25 percent to 65 percent, and the bottom rate by a factor of ten, from .4 percent to 4 percent. To raise taxes in a recession is suicidal. FDR compounded the felony by raising the top rate to 79 percent! Anxious to convict Smoot-Hawley, economists have ignored the critical role that the record tax hikes of the 1930s played in keeping America mired in depression until World War II pulled us out.

The contention that Smoot-Hawley triggered a global stampede to protectionism is another myth. The world was already far down that road before Smoot-Hawley was even on the table. In France the trend toward protectionism had begun in 1890; in 1918 Paris renounced all treaties based on the most-favored-nation principle. Yugoslavia, Hungary, and Czechoslovakia had higher tariffs after World War I than before. So, too, did Bulgaria and Romania. Italy, Spain, Belgium, Holland — and Germany after 1925 — had all raised tariffs above prewar levels.[37] Japan, India, Australia, and New Zealand had also adopted policies to curtail imports to protect the industries that had expanded during the war.

Even free-trade Britain was going protectionist. The 33¹/₃ percent duties levied on cars, motorcycles, and other manufactures by the McKenna Act of 1915 were expanded in 1921, by the Safeguarding of Industries Act and the Dyestuffs Importation Act, to industries vital to national security. The thinking behind Britain's return to protectionism:

> The new industries since 1915 would need careful nurturing and protection if foreign competition were not again to reduce Britain to a technological colony. All in all, although Britannia had been rescued from liberalism by the Great War, it was possible that she might abandon the hard road of rehabilitation and return to her old life.[38]

There was one major exception to this protectionist trend. In 1927 the League of Nations called an International Economic Conference, after which tariffs were lowered in almost all developed countries in 1928 and 1929.[39] As these tariff cuts came just *before* the 1929 crash, it would be more logical (though no less wrong) to blame worldwide tariff cuts, rather than Smoot-Hawley, for the crash and the Depression.

In his memoirs Cordell Hull recalls that when he arrived at his office as FDR's new secretary of state,

> I found in the files no fewer than thirty-four formal and emphatic diplomatic protests presented by as many nations following the passage of the Smoot-Hawley high tariff Act nor had their protests been confined to words. Goaded by what they regarded as almost an embargo keeping out their exports to the United States, they retaliated in kind.[40]

Eckes discovered this to be Hull hype. The real figure turns out to be three or four diplomatic protests. A few nations did retaliate but only against a few selected products, like autos.

In 1933 FDR and Hull began rolling back the Smoot-Hawley tariff rates — to below the rates of Fordney-McCumber. Yet, recovery did not come. By 1937 tariff rates had been slashed to some of the lowest levels of the twentieth century, but still prosperity did not come. That year a second wave of the Depression struck with unemployment rising to 17 percent.

What caused that?

Like all economic activity, trade did contract in the Depression. Import trade, however, contracted about the same for duty-free as for dutiable commodities covered by Smoot-Hawley. Smoot-Hawley thus had an imperceptible effect even on trade, let alone on a national economy of which foreign trade was but a tiny fraction.

As for Smoot and Hawley being punished by an enraged electorate, this, too, is bogus history. Willis Hawley, sixty-eight, lost in a primary in Oregon to a popular fellow twenty years his junior. His tariff had nothing to do with it. Hawley did not even go home to campaign. Among his problems, Hawley was a "dry" on Prohibition, while his rival was a "wet."

Reed Smoot went down to defeat in Utah in the New Deal landslide. But few survived that Little Big Horn. Smoot, however, ran *ahead* of both his governor and President Hoover. Like Hawley, he lost to a man twenty years his junior. Among Smoot's problems: at seventy, he was an apostle of the Mormon Church, whose people wanted him home. Both men went down to defeat without repudiating their work or renouncing their faith. Smoot remained a proud protectionist:

> This Government should have no apology to make for reserving America for Americans. That has been our traditional policy ever since the United States became a nation. We have refused to participate in the political intrigues of Europe, and we will not compromise the independence of this country for the privilege of serving as schoolmaster for the world. In economics as in politics, the policy of this Government is "America first." The Republican Party will not stand by and see economic experimenters fritter away our national heritage.[41]

Smoot left office, prestige intact, with the *New York Times* paying him tribute. Senator Reed Smoot, said the *Times*, was "a statesman of the highest type."[42] With his defeat, the bloodline going back to before the Civil War was broken. Justin Morrill had written Lincoln's tariffs that financed the war that saved the Union. Morrill moved over to the Senate Finance Committee in 1867, where he took the chairman's gavel from John Sherman in 1877, wielding it until his death in December 1898. The gavel was then passed to Morrill's protégé, Nelson Aldrich, who held it until 1911. Aldrich's principal lieutenant was Reed Smoot, who succeeded to the Finance Committee chair in 1923. With Smoot's 1932 defeat, the great era of protectionism, begun when Lincoln carried Pennsylvania and the nation on the tariff issue, came to a close.

Was Smoot-Hawley responsible for the rise of fascism and Hitler? The assertion is absurd. Hitler attempted his Munich Beer Hall Putsch in 1923, seven years before Smoot-Hawley. Had Hitler's coup succeeded, would Fordney-McCumber have been responsible? Did Mussolini march on Rome to protest U.S. tariff rates? Did any war criminal ever attribute the turmoil in Germany, or the fascists' anti-Western attitudes, to U.S. tariffs? No. Only Americans do that. The charge that Smoot-Hawley was responsible for the rise of fascism is an early and excellent example of the "blame America first" syndrome.

For what purpose this malicious and mendacious charge? The answer: moral extortion, to induce in Americans a sense of guilt, so that we never again raise tariffs to protect our nation and so that we shall assume our moral duty to make reparations to a world that suffered terribly because of the greed and selfishness of Republicans of the Roaring Twenties.

Smoot-Hawley was a "molehill, not a mountain," writes Eckes. Milton Friedman concurs with Dr. Eckes. In a December 1997 letter to the author, he said of Smoot-Hawley, "It played no significant role in either causing the depression or prolonging it." Yet, generations are still being indoctrinated in the myth. The hidden agenda: to ensure that no future generation ever again studies, learns, or embraces the ideas of those nationalist Republicans who, in the tradition of Lincoln, McKinley, Teddy Roosevelt, and Calvin Coolidge, put America first.

THE POLITICS OF PROTECTIONISM

The golden age of protection, from 1865 to 1913, which produced the greatest economic expansion in history, and its silver age, the Roaring Twenties, where annual growth rates reached 7 percent, were history. Americans would soon forget what protectionism had wrought and would come to believe the establishment line — that it was all a dark and sordid past, best forgotten, that can teach us nothing.

We have seen what economic nationalism did for the country. What did it do for the GOP? From 1860 to 1932 Republicans carried the White House in fourteen of eighteen elections. Eleven Republicans won in their own right: Lincoln, Grant, Hayes, Garfield, Harrison, McKinley, Roosevelt, Taft, Harding, Coolidge, Hoover. But only two Democrats won the White House in those seventy-two years: Cleveland and Wilson, both of whom won only because the Republican Party had split. So potent was the tariff issue that in 1872 the Democrats, weakened by identification with the Confederacy, pinned their hopes on a journalist! The high-tariff man: Horace Greeley.

From Lincoln to Hoover, Republican presidents were economic nationalists. These men made no apology for putting their country first. Foreign manufacturers and workers had no claim to equal access to U.S. markets, for they did not share the duties and burdens of citizenship. This land was our land. America was for Americans. Tariffs protected the home market, kept America first in industrial power, and made U.S. wages the envy of the world. Isn't that who the economy was for?

Isn't that what government was supposed to do?

In every GOP platform from 1884 to 1944, the party proclaimed its faith in protection. That U.S. citizens would be swarming over Capitol Hill, at six-figure salaries, paid by Toyota or Toshiba, doing the bidding of Japan, Mexico, or China, and that American businessmen would be pounding on executive desks for trade deals so they could shutter U.S. factories and open plants in Asia — these old Republicans would have regarded such as little short of treason. And political correctness would not have inhibited them from saying what they thought of this new breed.

Book Three

THE COUNTERREVOLUTION
AND THE
COMING OF A NEW POPULISM

Chapter 13

1933–93

> *The question . . . that is presented to every American is whether the United States will take the opportunity which is offered to shape her own life in her own way and in accord with her own ideals, or whether this opportunity will be thrust aside for an elusive and delusive old-world concept of sordid international shopkeeping.*[1]
>
> — Sam Crowther, 1933

The year 1933 marked the triumph of the free traders. In the decades to follow, Smoot-Hawley would become an epithet, a synonym for a selfish, crabbed conservatism, and a convenient stick to beat any who would dare urge a revival of economic nationalism. "What about Smoot-Hawley!" was the concluding crushing taunt in any argument on tariffs and trade.

For twenty years liberals who dominated the nation's politics, popular culture, and intellectual discourse drove home the lesson: Smoot-Hawley was a crime in the realm of economics as great as the appeasement of Hitler at Munich had been in the realm of politics. Tariffs were "beggar thy neighbor" economics in which the great republic that now led the Western democracies must never again indulge.

With America's victory in World War II, New Deal Democrats

resurrected the dream of Wilson and sought to create an International Trade Organization (ITO) with the power to enforce rules of worldwide free trade, over which no nation would be granted veto power. A postwar Republican resurgence killed the ITO, but free traders made a historic breakthrough with the election of Dwight Eisenhower. During the Eisenhower era, the Republican Party, America's bastion of economic nationalism, converted to free trade. A soldier all his life, Dwight Eisenhower put Allied solidarity in the Cold War before all else. By the end of his second term, Ike had "led Republicans from protectionism to Cobdenism."[2] Pre-Ike, free-trade presidents were the exception; post-Eisenhower, they were the rule.

Just as important were the Young Turks of the New Conservatism who would capture the Republican Party for Barry Goldwater in 1964 and for Ronald Reagan in 1980: free traders who read Milton Friedman and mocked William McKinley with the relish of a New Dealer. I know, because I was one of them.

Presidents Kennedy and Johnson came out of the FDR tradition and shared Eisenhower's conviction that opening America's markets, even if foreign governments refused to reciprocate, was essential to bind allies and neutrals to America's cause. Trade concessions were to them instruments of diplomacy; any casualties caused to U.S. industry or labor must be borne manfully in the name of fighting and winning the Cold War.

Presidents Nixon and Ford were in the Eisenhower tradition — as were their national security advisers Henry Kissinger and Brent Scowcroft. Foreign policy was what their presidencies were about; all else was subordinated to the higher cause of prevailing in the East-West conflict.

Ronald Reagan, however, was a man apart. Raised in a working-class Democratic home, he had been a union leader and was as visceral a patriot as any man to occupy the Oval Office. Though he made the case for free trade with the zeal of a convert, Reagan was also a "conservative of the heart." Convinced in the case of the Harley hog that Japan was unfairly destroying an American icon, he did not hesitate to take actions that horrified free traders. Reagan would go on to impose quotas on imported cars, steel, and machine tools and force Japan to share 20 percent of its home market for semiconductors with American producers.

His successor, George Bush, however, was an internationalist out of the Eastern schools and a reflexive free trader. Though his father, Prescott, had led the battle against JFK's free-trade policies, George Bush lacerated protectionism and isolationism with the relish of a New Dealer.

And so for sixty years, the free traders had it all.

What caused the disintegration of their coalition? First came the stunning collapse of the Soviet empire. With the Cold War's end came the breakup of the conservative-Republican coalition that had come together to fight that war. Second came the dawning on Americans that while the Soviet Union had paid the ultimate price of imperial overstretch, America had also paid an immense price. We had sacrificed our national interests in the cause of Allied solidarity, while Western Europe and Japan had made no comparable contributions and had prospered mightily at our expense.

At the end of sixty years of free-trade policies, America found itself as dependent on foreign imports, foreign markets, and foreign capital as it had been in the infant days of the new republic. In a few decades the globalists had reverse-engineered American history, inaugurated a new era of American dependency, and thrown away the gains of a century and a half of economic nationalism. The republic that had grown out of thirteen colonies of the British Empire to become the most self-sufficient nation in history was now a colony of the world — with trade deficits at Colonial levels, wages well below those of Japan, and a dependency on foreign manufactures greater than before the Civil War. What Washington, Hamilton, Madison, Jackson, Lincoln, and Republican presidents from the Civil War to the New Deal had achieved at enormous cost, America's elites had sacrificed on the altar of the Global Economy of their dreams.

Thus, many Americans began to demand that America's leaders start looking out for their own country first. President Bush denounced the new spirit of nationalism. Triumphant in the Gulf War, he defiantly strode before the United Nations on October 1, 1991, to call for a new world order of "open borders, open trade." On December 7 at Pearl Harbor, he damned "isolationism" and "protectionism" for a war begun at Pearl Harbor by the Japanese, to whom Mr. Bush was magnanimous. It was clear that economic nationalism would get no hearing in the presidential councils of George Bush. Message received. We gave our answer in New Hampshire three days after that Pearl Harbor speech. George Bush, I said

> is a man of graciousness, honor and integrity, who has given a lifetime to his nation's service. But the differences between us are now too deep. . . . He is a globalist and we are nationalists. He believes in some Pax Universalis; we believe in the Old Republic. He would put America's wealth and power at the service of some vague New World Order; we will put America first.

We did not prevail, but the breadth of the support we rallied in a ten-week campaign against the president of the United States astonished observers. Ross Perot would echo the theme of economic nationalism in an independent campaign that would win 19 percent of the national vote. In both parties now, economic nationalists were at war with free traders, and the stage was set for the first great political test of strength between them since the days of Smoot-Hawley. This was to be the Battle of NAFTA.

Chapter 14

COUNTERREVOLUTION

Labor Secretary Robert Reich, Senator Edward Kennedy, House Democratic leaders Richard Gephardt and David Bonior, and the labor movement all tried to raise the issue of jobs and wages. But the political establishment and the media didn't pay attention until the conservative commentator Patrick Buchanan started pounding podiums about it in his insurgency campaign for the Republican presidential nomination.[1]

— John J. Sweeney,
AFL-CIO PRESIDENT, 1996

With manufacturing jobs disappearing, family incomes stagnant, and wages slipping, the counterrevolution took a long time in coming. Such is the hold of ideology. After all, it took the communists decades after the failure of their idea was manifest for them to give up on it. Some still have not. But by 1991 the social consequences of America's embrace of the Global Economy began to be reflected in national politics. Economic nationalism powered our challenge to President Bush, the Jerry Brown campaign, and that of Ross Perot, who declared his candidacy for president the day after news hit of our near upset of George Bush in New Hampshire. The forces were in place for the first great collision between an establishment converted, whole and entire, to free trade and a new populism: the Battle of NAFTA.

All the King's Men

Like the Panama Canal controversy, the national debate over the North American Free Trade Agreement (NAFTA) was a robust affair, democratic politics at its best. Our attack on NAFTA was deliberately timed for late August, when the political and media elites had left Washington and the reporters who stayed behind would be casting about for a good story. Our press conference attracted fifty reporters and got extraordinary coverage. There was no answer from the administration. Throughout the summer, daily attacks on NAFTA received endless hours of air time, while its advocates seemed asleep. Like the rebels at Concord Bridge, the adversaries of NAFTA had stunned a sleepy establishment with their ferocity and number. Passage of trade deals had been routine. By mid-September a poll by the *Wall Street Journal* found that 36 percent of Americans were opposed to NAFTA, 25 percent for it.[2] Near panic took hold of both a media and political elite that had assumed easy passage. There were predictions that the pact was going down.

The lamentations began. NAFTA is George Bush's "boldest legacy," wailed the *Wall Street Journal.* Can this child of so much love be lost? Support for NAFTA, said Jack Kemp, is a "litmus test" for Republicans.

As despair spread, President Clinton, who had affected an almost diffident stance toward his own treaty, shoved his poker chips into the center of the table, assumed leadership of the campaign, and went all-out. With that decision, he solidified his hold on the American establishment. In July Henry Kissinger had promised the new president that if he took command in the NAFTA battle, a mighty coalition would form behind him, and his tenure "would be perceived as a seminal presidency whatever else transpires while he is in office."[3] It was an offer Clinton couldn't refuse. The White House bought in, and Kissinger delivered.

On September 14, 1993, the president held a White House rally for a NAFTA pact that had now been endorsed by all five ex-presidents; three of them were in the East Room. Gerald Ford, a top recruiter at Yale for the America First Committee, dragged out Smoot-Hawley for another thrashing, warning against any repetition of that "stupid, serious mistake."[4] George Bush denounced "those demagogues who appeal to the worst instincts that our special interest groups possess."[5] But Jimmy Carter stole the show. The assemblage rose as one in applause as Carter savaged Perot as a "demagogue . . . with unlimited financial resources . . . who is extremely careless with the truth, who is preying on the fears and the uncertainties of the American public."[6]

The establishment was united, with spirits buoyed by Clinton's rally. Leaving the White House, a pleased Senate minority leader spoke for the congressional Republicans. "President Clinton hit it out of the ballpark. We're getting back on the offensive," said Bob Dole.[7]

Closing ranks behind Clinton were every ex–secretary of state, the congressional leaders of both parties, the Heritage Foundation and Brookings Institution, the *Wall Street Journal* and *Washington Post*, the Council on Foreign Relations and the Trilateral Commission, the *New Republic* and *National Review:* all the king's horses and all the king's men.

Mexico City poured, by one estimate, $30–$50 million into the campaign for NAFTA, hiring an army of U.S. mercenaries — lobbyists, lawyers, ex–trade officials, consultants, PR specialists. As the essence of NAFTA was a fifteen-year phaseout of a puny 4 percent U.S. tariff on Mexican goods, and a 10 percent Mexican tariff on U.S. goods, why would both nations roll out their heavy artillery? Because just as the Battle of Gettysburg was about more than who controlled a small town in Pennsylvania, NAFTA was about more than tariffs. It was to be the first step toward a free-trade zone that would extend the U.S.-Canada common market to all of Latin America — and eventually the world.

KISSINGER'S NEW WORLD ORDER
VS.
"THE CAUSE OF EVIL"

To opponents, NAFTA was always about more than jobs going south; it was about American sovereignty going south. Under NAFTA, foreigners would be given inspection rights in U.S. plants, and transnational boards would be established to judge trade disputes. Opponents saw in NAFTA the first step toward a merger of the American and Mexican economies, a prelude to eventual merger of the two countries. Indeed, Kissinger conceded that there was larger game afoot; NAFTA, he wrote, represents the "architecture of a new international system," a great "step toward the new world order."[8]

As both sides came to believe that America's destiny might turn on the vote, rancor and bitterness intensified. The feline ferocity of NAFTA supporters was corroboration that something more was at stake than a phaseout of inconsequential tariffs. Echoing Carter on Perot, *Wall Street Journal* writer Paul Gigot accused me of "demagoguery," lying, hypocrisy, "raw anti-Mexican bias," and weaving a "web of distortion and ignorance." Buchanan belongs to the "Fear & Loathing branch of conservatism," Gigot wrote; his politics are "too crabbed, fearful and tribal" to be acceptable to the cosmopolitan Right.[9] The *New Republic* even sniffed out demonic roots in the anti-NAFTA coalition. In a cover editorial, it declared, "It may not be too great a flight of rhetoric to say that at this crossroads of post–cold war history, Pat Buchanan and Ross Perot represent the cause of evil."[10]

"Why the pro-NAFTA hysteria?" asked libertarian philosopher Murray Rothbard.[11] But Rothbard, a cherished friend of mine and passionate foe of NAFTA, knew exactly what the hysteria was about. For the first time in modern history, the U.S. foreign policy Establishment was heading for a humiliating repudiation. A populist-nationalist coalition was fixing to dynamite Henry Kissinger's new world order right off the rails.

By voting time in the House, November 17, 1993, a plurality of Americans wanted NAFTA defeated. Clinton prevailed with one of the most flagrant vote-buying sprees in history. Hours after NAFTA's victory, I wrote an assessment I believe still stands up today:

> In the end they had to buy it. In the end they won the bidding war, not the battle for hearts and minds. . . . The president's men won not by giving their countrymen the vision of a better future, but by buying up their representatives with deals on tomatoes, peanut butter, sugar, citrus, trade centers, C-17s and development banks. . . . The remarkable thing is not that the coalition of working men and women, populists and conservatives, was defeated, but that they came so close to recapturing the nation's destiny.[12]

As the bitter debate over war in the Persian Gulf had exposed an unsuspected rift in the Cold War consensus, NAFTA revealed that Americans are not sold on free trade. The Middle American coalition that propelled Richard Nixon to his forty-nine-state triumph in 1972, and Ronald Reagan to his forty-nine-state triumph in 1984, is shattered. Within both parties, nationalists are now in rancorous conflict with the globalists. And it is true not only of America. This is the new conflict of the age that succeeds the Cold War.

"A Transformational Moment"

One year after NAFTA came GATT.

All through 1993 the Uruguay Round of GATT negotiations, in their seventh year, seemed barren of issue, about to wrap up without agreement. But at the eleventh hour the Americans, as they had in all previous GATT talks, capitulated and made the critical concessions. When the pact was brought back, the United States had agreed to the creation of the World Trade Organization (WTO), which had the authority to determine when trade agreements were violated and the power to decide when punishment might be imposed. In the WTO — for the first time in any global organization — America was given neither veto power nor voting power comparable to its contribution, size, and strength. The United States, in the WTO, was the equal of Ecuador. That this new global supreme court of world trade was a leap forward to world government was conceded by Newt Gingrich:

> We need to be honest about the fact that we are transferring from the United States at a practical level significant authority to a new organization. This is a transformational moment. I would feel better if the people who favor this would just be honest about the scale of change.
>
> I agree . . . this is very close to Maastricht, and 20 years from now we will look back on this as a very important defining moment.[13]

How transformational a moment?

Where Harry Truman and Dwight Eisenhower had failed, Bill Clinton would succeed, with the collaboration of Republican leaders. Indeed, as far back as the days of Woodrow Wilson, an international trade court had been the dream of American globalists.

> Woodrow Wilson's 1918 plan for a World Trade Tribunal was part of his League of Nations Covenant. Thanks to Henry Cabot Lodge . . . and his allies, neither the League nor its Trade Tribunal were approved by the U.S. Senate, in one of the most courageous acts in history.[14]

Lodge's defiant stand had bought the Republic seventy-five years, before a Clinton-Gingrich-Dole coalition would agree to give up a measure of that national sovereignty for which the Founding Fathers had fought.

As in the NAFTA battle, pro-GATT forces charged opponents with appealing to fear, and then appealed to fear themselves. Peter

Sutherland, the general director of GATT, warned that a failure to ratify the treaty would put us on a glide path to war!

> If we had not cut the deal by December 15 [1993] the world overnight would have become a much more dangerous place. . . . It would have been carved up into spheres of influence, or regional trade blocs, which ultimately would have proved self-destructive . . . [and] would have quickly escalated to military conflict.[15]

Defeating the GATT deal was a harder sell than battling NAFTA. Few Americans knew what the General Agreement on Tariffs and Trade or the Uruguay Round was or that a new World Trade Organization had been created or what the WTO was. Perot did not believe that the GATT fight could be won. But once explained over radio and television, GATT was a loser for the administration. Grassroots support was nonexistent; the only enthusiasts were executives and lobbyists whose corporate interests had been protected at Geneva by Mickey Kantor. The longer Clinton delayed in bringing his 23,000-page treaty to a vote, the more ground he lost. The most resolute and courageous opponent was Senator Fritz Hollings of South Carolina. Confronted with Hollings's determination to hold hearings, and wary of another brutal NAFTA-type battle so close to November, the White House put off a vote until after the 1994 elections.

The elections proved an earthquake for Clinton, and a potential disaster for GATT. For the freshman class of the new Congress was full of young Republican trade hawks! If the White House and Gingrich and Dole did not want a crushing defeat, they had to get the GATT approved before the 104th Congress convened. A lame-duck session was called for the end of November. With the Republican leadership collaborating with the White House, our one-party government passed GATT. Gingrich and Dole denied their own freshmen a chance to vote on the GATT treaty and gave Clinton a victory that would start him back on the road to recovery and reelection. Greater love than this hath no party. In gratitude to its corporate contributors of soft money, the GOP gave Clinton a triumph that enabled him to strike a posture as a national and world leader.

"Yes, We Have No Bananas"

> *What all the wise men promised has not happened, and what all the damn fools said would happen has come to pass.*[16]
>
> — Lord Melbourne,
> British prime minister
> (on a failed reform)

In getting the GATT vote behind it in late November, the White House had been extraordinarily lucky. Had the president delayed a few weeks, GATT would have gone down. In mid-December Mexico City leaked word that it could not pay off its *tesebonos*, tens of billions of dollars of bonds due in 1995. Mexico's currency reserves had vanished. The peso collapsed, quickly losing half its value against the dollar. For the third time in a year, the U.S. establishment found its chestnuts blazing in the fire and populists howling, "Let 'em burn!"

With Kissinger's new world order shaken to its foundation, Clinton summoned Dole and Gingrich, who instantly agreed to rush through a financial bailout of the Mexican government — to enable Mexico to pay off the bonds held by now-panicked U.S. investors. The stake of Goldman, Sachs in the bailout was huge, as was Robert Rubin's. The early-nineties star of Goldman, Sachs, Rubin had led its clients into Mexico, had been the watch officer at the National Economic Council who failed to see the Mexican crisis barreling up the tracks, and was now the treasury secretary–designate, who would have to preside over a collapse of the house of cards he had helped erect.

* * *

When Dole and Gingrich arrived back on Capitol Hill to report on the bailout they had bought into, the GOP freshmen rioted. They had not been elected, they said, to vote $25 billion for Mexico on the say-so of Clinton and Rubin. Seeing that the bailout could not pass — 80 percent of the nation opposed it — the GOP leaders bailed out on the president. Clinton was forced to conduct a $20 billion raid on a Treasury fund created to maintain the exchange rate of the dollar. The White House then leaned on the IMF to lend Mexico another $17 billion. Eventually, a $53 billion bailout was wired together, even though Mexico did not use its full credit line.

Had the peso collapse occurred three weeks earlier, GATT would have been defeated and the WTO stillborn. Had Congress been told the truth in 1993 — that the tiny U.S. trade surplus with Mexico was due to an overvalued peso — NAFTA never would have passed.

LA RECONQUISTA

Two years after NAFTA, the predictions of its opponents had all come true. The U.S. trade surplus with Mexico had vanished; a trade deficit of $15 billion had opened up. Trucks heading north out of Mexico were hauling more and more manufactured goods, while those coming south carried machinery and equipment for the new factories going up, pointing to endless and deepening U.S. trade deficits. By 1997, 3,300 *maquiladora* factories were operating, employing 800,000 Mexican workers in jobs that not long ago would have gone to Americans.[17]

Only one-sixth of U.S. exports to Mexico are consumer goods; one-third are factory components. Another huge slice of our exports is parts sent south for assembly and reshipment back to the United States. Such exports translate into lost American jobs. Consider automobiles. In 1996 we exported 46,652 cars to Mexico, and Mexico exported 550,622 cars to the United States, *"more cars than the U.S.*

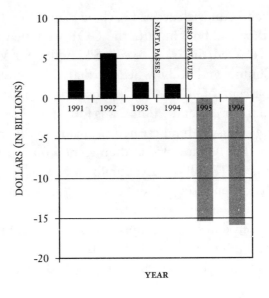

U.S. Trade Balance with Mexico

Source: U.S. Department of Commerce

exports to the world.[18] For every truck we export to Mexico, Mexico exports six to the United States.

Many American companies first went to Mexico to shed their high-paid U.S. workforce. Others followed because they had no choice if they wished to survive the low-wage competition. Realizing NAFTA had made Mexico a perfect launching pad into the United States, Japanese and Korean companies began siting plants south of the border. Along a seven-hundred-mile stretch from Tijuana to Ciudad Juárez, dozens swooped in to exploit Mexico's special trade relationship with the United States. Consumer-electronic giants Matsushita Electric Industrial, Mitsubishi Electric, Daewoo, and Sony have all built assembly plants there, transforming the region into a Silicon Valley of TV manufacturing. In 1997 more than 10 million sets will have been produced in northern Mexico.[19]

*   *   *

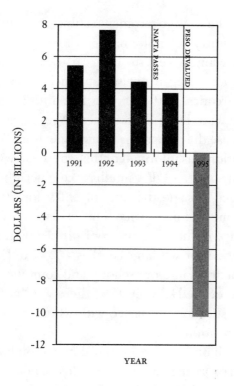

**Balance of Trade with Mexico in
Manufactures, 1991–95**

Source: U.S. Department of Commerce

During the NAFTA debate the *Wall Street Journal* had christened its opponents — Ross Perot, Ralph Nader, Jesse Jackson, and this writer — the "Halloween coalition." But in two years NAFTA did what the Halloween coalition predicted; it created a booming new Sun Belt, a giant new U.S. enterprise zone — in Mexico.[20] But even those new factories could not provide enough jobs for Mexico's millions of unemployed. Thus, even as U.S. jobs went south, Mexico's jobless continued to come north. By early 1995 illegal aliens were pouring across the U.S. border in record numbers to take jobs and get welfare benefits now worth twice as many pesos as in pre-

NAFTA days. The U.S. government estimates the number of illegal aliens in this country at 5 million.

The biggest winners were the drug cartels. Anticipating NAFTA, Mexico's drug lords began buying up trucking companies on the border and narcotics traffickers began shifting operations from Colombia. The U.S. Drug Enforcement Agency knew that the cartels planned to use the companies to smuggle drugs. When the Clinton administration was informed of this, the agency was told to shut up, according to retired DEA intelligence chief Phil Jordan. Post-NAFTA, Mexico became the port of entry for 70–80 percent of America's cocaine and marijuana. This crisis, said Teamsters president Ron Carey, is "blowing the roof off claims that the NAFTA trade deal is good for working families. . . . NAFTA has created a new pipeline of drugs into our schools and communities."[21] According to the head of the DEA, by 1997 there was "not one single law enforcement institution in Mexico with whom the DEA has an entirely trusting relationship."

Mexico is well on its way to succeeding Colombia as the leading narco-democracy in the Americas. Carlos Salinas, Mexico's president from 1988 to 1994, who negotiated NAFTA, the man Clinton had wanted to head the WTO, fled in 1995 and was sought for questioning in connection with his brother's alleged theft of hundreds of millions of dollars. It was the Salinas regime that Henry Kissinger had personally vouched for in his call for support of NAFTA:

> Salinas turned Mexico on its head. He . . . quelled corruption and brought into office an extraordinary group of young, highly trained technocrats. I know no government anywhere that is more competent.[22]

Has the standard of living of Mexico's workers risen? According to Alan Tonelson of the U.S. Business and Industrial Council, real hourly wages in Mexico, which fell 30 percent between 1980 and 1994, fell another 25 percent after devaluation.[23] Mexico's workers remain in a generation-long depression. In a sad little episode in 1995, Guillermo Lasso's veterinary practice for Cuernavaca's middle class collapsed with the peso. "People were just letting their dogs and cats die," he said. By mid-1997 Mexico's minimum wage had slumped to three dollars a day — less than thirty-eight cents an hour.[24] Writes scholar Mark Falcoff:

> 1995 was probably Mexico's worst [year] since the Great Depression, with at least 1 million Mexicans losing their jobs. Unofficial estimates hold that fully 18 million Mexicans, or almost half the economically active population, are underemployed. These frightening statistics portend a deep and profound social crisis. Urban crime has dramatically increased, with even formerly "safe" areas of the capital now pervaded by fear and trepidation.
>
> Mexico is also experiencing a quiet but acute public health crisis. Outbreaks of cholera and dengue fever increased *tenfold* between 1994 and 1995. . . . According to UNICEF, some 30,000 Mexicans died of malnutrition in 1995. If this is true, Mexico would be in the same category as Ethiopia, Kenya and Nigeria.[25]

Ultimately, NAFTA and the peso devaluation were about larceny on a global scale. Mexico's good people were robbed of half the dollar-purchasing power of the pesos they had sweated for and saved. American border towns lost loyal Mexican customers. American workers saw factories and jobs go south. All so a Mexican regime could run a $15 billion trade surplus with the United States — and raise the cash to pay off its New York creditors. Mexican and American workers lost, but the big banks were made whole, and the wages the transnationals pay their Mexican labor were sliced in half. No wonder America's financial elite finds a lot to like in Bill Clinton.

In early 1997 Clinton held a press conference to publicize Mexico's repayment, with interest, of the billions of dollars America had lent it in the bailout of 1995. To raise the money, Mexico had floated bonds with the Europeans, and Mexico City's external debt was now a larger share of the GDP than ever. And so the great global pyramid scheme goes on.

*   *   *

With one hundred thousand impoverished Mexicans pouring into the United States every month, Californians sought to stem the invasion by voting an end to welfare benefits for illegals. They were castigated by the press and political elites as "racists" and "nativists"; when Proposition 187 won in a landslide, the law was immediately suspended by the courts.

Mexican consuls in the United States began calling for public protests against any immigration controls, at demonstrations where the Mexican flag was a common sight. Counterdemonstrations by U.S. citizens demanding action to halt the invasion were broken up by militants, rioters, and thugs.

"You're Mexicans, Mexicans who live north of the border," President Ernesto Zedillo told Mexican-American leaders in Dallas in 1996.[26] Zedillo expressed hope that his new constitutional amendment, providing for dual citizenship, would enable Mexicans living in America to become a powerful force in shaping U.S. policy in Mexico's interests.

La Reconquista — the Spanish term for the recapture of Spain and the expulsion of the Moors in 1492 — is the term one Mexican diplomat used to describe his country's designs on the American Southwest. The vast majority of Mexican-Americans love this country and serve it honorably, especially in America's armed forces. The same is true of most who come here. But to the militant few whose number is growing, America is the occupying power. And the U.S. government shows little appreciation of the gravity of the situation, or what it portends for America.

A NEW ISSUE: TAINTED FOOD

Lately, a new concern has arisen from the explosion of imports, and it has been exacerbated by the hysteria in Europe over "mad cow disease" discovered in cattle in the United Kingdom. That concern is disease.

In the summer of 1996, 1,450 Americans came down with severe stomach disorders that were traced to Guatemalan raspberries that had been irrigated or sprayed with water contaminated by cyclospora, a rare waterborne parasite. A few months later, 175 Michigan children came down with hepatitis A, which was traced to Mexican strawberries in school lunches, strawberries that had been mislabeled as American-produced.

Public interest groups began to speak up. "Promoting international trade is a worthy cause, but the health of the American people has to come first," said Bruce Silverglade, president of the Center for Science in the Public Interest. Americans are becoming "a bunch of guinea pigs, and there's no possible way under current trade agreements for these risks to be controlled," added Rod Leonard, executive director of the nonprofit Community Nutrition Institute.[27]

In mid-1997 at least 126 D.C.-area residents had become ill, including thirty members of the Washington Symphony Orchestra, with intestinal disease caused by cyclospora from basil and pesto out of the upscale Sutton Gourmet.[28] The source was traced to a kitchen and Salvadorean immigrants carrying the parasites in their systems. Cyclospora was first identified in Papua, New Guinea, in 1979 and has now become "a serious health problem," said David Portesi, an epidemiologist with the Maryland Department of Health. "We're not talking about some twenty-four-hour bug here, but something that can disable you for thirty days or more with serious diarrhea and dehydration."[29]

While more than nine thousand Americans die each year from foodborne illnesses, few — if any — deaths have resulted from imports. Yet, these episodes raise alarms. "The surge in global trade and travel . . . is creating a huge health threat in the United States" is how Reuters news service summarized a 1997 report of the Institute of Medicine of the U.S. Academy of Sciences. Among the germs and medical threats listed, besides cyclospora, are new infections such as the Ebola virus; mosquitoes capable of carrying dengue fever, viral encephalitis, and yellow fever, introduced in tire imports from Asia; and pesticides banned in the United States but discovered on imported food.[30]

With foreign food flooding into the United States — 70 percent
of our winter fruits and vegetables now come from Mexico — these
episodes are certain to increase. Declares Nicholas Fox, author of
Spoiled:

> We demand cheap food, we demand fresh fruits and vegetables all year
> round. . . . We have to understand that when we import fresh fruit and
> vegetables we are importing the environment in which that food was
> grown. We are consuming that environment, and the sanitation and
> working conditions of that environment.[31]

"Greater reliance on food imported from countries that have less
stringent sanitary and pesticide regulations means a greater likeli-
hood of epidemics," warns the *New York Times'* Marian Burros.[32]
The free-trade *Economist* fears that the trend toward globalism could
be derailed: "Quarrels over food safety will blow a hole in free trade
unless governments put more trust in science, and in consumers."[33]
As Ms. Burros suggests, it cannot be long before some future
episode brings this issue to critical mass. Indeed, it seems almost remarkable that in thousands of restaurants Americans are eating vegetables and salads whose ingredients come from countries where
American tourists are warned repeatedly not to drink the water. And
whether the risk we are taking is great or small, it must be placed on
the liability side of the ledger of NAFTA and GATT.

OVER THE TOP

In the fall of 1997, President Clinton went to the Congress to ask for
renewal of "fast-track" authority, the presidential power to negotiate trade treaties that are exempt from all congressional amendment.
His purpose was to win a free hand from Congress to extend
NAFTA to all of Latin America. Fast track was the highest priority
of the administration, and the president began the battle with the
leadership of both houses squarely behind him.

Like NAFTA and GATT, fast track was powerfully endorsed by all the ex-presidents and secretaries of state, all major newspapers in the New York–Washington corridor, all the major think tanks. The bill was the top priority of the Business Roundtable, whose membership had lavished millions in "soft money" on both parties for purposes such as this. Yet, as with NAFTA and GATT, the same coalition of populists, environmentalists, union leaders, and conservatives formed up to fight fast track to the last ditch. Now backing the coalition, according to a *Business Week* poll, was a clear majority of Americans, 54 percent of whom opposed extending NAFTA to Latin America, with only 34 percent in favor.[34] By equal margins, Americans opposed renewing fast-track authority for the president.

The free traders had lost the country.

As Congress neared adjournment in early November, it became clear that Mr. Clinton was coming up short, that fast track was about to be derailed, that for the first time since the Eightieth Congress killed the ITO, a major bill to expand global free trade was going down. Panic set in; and the White House went all-out, using the tactics that had prevailed in NAFTA. "The bazaar is open!" one congressman chortled to this writer.

On Friday, November 7, a visibly unsettled president asked that the vote be postponed for forty-eight hours; he was nowhere near the numbers needed. All weekend, the House was in rancorous session, with the GOP leadership threatening opponents with the loss of committee assignments, as White House aides and cabinet officers cut any deal that could bring them closer to the magic 218 needed for passage. This is a "no-brainer," an exasperated president declared; members of Congress must not give in to intimidation. The Clinton suggestion that a vote against fast track was a mark of political retardation or cowardice infuriated those standing up to the incessant pounding of the national establishment. Republican House members called into a midnight conference by the speaker had to pass through a gauntlet of corporate lobbyists demanding that they support fast track.

The lines held. In the early hours of Monday morning, Speaker Newt Gingrich announced that the White House was "pulling" the bill. The votes weren't there. Fast track was dead! It was a stunning defeat for global free traders, one that they did not even bother to disguise. And it was the triumph of five years of labor by a coalition that spans the political spectrum, from unionists and environmentalists to the Reform Party and conservatives like Congressmen Duncan Hunter and Gerry Solomon.

Fast track was defeated for many reasons. But ultimately, it was rejected by Congress because Mr. Clinton and the free traders had lost the country. The special interests might try to punish congressmen who voted against fast track, but it was clear by 1997 that the people would not. Indeed, by now, calling one's opponent a protectionist, or invoking the Smoot-Hawley bogeyman was not enough. Through years of persuasion, employing the evidence of the eyes, the coalition had turned the American people into skeptics of globalism. Mr. Clinton vowed to come back early in 1998, to renew the battle for fast track, but in the Republican caucuses in the Senate and House there seemed to be no stomach for the battle, and no confidence it could be won.

Neither NAFTA nor GATT would pass today. Economic nationalists are stronger and more evenly matched against free traders, just as those who demand a new foreign policy, rooted in U.S. national interests, are gaining ground on the globalists. The twentieth-century triumphs of Wilson and FDR may not have been forever after all. During the NAFTA debate, historian Arthur Schlesinger yielded to a keening lament:

> Can this reversion to isolationism be arrested? Or must we abandon the Wilsonian dream, forget the hope of an international peace system and return to the old *sauve qui peut* world? For the idea of a new world order becomes meaningless if the most powerful nation on the planet is not fully committed.[35]

Schlesinger's "Wilsonian dream . . . of an international peace system," however, was always only that — a dream. What he bemoans, the *"sauve qui peut* world" of nations that see one another as rivals and antagonists in an endless struggle for primacy, is the real world, the only world we shall ever know. Leaders who have acted on that truth have done far better by their people than dreamers who have believed that with goodwill and hope, a utopian world can be created this side of the grave. If the edifice we erect is constructed on the gossamer stuff of dreams, not the hard rock of reality, it will come down in ruins for us, as it did for Wilson.

Plowing Up a *Field of Dreams*

In the summer of 1945, during a strike at the foundry where he worked, Fred Ertl went down to the basement of his Dubuque home and began to make toys. Using aluminum scrap from war surplus pistons, he melted the metal in a potbelly furnace and cast it into sand molds. With his four sons helping out, Fred bolted the parts into toy tractors. His wife Gertrude painted the toys on the kitchen table and kept the books. Fred's two eldest boys — with sixteen-year-old Fred, Jr., at the wheel of the family's Olds — drove all over Iowa delivering Ertl toys to hardware stores and retail outlets.[36]

With the beginning of the baby boom, postwar America was wild for toys. Ertl's became almost as popular and collectible as Lionel trains. "These are products that bring enjoyment to old and young alike and that aren't thrown away," said a proud Fred Ertl, Jr., in 1992. "Our products from day one are still in existence in many places."[37]

In 1959 Ertl Toy, with fifty employees, moved thirty miles west to Dyersville. Its workforce rose to eleven hundred in a town of just four thousand. The Farm Toy Museum, featuring Ertl miniatures of John Deere tractors, opened. Dyersville declared itself the "Farm

Toy Capital of the World."[38] The tiny Iowa town became the setting for Kevin Costner's *Field of Dreams*.

In 1967, however, Fred, Sr., who had suffered from colon cancer, sold the family business to Victor Comptometer for retirement money and to avoid inheritance taxes. If you die with a successful family business in America, inheritance taxes can take half and kill it. "You have to sell when you retire, or it's sold when you die. You've already paid taxes on that money and you have to pay again when you die," said Iowa state representative Joe Ertl.[39]

Victor Comptometer sold out to Kidde in 1977. Ten years later, Kidde was bought by Hanson Industries, U.S. subsidiary of Hanson PLC, the British conglomerate that had bought out Eveready, Smith-Corona, Jacuzzi, and Kaiser Cement. Hanson PLC is run by Lords James Hanson and James White. Having swallowed more than it could digest, Hanson "demerged" thirty-four of its U.S. companies in 1995 into U.S. Industries. The goal: squeeze the new company's profit-making enterprises to cover the debt-ridden ones. A business journal defined the process as follows:

> Hansonization . . . is a simple, although sometimes brutal process. After buying overstuffed, poorly run businesses at a reasonable price, officials whack away at the fat, impose stiff new budgets, retain able managers and then let them run it. If they do a good job, they get good bonuses. If they don't, they get the axe.[40]

After buying out Smith-Corona in 1986 for $930 million, Lords Hanson and White tore the company apart and spun off most of its pieces for $960 million within a year.

The managers at Ertl Toy knew the meaning of Hansonization: cut costs or get the axe. They decided to "whack away the fat" by lopping off hundreds of nine-dollar-an-hour Iowa workers and shifting production to a part-time Ertl plant in Tijuana, where Mexicans will assemble toys for $1.50 an hour. Ertl Toy, with more workers in Dyersville than the next ten largest companies combined, shut down one of its two plants and let three hundred people go. Chief executive George Volanakis explained, "Due to high labor and material costs and competition, we were forced to move these jobs to Mexico."[41] In shipping those three hundred jobs to Mexico, Volanakis did well by the lords. Saving $7.50 an hour in wages per worker adds up to $2,250 an hour saved, $90,000 less per week in wages, $4.68 million in annual savings — from ditching Dyersville.

To mock their loss and hide their pain, the discharged workers came to Ertl's 1995 Halloween party — wearing sombreros. They did not need a course in global economics to understand what NAFTA had done to their families and their field of dreams.

Chapter 15

A NEW NATIONALISM

*The true way to protect the poor is to protect
their labor. Give them work and protect
their earnings; that is the way to benefit the
poor. Our artisans . . . were the first to be
protected by the Constitution. . . . The free
labor of the United States deserves to be protected, and, so far as any efforts of mine can
go, it shall be.*[1]

— Daniel Webster, 1828

*The nationalist has to offer no arguments
except those which boil down to a love for his
native land to the exclusion of all others.
And this love somehow is supposed to be un-
worthy.*[2]

— Samuel Crowther, 1933

Stuck in traffic on the way to the Republican National Convention in San Diego in 1996, I noticed a truck circling, with billboards
on either side. One read, "Don't Forget Working Men and
Women!" The other, "America Needs a Pay Raise!" The signs pin-
point what has gone wrong: real wages are what they were during
the presidency of Lyndon Johnson; wages in retail are what our
grandparents used to earn. This wage stagnation has forced into the
job market millions of wives and mothers who would prefer to stay
at home, to have children or to raise their children, adding to the
stress and strain of middle-class life. In 1947, 30 percent of our population was employed, earning 44 percent of the GDP. Forty-four

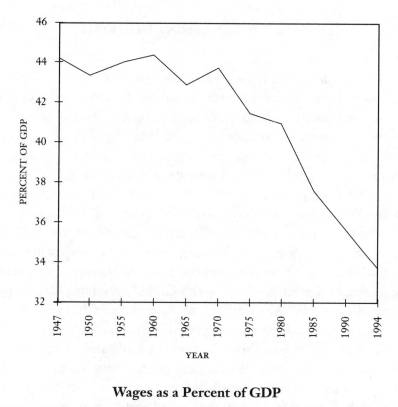

Wages as a Percent of GDP

Source: *President's Economic Report, 1995*

percent is employed now, but wages are only 34 percent of the GDP.[3] As Affluent America takes stride after stride into prosperity, Middle America remains on a treadmill.

In devising new policies, however, we cannot wrench America violently off the course on which she has been set. Traditionalists don't do that. We must build on what we inherit and proceed from where we are. But those who say our course is forever set speak out of timidity or self-interest. We are, after all, Americans. We can change course. We can turn the ship a degree at a time so that, in a few years, we are headed toward a safer, more secure harbor.

TOWARD ONE NATION, INDIVISIBLE

It is time we looked at the world from a new perspective, a perspective of enlightened nationalism. Clichés about a "new" Global Economy aside, there has always been an international economy — ever since Columbus stumbled onto the Western Hemisphere while seeking new trade routes to the East, in the hire of a nation-state, Spain. The Dutch East India Company was founded in 1602 to displace the Portuguese in the lucrative Far Eastern trade, and the Dutch West India Company in 1621 to capture the American trade.

The U.S. economy, however, is more than simply a part of the international economy, and its purpose is not to prosper mankind — but Americans first: our workers, farmers, businessmen, manufacturers. And what is good for the Global Economy is not automatically good for America, any more than what is good for our transnational elite is necessarily good for the United States.

We need a new patriotism. In devising trade and tax policies for the twenty-first century, the national interest, not the gratification of consumer demands, must be the paramount consideration. Rather than global free trade, the United States should promote regional trading zones. The United States–Canada is one such zone, East Asia another, the European Union another; MERCOSUR, led by Brazil and Argentina, is another. Nations inside these blocs are far more compatible than, say, America and China. They share common geography, comparable economic and social systems, a common history and culture. A regional trading bloc is more natural and organic than a global regime, and nations within these zones are in similar stages of development.

With so many forces — social, cultural, and ethnic — pulling us apart, Americans constantly need to nurture the bonds of union. One of the most powerful cements is peaceful commerce. "The fundamental bond that unites men into a society," wrote von Mises, "is the interpersonal exchange of goods and services."[4] Why are we rapidly dissolving those bonds with our fellow Americans? Before 1965 foreign trade accounted for 10 percent of the GNP; by 1995, 23 percent; in a dozen years it will account for 36 percent! Why are so many of our automobiles, TVs, VCRs, radios, shoes, cameras, clothes, toys, and telephones made overseas when there is nothing we Americans cannot make here? Comes the response: we buy from abroad because it is cheaper. But when American workers lose high-paying manufacturing jobs, the nation pays — in lost taxes those workers would have paid, in unemployment benefits for our jobless, in welfare and food stamps for those who quit looking for work. When company towns become ghost towns, when wives with young children are forced into the job market to make up the lost family income, America pays. Broken homes, uprooted families, vanished dreams, delinquency, vandalism, crime — these are the hidden costs of free trade. And if not families and neighborhoods, what in heaven's name is it that we conservatives wish to conserve?

A tariff, satirist Ambrose Bierce once mocked, is a "scale of taxes on imports designed to protect the domestic producer against the greed of his consumer."[5] Behind Bierce's crack lies the notion that citizens ought not care where their merchandise is produced. But the jobs and families of our fellow Americans depend on our buying U.S.-made goods, and every product MADE IN THE USA carries in its price the cost of the taxes that fund Medicare and Social Security for our elderly and provide for the defense of our freedom.

What Is a Nation?

Although we cannot return to the days of McKinley and Morrill, we can learn from American history. We can apply to our own situation the guiding principles of Washington, Hamilton, Jefferson, Madison, Jackson, and Lincoln. George Bush is not necessarily a wiser man than Prescott Bush, and Bill Clinton's globalism is not necessarily a superior guide to the future than Theodore Roosevelt's nationalism.

Nor are these ideas unique to America. All nations can benefit from greater emphasis on what is best for their own people, rather than sacrificing their unique character to the gods of globalism. If it is Japan's desire and tradition to be self-sufficient in rice, why insist that Japan open its market to imported rice? If the French wish to subsidize farmers to preserve their countryside, why shouldn't they? If Canada wishes to retain her cultural identity and restrict the flood of U.S. magazines, TV shows, and films, why are Canadians wrong? When the WTO ruled against Canada's right to use a tariff to protect its magazines from being swamped by American publications, Heritage Minister Sheila Copps declared, "We will not take this sitting down!" She was right. Traditionalists should have stood with Ms. Copps and Canada. Who are these nameless, faceless global bureaucrats of the WTO to tell Canada that it cannot act to preserve its unique identity, culture, and heritage? What Canadians are told to do today, we Americans will be told to do tomorrow.

What, after all, is a nation? French historian and philosopher Ernest Renan described it a century ago:

> A nation is [a] living soul, a spiritual principle. Two things, which in truth are but one, constitute this soul, this spiritual principle. One is in the past, the other in the present. One is the common possession of a rich heritage of memories; the other is the actual consent, the desire to live together, the will to preserve worthily the undivided inheritance which has been handed down. Man does not improvise. The nation, like the individual, is the outcome of a long past of efforts, and sacrifices, and devotions. . . . To have common glories in the past, a common will in the present; to have done great things together, to will to do the like again, — such are the essential conditions for the making of a people.[6]

Enlightened nationalism is not some blind worship of the nation. It is not a nationalism that wishes to denigrate or dominate others. It is a passionate attachment to one's own country: its history, heroes, literature, traditions, culture, language, and faith. It is the spirit that enables a people to endure, as the Polish people endured, under occupation and oppression, to rise again to live in the sunlight. Intellectuals, writes Regis Debray, "forget that nations hibernate, but empires grow old . . . that the American nation will outlast the Atlantic empire as the Russian nation will outlast the Soviet Empire."[7]

This community called a nation is more than any "division of labor," or "market" that may encompass it. Adds Renan:

> Community of interests is assuredly a powerful bond between men. But nevertheless can interests suffice to make a nation? I do not believe it. Community of interests makes commercial treaties. There is a sentimental side to nationality; it is at once body and soul; a *Zollverein* is not a fatherland.[8]

An economy is not a country. A nation's economic system should reinforce the bonds of national unity, but the nation is of a higher order than any imaginary construct of an economist. A nation is organic, alive; it has a beating heart. The people of a nation are a moral community who must share values higher than economic interest, or their nation will not endure. As scholar Christian Kopff asks, "What doth it profit a man if he gain the whole world, and suffer the loss of his country?"[9]

What is wrong with the Global Economy is what is wrong with our politics; it is rooted in the myth of Economic Man. It elevates economics above all else. But man does not live by bread alone. In a true nation many things are placed on a higher altar than maximum efficiency or a maximum variety of consumer goods. Once, conservatives understood that.

A HUMANE ECONOMY

Neither the national economy nor the free market is an end in itself. They are means to an end. A national economy is not some wild roaring river that must be allowed to find any course it will, to be admired for its raw power and beauty. It is to be tamed for the benefit of the nation. The same holds true for the market. While an unfettered free market is the most efficient mechanism to distribute the goods of a nation, there are higher values than efficiency. To worship the market is a form of idolatry no less than worshiping the state. The market should be made to work for man, not the other way around. "What is the market? It is the law of the jungle, the law of nature. And what is civilization? It is the struggle against nature." So declared France's Prime Minister Edouard Balladur at the close of the GATT negotiations of 1993; he is right.[10]

In devising new policies, let us marry the patriotism of Theodore Roosevelt to the humane vision of Wilhelm Roëpke, the student of von Mises and refugee from Hitler whose vision informed the postwar miracle of Ludwig Erhard. Roëpke "saw the market as but one section of society . . . 'whose existence is justifiable and possible only because it is part of a larger whole which concerns not economics but philosophy and theology.' . . . There is more to the whole of life . . . than maximizing GNP."[11]

> The market is not everything. It must find its place in a higher order of things which is not ruled by supply and demand, free prices, and competition. It must be firmly contained within an all-embracing order of society in which the imperfections and harshness of economic freedom are corrected by law and in which man is not denied conditions of life appropriate to his nature.[12]

What do we mean by "economic nationalism"? We mean tax and trade policies that put America before the Global Economy, and the well-being of our own people before what is best for "mankind." Trade is not an end in itself; it is the means to an end, to a more just society and more self-reliant nation. Our trade and tax policies should be designed to strengthen U.S. sovereignty and independence and should manifest a bias toward domestic, rather than foreign, commerce. For, as von Mises said, peaceful commerce binds people together, and Americans should rely more on one another.

A humane economy will harness the mighty engine of a free market for higher ends than maximum efficiency or maximum output. Neither the goodness nor the greatness of a nation is measured by its GDP. America was a good country before it became a great nation. Efficiency does not come first. The good society, a decent income for all our families, the good life for all our people, come first. For what is man? As Roëpke wrote:

My picture of man is fashioned by the spiritual heritage of classical and Christian tradition. I see in man the likeness of God; I am profoundly convinced that it is an appalling sin to reduce man to ends (even in the name of high-sounding phrases) and that each man's soul is something unique, irreplaceable, priceless, in comparison with which all things are as naught. I am attached to a humanism which is rooted in these convictions and which regards man as the child and image of God, but not as God himself, to be idolized as he is by the hubris of a false and atheist humanism.[13]

What are the goals of a new nationalism and humane economy?

1. Full employment, with our working people as well compensated and rewarded as any on earth
2. A wider, deeper distribution of property and prosperity
3. A standard of living that rises each year, and a "family wage" that enables a single parent to feed, clothe, house, and educate a large family in decency
4. A tax system that leaves Americans with the largest share of the fruits of their labor of any industrial democracy
5. Diminished dependence on foreign trade for the necessities of national life, such as oil
6. Restoration of America's lost sovereignty
7. Self-sufficiency in all areas of industry and technology vital to the national security
8. Maximum freedom for citizens and private institutions — consistent with a moral community and the common good

"Cast Down Your Bucket Where You Are!"

On September 18, 1895, Booker T. Washington delivered an address to the Atlanta Cotton States and International Exposition. The African-American founder of Tuskegee Institute began with a story:

> A ship lost at sea for many days suddenly sighted a friendly vessel. From the mast of the unfortunate vessel was seen a signal, "Water, water; we die of thirst!" The answer from the friendly vessel at once came back, "Cast down your bucket where you are." A second time the signal, "Water, water; send us water!" ran up from the distressed vessel, and was answered, "Cast down your bucket where you are." And a third and a fourth signal for water was answered, "Cast down your bucket where you are." The captain of the distressed vessel, at last heeding the injunction, cast down his bucket, and it came up full of fresh sparkling water from the mouth of the Amazon river.[14]

Washington then interpreted his imagery. In seeking workers for your new factories, he pleaded with the industrialists, look to my people! Look to the people who were loyal to you even in the days of civil war and reconstruction: "Cast down your bucket where you are!"

> Cast it down among the eight millions of negroes whose habits you know, whose fidelity and love you have tested in days when to have proved treacherous meant the ruin of your firesides. Cast down your bucket among these people who have, without strikes and labour wars, tilled your fields, cleared your forests, [built] your railroads and cities, and brought forth treasures from the bowels of the earth and helped make possible this magnificent representation of the progress of the South. Casting down your bucket . . . you will find that they will buy your surplus land, make blossom the waste places in your fields, and run your factories.[15]

Do not wait, said Washington, for the arrival of "those of foreign birth and strange tongue and habits." [16] Take my people first!

America did not listen. The millions of new jobs in burgeoning industries went to immigrants who poured into the United States between 1890 and 1920. These men and women enriched our country, true, but they also moved ahead of the black men and women who had been here for generations. In 1924, however, under Calvin Coolidge, the United States imposed a moratorium on immigration. It would last four decades. And while it did, Booker T. Washington's prediction of 1895 came to pass. As Vernon Briggs, an expert on the economic impact of immigration, wrote in 1992:

> The rapid decline in the level of immigration from the late 1920s to the late 1960s provided the opportunity for the nation to look internally to unused and underused subgroups of the population to draw upon for labor force needs.... With immigration levels sharply reduced ... women, minorities, disabled persons, youth and rural migrants did enter occupations and industries as well as move to geographical areas where they had not been present before.[17]

Then history repeated itself. No sooner had the Civil Rights Act of 1964 been passed than America threw open its doors again — with the Immigration Act of 1965. In thirty years, 30 million immigrants, legal and illegal, poured in. These immigrants do not, by and large, compete with our professionals: lawyers, journalists, brokers, doctors. These hardworking men and women compete with our native-born for a shrinking number of industrial jobs. And this huge and rapid increase in the supply of labor has cut the price of labor. If workers' wages are to take a sharp upward turn, America must return to normal growth in its labor force.

Editorial-page boosters of open borders refuse to recognize that there is another America out there, of men and women who never finished college or never went to college. An assembly line may mean "dead-end" jobs in "dinosaur" industries to America's elite, but for millions of our people, they are the yellow brick road to the American Dream. We can't write off these Americans.

*   *   *

On my way home from the Houston convention in 1992, I was having my bags checked at the airport. I saw your speech, the black porter said; *I* liked it. He told me he was a Christian and a grandfather. When I handed him a tip, he waved it off. "Just one thing," he said, "don't forget the black folks!" He is right. We must put our own people first — black and white, Hispanic and Asian, immigrant and native-born. Because they belong to the American family, they have first claim on our compassion and concern; and it is un-American to force members of one's own family into a global hiring hall to compete against foreign workers who make five dollars a day.

To ease America's social crisis and increase demand for blue-collar workers, America must halt illegal immigration and impose limits on legal immigration. Nor is there anything un-American about a moratorium, or a "time-out," on immigration. As we have seen, after the Great Immigration of 1890–1920, the United States imposed a moratorium under Presidents Coolidge, Roosevelt, Truman, and Eisenhower. In 1953 Eisenhower directed the repatriation of all aliens with no legal right to be here. There was nothing racist, immoral, or xenophobic in this. Eisenhower was enforcing the law, as he had taken an oath to do. The president knew that a country that cannot control its borders isn't really a country anymore.

By three-to-one, Americans support a moratorium. Who are the strident opponents? Cultural, social, and economic elites who do not compete with immigrant workers and benefit from an endless supply of low-wage labor. Working Americans are betrayed by these elites.

Tariffs — or Income Taxes?

I don't know much about the tariff. But I know this much. When we buy manufactured goods abroad, we get the goods and the foreigner gets the money. When we buy the manufactured goods at home, we get both the goods and the money.[18]

— Abraham Lincoln

In the last two hundred years there has not been one credible intellectual argument for protectionism anywhere in the world.[19]

— Senator Phil Gramm

Out of embarrassment of the party's past, ignorance, or ideological rigidity, many Republicans will not even discuss tariffs, as though to do so were an occasion of sin. When he dropped out of the New Hampshire primary in 1996, Senator Gramm declared, "Our party can never follow the path of protectionism. It is a dagger in the heart of everything we stand for around the world."[20] There has always been a "recessive gene in the American character that has found protectionism appealing," he added, vowing to "fight it . . . until I am lowered in the grave. . . . I cannot and will not support someone who's a protectionist. . . . It's a litmus-test issue for me."[21]

Gramm's line in the sand would have ruled out support for every Republican president before Eisenhower, including Lincoln and Theodore Roosevelt, both of whom had that "recessive gene" in their DNA. Gramm calls all impediments or hindrances to trade "immoral." "They limit my freedom," he says. "If I want to buy a shirt in China, who has the right to tell me as a free person that I can't do it?"[22] The freedom that trade brings, says Gramm, "[is] the greatest catalyst for human happiness and morality in history."[23]

Quite a claim — one that would seem to accord an earlier gospel a diminished place. Yet, Gramm speaks for the party elite. "Denying trade is a violation of human rights, and a most reprehensible one," thunders rising GOP congressman David Dreier.[24] Dick Armey calls free trade a "basic human right," as does the libertarian scholar Jacob Hornberger. Every person on earth, writes Hornberger, has a

> God-given right . . . to enter into mutually beneficial exchanges with others anywhere in the world. . . . They have the right to travel and move without political restriction. It is the duty of government to protect, not regulate or destroy, these inherent fundamental rights.[25]

But if this right is "God-given," the Founding Fathers trampled all over it. The Constitution declares that Congress "shall have Power" to lay "Duties" and "Imposts" and "regulate Commerce with foreign nations." The second bill that President Washington signed was the Tariff Act of 1789. In 1807 Jefferson embargoed all trade with Europe. Tariffs were the preferred taxes of Madison, Monroe, Jackson, Lincoln, and Theodore Roosevelt. For Republican leaders to declare free trade a "God-given" or "moral" right — i.e., one that cannot be compromised — is not only a repudiation of America's legendary leaders, it imperils the future of the party when, according to the *Wall Street Journal*, two-thirds of our people believe these NAFTA and GATT trade deals are unfair to American workers.

Free-trade Republicanism not only departs from party tradition, it denies us that form of taxation most consistent with the party philosophy of limited government. Why cannot free-market economists see that?

"Protectionism is purely and highly socialistic," railed the American economist Francis A. Walker in 1887.[26] Walker is echoed by two giants of twentieth-century free-market economics. In *Free to Choose*, Milton Friedman titles his chapter on tariffs "The Tyranny of Controls." Von Mises equated protectionism with statism:

> A nation's policy forms an integral whole. Foreign policy and domestic policy are closely linked together, they are but one system. Economic

nationalism is the corollary of the present-day domestic policies of government interference with business and of national planning as free trade was the complement of domestic economic freedom. . . . The trend toward [protectionism] is . . . the outcome of the endeavors to make the state paramount in economic matters.[27]

Intending no disrespect, this is nonsense. In the nineteenth century, when tariffs ran as high as 50 percent, there was far greater economic freedom than today, when tariff rates approach zero. For our first fourteen decades, high tariffs and small government went hand in hand. The most protectionist president of the twentieth century, Coolidge, cut spending to 3 percent of the GNP. Wilson, our first free-trade president, gave us the income tax, took us into World War I, and left the nation with a national debt that has never been repaid; the greatest free trader of all, FDR, was the godfather of Big Government. Do economists read history?

The libertarian retort: tariffs are taxes! Of course they are, but every government imposes taxes, for every government needs revenue. But are not tariffs a superior way to raise revenue than income taxes? Lincoln thought so. He argued that having customs officers collect duties at ports was a less expensive and intrusive way to raise revenue than having citizens "perpetually haunted and harassed by the tax-gatherer."[28] Our federal income tax system requires more than 100,000 IRS agents. Even a national sales tax would require tens of thousands of IRS agents poring over the cash receipts of millions of businesses. Tariffs, however, can be collected by U.S. customs agents. And unlike an income tax, which is mandatory — you pay, or go to jail — a tariff is a discretionary tax. As Lincoln said, with a tariff, "the man who contents himself to live upon the products of his own country pays nothing at all."[29]

Who Pays the Tariff?

Often, foreign regimes will swallow a tariff rather than risk losing their U.S. market. Assume a pair of running shoes cost $5 to produce in China and is sold in the United States for $100. The manufacturer in China realizes a profit of $95 on each pair. A U.S. tariff of $20 on each $100 pair of shoes would surely be swallowed by the manufacturer. To try to pass the $20 cost of the tariff onto consumers, by raising prices to $120 a pair, would risk losing market share to $100 shoes made elsewhere. By paying the tariff, the manufacturer in China lets its profit fall to $75 a pair, still a 1,500 percent profit. But the U.S. Treasury would realize $20 on each pair of shoes. China could thus help subsidize the U.S. Pacific fleet, while U.S. consumers pay no more for their running shoes.

In his 1995 confrontation with Japan, Clinton threatened to impose a 100 percent tariff on Lexus sedans. Japan publicly hinted that it might absorb that huge tariff — just to retain Lexus's share of the U.S. market.

The cost of a tariff, it is said, falls on consumers. Often that is true. But what tax ultimately does not fall on consumers? Where does GM get the money to pay its corporate taxes, if not from the buyers of GM cars?

A tariff discriminates against foreign goods, it is said. But every tax discriminates against some economic activity. A sales tax discriminates against consumption; a capital gains tax against investment, an income tax against work. What is so sacrosanct about imports? And what is the alternative to tariffs? In 1913 it became a federal income tax that invades the privacy of our people, consumes our substance, and diminishes our freedom in ways never dreamed of by the royal tyrant against whom Jefferson declaimed in America's Declaration of Independence.

Given the size of the U.S. government today, critics argue, tariffs could never provide all the revenue needed. True, but tariffs could provide *some*. Why not transfer some of the cost of government off the incomes of U.S. workers and onto the imports of foreign manufacturers? Why not shift part of the burden of taxation off U.S. companies that stay home and onto U.S. companies that move overseas? Why not put the full dinner pail for the American worker ahead of the free lunch for the American consumer?

The old Republicans taxed work, savings, and investment at 0 percent, and foreign goods at 40 percent. We do the opposite. We tax the return on savings and work at 40 percent, and foreign goods at 0 percent. Thus are we starved for savings — and swamped with foreign goods.

Are tariffs xenophobic? Only if it is xenophobic to put America first. A tariff does not deny foreign merchants access to U.S. markets; it merely imposes on them a price of admission into a lucrative market, which was, after all, created for the benefit of Americans. Under a fair tariff, foreign firms that manufacture here would be treated like American companies. Toyotas made here would compete on an equal basis with Fords made here, and Toyotas made in Mexico would compete with Fords made in Mexico. That is free and fair competition. But to have a Toyota made in Mexico, where autoworkers may earn six dollars an hour, compete against a Ford made in Michigan, where autoworkers may make thirty-five dollars an hour in pay and benefits, is unfair to American workers.

Under such a tariff system, U.S. companies that shifted factories overseas would be treated as foreign companies. The only bias in such a system is one in favor of products MADE IN THE USA, by people who live in the U.S.A. That is not discrimination; it is patriotism.

In any poker game there is an ante. Before every hand, each player throws the same number of chips into the pot. In America's free market, the pot is the greatest on earth, and the ante is the burden of taxes and the cost of regulations. Every U.S. company pays this ante; to allow foreign companies to enter the U.S. market without paying this ante does violence to the Fourteenth Amendment concept of equal justice under law. How can we impose an ante on

foreign firms and runaway factories to make them pay equally for
the privilege of competing in the U.S. market? Said Adam Smith:
The government should impose a tariff.

A REVENUE TARIFF

America should declare to the world in a way it will understand that
the present global regime *must* be revised, that we no longer intend
to make the world prosperous at the expense of our own country. A
15 percent revenue tariff on all imported manufactures and goods in
competition with U.S.-made goods would be a fitting way to declare
our economic independence.

As part of the "Nixon Shock" of August 15, 1991 — to jolt the
world into understanding that the United States could no longer
continue under the Bretton Woods agreement — a 10 percent tariff
was imposed on Japan. Thus, we need not go back to the Tariff of
1816 to find a precedent for unilateral American action in defense of
our economic security. Unlike Clinton's threat of a 100 percent tariff on Lexus cars, a 15 percent tariff would not destroy U.S. businesses set up in good faith. The tariff could be imposed in stages:
5 percent immediately, 5 percent in six months, the final 5 percent a
year later, giving merchants eighteen months to adjust. If Ronald
Reagan could impose a 50 percent tariff to save Harley-Davidson,
surely we can impose a 15 percent tariff to inaugurate a new industrial age in the United States.

The revenue tariff should be high enough to generate a powerful
stream of revenue, but low enough not to destroy trade. With U.S.
merchandise imports now exceeding $700 billion a year, this 15 per-
cent tariff would yield a cornucopia of revenue while giving U.S.
products a marginal new advantage in their home market. *Every dollar in tariff revenue could be used to cut taxes on income, savings, and investment.*

A shift in taxation away from incomes, onto foreign goods, is how Bismarck built the German nation. In a December 15, 1878, letter to the Reichstag, the chancellor spoke of a crisis in the German middle class, similar to our own, and how he proposed to emulate the Americans:

> It is no accident that other great States — especially those in a very advanced stage of political and economic development — prefer to try to cover their expenditures by the proceeds of duties and indirect taxes. . . . In the greater part of Germany the direct taxes . . . have reached a level which is oppressive and appears to be economically unjustifiable. Those people who suffer most from these taxes are those members of the middle class. . . . Reform of the taxation . . . must begin with the revision of the tariff on as broad a basis as possible so as to benefit this class of the community. *The more money that is raised from tariffs the greater can — and must — be the relief in direct taxes.* . . . (Emphasis added.)
>
> It should be based on the principle of imposing import duties on all goods which cross our frontiers.[30]

Bismarck's idea: raise tariffs on goods entering Germany and use the tariff revenue to cut direct taxes on the people. High tariffs would also give Germany leverage in "fresh negotiations with foreign countries concerning new commercial treaties."[31] Bismarck was an apt pupil of the economic nationalists who made America the world's greatest industrial power. Under Bismarck's policy, Germany increased its share of world production from 8.5 percent in 1880 to 14.8 percent by 1913.

In 1880 Germany and the United States together had less than a fourth of world output. By 1913 the two countries had nearly half, while free-trade Britain's share was sliced from one-fourth to one-seventh.[32] The great unacknowledged truth of the second half of the nineteenth century — and of the second half of the twentieth century — is that the nations that followed the free-trade dogma of the classical liberals lost ground to the nations that pursued the Hamiltonian policy of economic nationalism.

Reciprocity with the European Union

Europe would howl, but even under the old GATT rules a nation running a chronic trade deficit may use tariffs to end the hemorrhaging. And our response should satisfy Europe. Believing in fairness, we accept full reciprocity: a 15 percent EU tariff on all manufactured goods made in the United States.

Lincoln called the cost of ocean transport "useless labor." Much of this useless labor can be done away with if European companies that wish to sell in America produce in America, and vice versa. Ford and GM have always built cars there; Europeans forced them to. When U.S. companies feared a protectionist Common Market, they created European subsidiaries to avoid being frozen out. Turnabout is fair play. Let BMW and Mercedes make their parts and assemble their cars here in the United States if they wish to sell here on equal terms. As for those who prefer the cachet of European-made goods, they ought not be denied the freedom to buy. But a 15 percent tariff does not amount to persecution of elites who call 55 percent inheritance taxes "progressive." That new BMW can be built in South Carolina as easily as in Bavaria.

Americans may face a social crisis, a racial crisis, a crime crisis. We do not face a crisis of consumer goods. There is nothing made anywhere that we cannot make here. America-Canada and the EU are huge and self-sufficient markets, with similar laws and regulations. Their standards of living and wage rates are comparable. A reciprocal trade agreement could strengthen and solidify both blocs.

Would reduced imports cost us our technological edge? History proves otherwise. The telegraph, electric lightbulb, telephone, "horseless carriage," and airplane made societal impacts as dramatic as the computer. Yet, Americans invented and exploited them as no other nation, behind a tariff wall built by Justin Morrill, Bill McKinley, and "Pig Iron" Kelley.

With the U.S. market alone almost as large as the European

Union, we can support and sustain a diversity and level of production no other country can match. The small and medium-sized nations of Europe have no alternative but to create interdependencies. Germany is, after all, smaller than Oregon and Washington; the United Kingdom is smaller than Mississippi and Alabama; and Japan is smaller than Montana and less endowed with natural resources.

> The free-trade philosophy is a philosophy for small countries. When a country lacks the resources within its borders to meet its people's need, it must trade extensively. . . . The United States, however, has both a plentiful supply of resources and a huge market within its own borders. Its economic philosophy should be geared to its own size and needs. It should buy from abroad what it needs, not items it can make at home. It should sell abroad surplus products, not products in short supply here.[33]

And there is a larger issue. If this greatest of nations is ensnared in the Global Economy, and unable to break free, no nation will ever escape. But if America can restore her national sovereignty and independence, nations all over the world will one day be able to do so. Truly, we are deciding not only for ourselves alone but for all mankind.

An Equalization Tariff

In many Asian and Latin American countries, wages are 10 percent of what they are here. Many of these countries subsidize exports. They have little or no regulation of their labor environment. Production can be done at a fraction of our cost. While a 15 percent tariff might give American products a marginal advantage over European rivals, it would be brushed aside as an inconsequential cost in Asia. Thus, the United States should apply to the imports of low-wage countries the Roosevelt Rule, enunciated in TR's Seventh Annual Message to Congress, in 1907:

There must always be as a minimum a tariff which will not only allow for the collection of an ample revenue but which will at least make good the difference in the cost of production here and abroad; that is, the difference in the labor cost here and abroad, for the well-being of the wage-worker must ever be a cardinal point of American policy.[34]

This is sound Republican doctrine. Similar language may be found in a dozen party platforms. Roosevelt's first principle of trade argues for a tariff on all imported manufactures from Asia, Africa, and Latin America to protect the wages of American workers. In Europe and Canada, U.S. wage levels are competitive. They are not, and ought not be, competitive with men and women forced to work for ten dollars a day in Mexico or two dollars a day in Asia. The wage differential between American workers and Asian, African, and Latin American workers should serve as the basis for a protective tariff on all products imported from the Third World that compete with products made in America.

A Global Economy in which U.S. free labor in protected workplaces is forced into Darwinian competition with conscript labor, working under hellish conditions, for statist regimes, is an abomination, a crime against American labor! We must stop turning a blind eye to what we are subsidizing overseas and to what we are destroying at home. Let us junk an unjust system that has American women earning six dollars an hour cutting T-shirts in Rayne, Louisiana, competing with Honduran women making fifty cents an hour, and replace it with a just system whereby North Americans compete with North Americans, Europeans with Europeans, Asians with Asians, Latin Americans with Latin Americans.

An equalization tariff would send a long-overdue message to our transnational elites that would read thus:

We will not bind you to America. If you wish to shut down here, and go to China — go to China! But your products will not re-enter the United States duty-free. They will carry a tariff to make up the difference between the cost of the Chinese labor you hired, and the cost of the American labor you left behind.

Any windfall profits that transnationals derive from firing Americans and hiring low-wage foreign labor would be recaptured by the tariff and returned to our own people in tax cuts. An equalization tariff would make U.S. labor competitive *in price* with Asian labor and put the profit back into patriotism. Transnationals would have no incentive to take factories out of the United States but rather a powerful incentive to bring them home.

The curtain would fall on the golden age of a transnational elite that prides itself on being above community and country. No longer would governors of American states have to go to foreign nations to offer tax bribes to Germans to build in South Carolina, or to Japanese to build in Tennessee. Representatives of these countries would be showing up, hat in hand, in Columbia and Nashville. The rules of international trade have been fixed in favor of the globalists for too long. But America has the power to rewrite the rules — to reward those who stay in America and to tax the products of those who turn their back on America. Greed being their motivation, they will hurry home again of their own accord.

Finally, the president must have authority, with the consent of Congress, to raise tariffs on any country that devalues its currency to seize unfair advantage over U.S. producers. To watch the value of the dollar rise by 50 percent against the yen in the same period in which Japan ran up $100 billion in trade surpluses at U.S. expense is to appreciate that something other than market forces are at work here. In coping with unfair trade practices, the president and Congress need a full toolbox.

CANADA AND JAPAN

Should any country be exempt from the 15 percent tariff? Yes, Canada — if Canada adopts the same external tariffs. In NAFTA, Canada married her economy to ours, to the economic benefit of Ottawa. The United States today takes 80 percent of Canadian exports, and Canada's merchandise trade surplus with the United States in 1996 was $23 billion.[35]

However, Canada would have to choose to remain inside the U.S.-Canada free-trade zone and accept the U.S. tariffs, or go outside. If Canada chose to depart, the 15 percent tariff on all manufactured goods would be applied to Canadian goods as well. With the United States far and away Canada's biggest customer, and with that surplus on the line, Canada would surely choose to remain inside a U.S. free-trade zone. But Canada would have to choose.

As the United States strengthens ties to Canada, we should put an early end to our huge, chronic trade deficits with Japan.

The Japanese are a proud people. It is unseemly and destructive to be endlessly hectoring them to open their markets, buy our rice, remove nontariff barriers, adopt free trade. Japan does not practice free trade for a simple reason: Japan does not believe in free trade. Japan puts its national interest in manufacturing and technology ahead of a free-trade ideology that has America in its grip. Japan is different because it prefers to be different. We should respect that. But while Japan's economic structure is no business of the United States, our trade deficits are our business. We should notify Japan that if an end to these trade deficits cannot be achieved through negotiation, it will be attained through unilateral U.S. action.

A horrendous imbalance in autos and auto parts is central to the U.S. trade deficit with Japan. America should follow the Harley formula and impose a special tariff on imported Japanese autos and auto parts, on top of that 15 percent revenue tariff. The Japan Tariff should lead to the rapid U.S. recapture of much of Japan's present 30 percent of the U.S. auto market.

To avoid the tariffs, Japan could shift production of parts and the assembly of autos to the United States, where MADE IN THE USA Japanese cars would be treated exactly like Fords or Chevrolets made in Michigan. Toyota, Nissan, BMW, and all foreign car makers would be welcome here, but to avoid tariffs they would have to produce here. The same would hold for GM, Chrysler, and Ford. Fords made overseas would face the same tariff as Mazdas made overseas. America would have the most competitive auto market on earth, but every company, foreign-owned or U.S.-owned, would play by the same rules, pay the same taxes, abide by the same laws, employ the same high-wage, high-quality North American labor. Jobs in the U.S. auto industry would explode.

Japan is a great nation, and its people have wrought a great miracle. But the present unequal relationship cannot continue. Our sales to Japan in 1995, $65 billion, were 1 percent of our GDP; Japan's sales to us, $125 billion, were 4 percent of its GDP. With an economy twice as large as Japan's, we still spend six times as much on defense. We remit annually to Tokyo tens of billions of dollars in interest payments on the hundreds of billions of dollars of Treasury debt Tokyo now holds as a result of having run up decades of trade surpluses at the expense of American workers. Historians will marvel that America let this happen.

Even the American Chamber of Commerce in Japan (ACCJ) is showing signs of despair. According to the ACCJ, only thirteen of forty-five U.S.-Japan trade agreements since 1980 were successful in helping U.S. businesses penetrate Japan's market. Ten were total failures. Said ACCJ president Bill Beagles:

> For many years, the American view was that a trade agreement with Japan spoke for itself. . . . However, the U.S. Government and American industry came to realize that this is not the case. An apparently successful negotiation may not necessarily produce the expected market result.[36]

This is unhealthy. As a First World nation, Japan has much in common with the United States. Our strategic interests are in harmony, and the possibility remains for a close relationship. But it is not 1950 anymore. Reciprocity is required. If Japan can begin to harmonize her trade policies with ours, open her markets to our manufactures and agricultural products as we do for Japan's, there is no reason we cannot establish with Tokyo the same defense and trade relationship we have with Europe. There is no reason we cannot grow closer rather than drift farther apart, because of chronic trade deficits most Americans see as due to unfair, and ungrateful, Japanese practices.

OUR CHINA PROBLEM

China is fast becoming America's number one trade problem. In its drive for dominance in Asia, Beijing has exploited slave labor, consumed all the Western credit it could extort, stolen U.S. intellectual property, and strong-armed American companies like Boeing and McDonnell Douglas to manufacture in China as the price of a deal. "Forced technology transfers" are a routine demand in dealing with China. "When you invest in China," says one auto company executive, "China assumes it owns all of your intellectual property."[37] The Manufacturing Policy Project puts the piracy rate of U.S. intellectual property in China at 98 percent. "Three days after Microsoft introduced Windows 95 in the United States for $89.95, copies were available throughout Asia for $4 or less."[38]

Following the path to power laid out by Friedrich List, China treats the United States, the world's most advanced nation, like a colony, a source of raw materials and a dumping ground for manufactures. China sends us up to 40 percent of its exports — much of it high-tech manufactured goods — but buys less than 2 percent of our exports. While China runs a trade surplus in manufactures with the United States of more than $35 billion yearly, prominent among U.S. exports to China are fertilizers, food residue and waste, ore slag and ash, wood pulp, animal and vegetable fats, meats, live animals, and cereals — the technology for which was given a while ago by Squanto to the Pilgrims. The one high-tech export for which America runs a large trade surplus is aircraft; but once China masters the

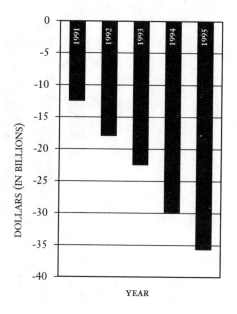

**Balance of Trades with China in
Manufactures, 1991–95**

Source: U.S. Department of Commerce

U.S. technology it has extorted, Beijing will begin building its own planes. For that is the way of economic nationalists.

From 1991 through 1996, China piled up $157 billion in surpluses trading with the United States. Its 1996 surplus of $40 billion was almost as large as the Pentagon procurement budget. In October of 1996 China invested $11.8 billion of its surplus in U.S. bonds, making China the third-largest buyer of U.S. debt, after Japan and Britain.[39] By September of 1997 China had amassed more than $130 billion in foreign currency reserves, the world's largest hoard after Japan's.[40]

For a century Americans have been transfixed by the great "China market"; it was one of the reasons business groups urged McKinley to annex the Philippines. But the China market proved a mirage then, and it is a mirage now, a corporate illusion. If China

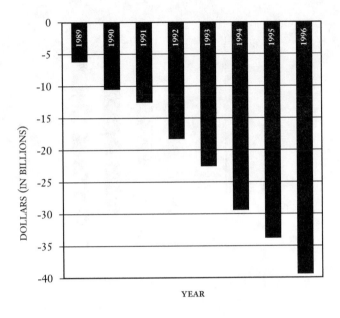

U.S. Trade Deficit with China, 1989–96

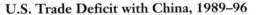

Source: U.S. Department of Commerce

vanished, the U.S. economy would not feel a breeze. Our sales to China in 1996 ($11.9 billion) were one-fifth of 1 percent of U.S. GDP. We sold more to Singapore. But China's sales to the United States — $52 billion worth of toys, textiles, shoes, bikes, computers, etc., in 1996 — were a crucial share of its entire economy and were the primary source of China's hard-currency reserves.

The United States has the whip hand in this relationship, and it is time we used it. For China is not only a trade problem, it is a national-security problem. China is using the hard currency from its U.S. trade surpluses and international bank loans to buy submarines, destroyers, antiship missiles, and fighter aircraft from Russia and to build long-range missiles to reach the west coast of the United States. Yet, America permits China to launch U.S. satellites on Long March rockets, thus subsidizing the development of the Chinese strategic missile force.

America is taking a terrible risk feeding a regime, the character of which may be seen in its treatment of dissidents, Tibetans, Christians, and women pregnant with any child conceived in violation of China's barbaric one-couple, one-child policy. While America should seek no confrontation with China, we should treat Beijing as the great power it has become.

We cannot practice true free trade with a nation that has no independent judiciary, where labor is conscripted, corruption is endemic, U.S. goods face a 17 percent value added tax and a 23 percent tariff, and many of whose corporations are government fronts.[41] The United States should cancel China's most-favored-nation status and negotiate a reciprocal trade agreement that recognizes our different societies and conflicting interests.

What About Mexico?

Mexico is another special case. We share a two-thousand-mile border, 10 million Americans trace their ancestry to Mexico, and our destinies are not separable. But NAFTA is not sustainable. NAFTA puts U.S. blue-collar workers into competition for manufacturing jobs with Mexican workers who earn 10 percent of their wages. American farm labor, paid a minimum wage near five dollars an hour, now competes with Mexican farm labor paid fifty cents an hour. American employers now hang over the heads of their workers this constant threat: accept reduced pay, or we go to Mexico!

What makes the threat credible is that hundreds of companies have already done so. Under the *maquiladora* program, tax concessions are offered to U.S. companies that site factories in Mexico to ship products back to the United States. New plants are opening at the rate of two a day. From San Diego to Brownsville, the Mexican side of the border is littered with signs of Fortune 500 corporations. Xerox, Zenith, Chrysler, GM, Ford, IBM, Rockwell, Samsonite, and GE have all sited plants south of the Rio Grande.[42] By moving to Mexico, they evade U.S. laws on child labor, worker safety, minimum wages, and health and pollution standards, as well as U.S.

taxes; their products come back to undercut those made in factories that stayed in America and obeyed the laws of the United States.

The Japanese are also exploiting NAFTA. Matsushita, Hitachi, Sony, and Sanyo have assembly plants in Tijuana. Toshiba's is in Ciudad Juárez. Japanese and Korean companies are also building auto plants there. This Japanese investment in Mexico represents a shift of capital away from the United States. The CEO of the Japanese Chamber of Commerce in Mexico describes how it works: "Japanese investments reaching Mexico do not come directly from Japan. It is the United States [subsidiaries], the son, who is investing in Mexico, the grandson of the main office." [43]

President Clinton points with pride to the growth of U.S. exports to Mexico. But prominent among those exports are parts for assembly into products for shipment back to the United States and capital equipment for factories being built in Mexico. Such exports destroy American jobs.

NAFTA must be renegotiated, or America's new Sun Belt will be south of the Rio Grande, and the consequences will be social and political as well as economic. Export the future of our working young, and those whose dreams have been destroyed will be heard from.

America's merchandise trade deficit, an all-time record of $191 billion in 1996, is a cancer. Either we cut it out, or it will kill America. History teaches that when a nation's manufacturing sector has entered a period of relative decline, that nation is in decline. Who profits most from the record U.S. trade deficits?

U.S. Merchandise Trade Deficits
(By Country, 1996)

Japan	$47 billion
China	$40 billion
Canada	$23 billion
Mexico	$17 billion
European Union	$14 billion
Taiwan	$12 billion
Malaysia	$ 9 billion

The policies outlined earlier can zero out these appalling numbers within a decade!

Our traditional industries are not in decline because manufacturing is obsolete in a postindustrial society. Americans still use manufactured goods in record numbers. We simply no longer make them all here. *The United States has been deindustrializing as a producer, not as a consumer.* America now imports more than a third of the goods it uses, worth more than $700 billion in 1996, triple their value in 1980. The world's largest growth market for U.S. products is here at home, a market that foreign interests control only by default. Automobiles, consumer electronics, industrial machinery, chemicals, clothing, telecommunications equipment, computers — these are at the core of America's trade crisis.

The idea of a "postindustrial economy" is nonsense. When the United States shifted from an agricultural to an industrial economy, America did not stop producing food. The factory did not replace the farm; it was built alongside it. Industry reinforced agriculture with machinery, fertilizer, improved transportation. America became the largest and most advanced industrial economy while remaining the largest and most advanced agricultural economy. Until the 1970s America's output of both farm and factory dominated the world economy. American agriculture still dominates. Only industry has lost ground — and not to some Third Wave service economy but to other industrial economies.

A third of the U.S. market for manufactures has been captured by foreigners. Let us take it back for Americans! A 15 percent tariff on all manufactures from First World countries, plus an equalization tariff on the products of low-wage nations, will erase these deficits and reindustrialize America within a decade. The reward: millions of high-paying manufacturing jobs for all our workers — immigrant and native-born, black and white, Hispanic and Asian — an easing of our social crisis, and trade and budget surpluses as America's workers find higher-paying jobs and contribute more to Social Security and Medicare, deficit reduction and tax reduction.

Free traders will cry, "But you are risking a trade war!" This is a fear rooted in ignorance and timidity: even if we eliminate our trade deficit, we will remain the world's leading importer. What foreign nation would offend its best customer? Our forefathers broke all ties with the mother country and risked their lives to achieve the economic independence we are piddling away. We need less of the gauzy spirit of globalism and more of the patriotic spirit of old George Meany:

> Practically every country in the world . . . has some type of restriction, some type of barrier, some type of subsidization for their own people, that gives their own manufacturers and workers an unfair advantage over the American worker. . . . When have we ever retaliated against the unfair barriers put up by these other countries which go back many, many years? And if we are to have a trade war, if that's the only answer, I imagine if we had an all-out trade war we would do quite well for one simple fact: We have the market. We have the greatest market in the world right in this country.[44]

Amen. Let us emulate our greatest leaders and use our control of that national market to achieve our national aims. After the Revolution, the War of 1812, the Civil War, and World War I, tariff revenue helped erase America's deficits and pay down America's debt. What is the alternative but more years of receding wages and rising tempers among American workers, until the social fabric is torn irreparably, the bonds of patriotism no longer hold, our vitality vanishes, and our economic divisions manifest themselves in class conflict between Industrial America and Third Wave America? We have nothing to lose by trying — except those policies that have put us on the slippery slope to national decline.

What to Do with the WTO?

The World Trade Organization was erected on ideas American patriots must reject. It subordinates everything to the demands of trade. It exercises a supranational authority in conflict with our forefathers' vision of an America forever sovereign and independent. Its dispute-resolution procedures shift to Geneva decisions that ought to be made in Washington. And if we refuse to abide by the WTO's edicts, America can be chastised and fined.

Run by nameless, faceless, foreign bureaucrats, the WTO is the embryonic trade ministry of a world government. There is no place for such an institution in a world where free nations negotiate their trade agreements in good faith and themselves oversee the execution of those agreements. The WTO is a monument to the one-world vision of Wilson and FDR. Our withdrawal — after the required six months' notice — would be an unmistakable signal that America is back and that this nation is again the independent self-reliant republic the Founding Fathers intended it to be.

Keeping Capital at Home

In a 1952 address to the University Club of Milwaukee, Ludwig von Mises declared that the "essence of Keynesianism is its complete failure to conceive the role that saving and capital accumulation play in the improvement of economic conditions."[45] He admonished Americans to appreciate the role that capital had played in creating their unrivaled prosperity:

> The average standard of living is in this country higher than in any other country of the world, not because the American statesmen and politicians are superior to the foreign statesmen and politicians, but because the per-head quota of capital invested is in America higher than in other countries. . . .
>
> Do the American voters know that the unprecedented improvements in their standard of living that the last hundred years brought was the result of the steady rise in the per-head quota of capital invested? Do they realize that every measure leading to capital decumulation jeopardizes their prosperity?[46]

Von Mises, a free-trade libertarian, is toasting a century in which the United States was the most protectionist nation on earth. Hamilton was right: protectionism went hand in hand with record capital accumulation. A primary reason that America's growth rates have been anemic in recent decades, and our recoveries not as robust as they once were, is the $2 trillion in trade deficits this generation has run up. Too much of the seed corn of the U.S. economy is now being exported all over the world. As Sir James Goldsmith warned in 1995,

> Today, capital is being transferred to the developing world in massively increasing amounts. In the period 1989–1992, the average capital transferred per year to emerging countries was 116 billion dollars. In 1993, the figure was 213 billion dollars and in 1994 it was an estimated 227 billion dollars. East Asia leads the field, with a rise in the annual rate of direct investment between 1984 and 1994 of 1100 percent.[47]

How can the United States halt the hemorrhaging of capital? First, consider how America's capital goes abroad. There are several primary vehicles for the "decumulation" of American capital:

- Imports — $2 trillion in trade deficits in twenty years
- Foreign investments by corporations, pension funds, etc.
- Foreign aid, perhaps $1 trillion in the Cold War
- IMF, World Bank, and international bank loans
- U.S. private bank loans
- U.S. overseas defense expenditures
- Illicit trade (drugs)
- Illicit wealth transfers to evade taxes

Each of these problems can be dealt with by strong action.

IMPORTS: A 15 percent tariff on all products that compete with U.S.-produced goods and a wage-equalization tariff on manufactures from low-wage countries would rapidly erase the U.S. merchandise trade deficits. Instead of capital going abroad to build plants for the assembly of goods to be sent back to the United States, capital would come home to expand U.S. industries and create American jobs. The deep tax cuts on investment and savings that the new customs revenue would finance would make America the most attractive investment site of all the industrial democracies.

FOREIGN INVESTMENT: Again, the tariffs, which would wipe out the admission-free access that foreign countries now have to the U.S. market, would have a chilling effect on the plans of transnational corporations to invest abroad or to move factories abroad. Comparative advantage would come home.

FOREIGN AID: Annual wealth transfers to foreign regimes like Egypt ($18 billion in cash reserves), Israel (a median income above $16,000), Greece, Turkey, Russia, and Pakistan make little sense. The Cold War is over; it's time for relics like foreign aid to be entombed. We cannot bribe nations to embrace free enterprise, and we ought not pay nations not to fight one another.

INTERNATIONAL BANKS: Far more serious is backdoor foreign aid, the scores of billions of dollars funneled yearly to foreign regimes through the IMF, World Bank, Asian Development Bank, etc. These relics of our "Marshall Plan mentality" have become global-socialist centers for the redistribution of American wealth.

Why should U.S. taxpayers guarantee loans to India or China, the leading beneficiaries of the World Bank? If these governments have worthwhile projects, let them finance the projects themselves. Didn't we when we were a developing nation? American-taxpayer guarantees for World Bank and IMF loans reward nations whose policies rarely merit such rewards.

PRIVATE BANK LOANS: Although America cannot and ought not impose controls on the foreign loans or investments of America's big banks, investment banks, mutual funds, and pension funds all should be put on notice: the next time there is another default, another Mexico, another meltdown in Asia, those who made the profits take the loss. This is neither harsh nor punitive. Private banks and overseas investors must begin to realize that there is no global bankruptcy court to bail them out. Once they know their investments are no longer risk-free, the market will solve this problem.

OVERSEAS DEFENSE EXPENDITURES: John Foster Dulles once said that a day was coming when the United States would have to conduct an "agonizing reappraisal" of commitments to defend nations that refused to bear their fair share of the cost of their own defense. With the Cold War over, that reappraisal is long overdue. NATO should not be expanded; new nations should not be added to the roster of those we are already committed to defending. And Europe should begin to bear the full economic cost of its own defense. While the United States retains a vital interest in preventing a hostile regime — a Hitler or Stalin — from overrunning Europe, that threat has never been more remote. England and France have nuclear deterrents; Germany is united and democratic; Russia is smaller than it was in the days of Peter the Great. No threat to any vital U.S. interest remotely exists in Europe. It is time to bring U.S. troops home and revise NATO so that America is no longer committed to go to war because some ancient border has been breached or because a forgotten trip wire has been activated in some forsaken corner of the old continent. The proper role of America in Europe is not to be a frontline fighting state but to be the "strategic reserve" of the West, which has restored to itself full constitutional freedom to decide when, where, and whether to involve itself in Europe's twenty-first-century wars.

The new relationship of America with Europe should be modeled on our *military* relationship with Israel. Where the Israelis provide the troops to maintain their own defense, the U.S. provides access to its advanced weapons. Israel gives us no veto over what it does in its own interests; and we give Israel no ironclad guarantee that any war Israel decides to fight will be our war as well.

In Asia the great threat to stability and security is almost certain to come from China. But Beijing is already contained — by geography: Islam to the west; a nuclear-armed Russia to the north; India and Vietnam to the south; Korea, Japan, and the U.S. fleet to the east. Any Chinese military move would trigger an arms race across East Asia. Here, again, the United States should play the role of arsenal of democracy and sell to the nations of Asia the modern weapons they need to resist intimidation or defend against Beijing's encroachments — while they provide the troops themselves. No more Koreas, no more Vietnams.

When the nations of Europe and Asia understand that they, not we, are primarily responsible for their security, they will cease acting like dependencies and begin acting like independent nations. It is past time prosperous allies began paying the cost of their own defense. Defense of the West can thus begin to enhance, rather than drain, America's vitality.

ILLICIT DRUGS: Seventy to eighty percent of the marijuana and cocaine that enter the United States, to destroy the soul of America's young, pass through Mexico. To secure our southern border from this deadly traffic, we should cancel that provision of NAFTA which permits Mexican trucks on America's highways. Second, we should expand the U.S. Border Patrol. Third, we should lengthen the triple fence already built at San Diego, which has begun to cut back illegal immigration and complicate life for drug smugglers. Fourth, we should demand of Mexico greater cooperation in running down narcotics traffickers, and greater freedom and protection for U.S. agents operating in Mexico. Finally, though the U.S. military does not belong in a policing role, American troops brought home from abroad should be moved to a southern border that is certain to be a crisis area in the twenty-first century.

ILLICIT WEALTH TRANSFERS TO EVADE TAXES: The scores of billions of dollars in tariff revenue should be used to virtually eliminate taxes on savings, capital gains, and inheritances. With taxes on capital at zero in the United States, departed capital would come running home and new capital would come pouring in. Finally, the Republican Party should heed the advice the Austrian champion of free markets, Ludwig von Mises, gave in that Milwaukee address:

> No party platform is to be considered as satisfactory that does not contain the following point: As the prosperity of the nation and the height of wage rates depend on a continual increase in the capital invested in its plants, mines and farms, it is one of the foremost tasks of good government to remove all obstacles that hinder the accumulation and investment of new capital.[48]

STRATEGIC INDEPENDENCE

> It is of importance that the kingdom should depend as little as possible upon its neighbours for the manufactures necessary for its defense; and if these cannot be maintained at home, it is reasonable that all other branches of industry be taxed in order to support them.[49]
>
> — Adam Smith

At the end of World War II, the United States had a nearly autarkic industrial base; we produced everything needed for our national defense. That day is gone. In 1982 we began to run manufacturing trade deficits; by 1986, deficits in the trade of high-technology

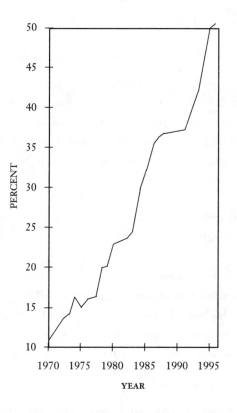

PERCENT

YEAR

Manufactured Imports as a Share of U.S. Manufactures

Source: U.S. Department of Commerce

goods. American dependence on foreign sources for items critical to our advanced weapons systems has created a vulnerability unknown since American doughboys had to use French artillery and tanks, British machine guns, and fighter planes built by our allies — even though our own Wright brothers had invented the airplane. A decade ago, Admiral James Lyons, commander of U.S. Pacific forces, warned, "All of the critical components of our modern weapons systems, which involve our F-16s and F/A 18s, our M-1 tanks, our military computers — and I could go on and on — come from East Asian industries. . . . Some day, we might view that with concern and rightly so."[50] Lyons was echoed five years later by former chairman of the Joint Chiefs of Staff Admiral William Crowe, Jr.:

> The gulf war was unique because America enjoyed the unanimous support of all its allies. Even so, cooperation was difficult. . . . The U.S. defense industrial base is already in danger of becoming too dependent upon foreign sources for strategic supplies. What if the next time we are called upon to respond, our allies decide it is in their best interest to sit it out?[51]

Former Commerce official Erik R. Pages writes of the difficulties to which Crowe alluded:

> The Bush Administration was forced to intervene with foreign governments on over thirty occasions to guarantee delivery of critical military parts. As one high-level administration official commented: "If the foreign governments were neutral or were not disposed to help us out, we could have run into some real problems. We were sweating bullets over it and the military was sweating bullets too."[52]

Peacetime America may ignore such concerns, but it is a dangerous vulnerability when technology is vital to national power, crucial to military victory, and essential to saving the lives of Americans sent into combat. We got a glimpse of what might happen during Vietnam, when Japan withheld the transfer of Sony TV cameras for missile guidance.

Foreigners today control the U.S. companies responsible for the heat shield of the D-5 Trident missile and the flight controls of the B-2 bomber, the F-117 Stealth, and the F-22, the backbone of the twenty-first-century air force.[53]

Overseas factories are far more vulnerable to espionage, labor problems, sabotage, political dictation — and attack by enemy or terrorist forces. There is no guarantee that U.S. secrets are safe abroad. A clear and present danger exists when corporations with allegiance to no country gain virtual monopolies over items critical to U.S. security. During World War II, Stalin's spies and our own homegrown traitors looted vital defense secrets, including those related to the atom bomb. Given this experience, for us to allow technology indispensable to our security to be kept outside the United States, vulnerable to theft or denial, is perilous folly. The time to end foreign military dependence is when new weapons systems are in the design stage. America should guarantee that no foreign dependency is built into any future generations of weapons. When it comes to technology vital to national defense, "Buy American" and MADE IN THE USA are the rules that should apply.

The world is a dynamic place. No nation can ground its security in existing technological superiority. Superpowers that rest on their laurels invite the fate of the first global powers of the modern era: Holland and Spain. When Treasury's Richard Darman blurted, "Why do we want a semiconductor industry? We don't want some kind of industrial policy in this country. If our guys can't hack it, let 'em go," his was the smug voice of the elites of numerous nations that are no longer counted as great.[54]

Unfortunately, President Clinton subscribes to the Darman view. His administration is outsourcing to foreign producers more components of U.S. weapons systems than ever before. This penny-wise, pound-foolish policy strikes at the heart of America's security and independence and ignores a truth taught by Adam Smith: "The great object of the political economy of every country is to increase the wealth and the power of that country."[55]

A Simpler, Fairer Tax Code

> *The ideal tax code must include five basic principles: Be fair, be simple, get at the underground economy, encourage savings and investment, and help our balance of trade.*[56]
>
> — Congressman Bill Archer, Chairman, House Committee on Ways and Means, 1996

The tariffs recommended above would provide the Treasury with perhaps hundreds of billions of dollars a year in revenue, to cut or to eliminate taxes on income, savings, and investment.

Another idea that ought to be considered is replacing the U.S. corporate income tax with a corporate revenue tax — to end the flagrant tax evasion of foreign companies operating in the United States. Using a scheme called "transfer pricing," foreign producers overcharge their U.S. subsidiaries for parts, guaranteeing no U.S. profit and no U.S. corporate tax. This gives foreign regimes an unjust advantage over U.S. industry.

European companies operating here regularly report profits half those of U.S. companies; Asian companies regularly report profits one-tenth those of U.S. companies.[57] The United States is, to put it bluntly, being swindled.

But transfer pricing can be defeated by a revenue tax. For example, a 4 percent corporate revenue tax would net $4 million in taxes from a Toyota assembly plant that sold $100 million worth of cars, regardless of any games played with inventory or parts. Foreign companies could no more avoid a revenue tax than a sales tax. American companies would be placed on an even footing with foreign firms that use accounting tricks to give themselves the "comparative advantage" of not paying U.S. income taxes.

In 1995 U.S. corporations paid $140 billion in taxes on $550 billion in profits, with the profits determined by a tax code of thousands of pages of exemptions, credits, deductions, and a depreciation schedule that even IRS agents have difficulty deciphering. However, the gross revenue of all U.S. corporations was $3.55 trillion. A 4 percent corporate revenue tax would have yielded the same $140 billion as the corporate income tax. To provide a break for small businesses, which have created almost all of the 30 million new jobs since 1981, the corporate revenue tax could be raised to 5 percent for large corporations, but the first few millions of dollars of revenue could be taxed at 0 percent, 1 percent, or 2 percent.

Converting to a corporate revenue tax would eliminate the jobs of thousands of lobbyists engaged today in the glorified bribery of our lords temporal with campaign contributions in return for "corporate welfare." By switching from a complex income tax to a simple revenue tax, tens of thousands of accountants, tax lawyers, and IRS agents could be shifted to more productive work. American businesses would save billions in accounting costs — another "comparative advantage."

Then, in place of the *personal* income tax, the nation should look to a flat tax, or a national sales tax (NST). What would an NST accomplish?

- End all federal taxation of salaries, wages, dividends, interest, gifts, estates, and capital gains
- Save 5.4 billion work hours spent filling out tax forms
- Eliminate the IRS
- Eliminate the need for hundreds of thousands of accountants, bookkeepers, tax lawyers, and trust lawyers, turning them loose for more productive work
- Eliminate thousands of lobbyists now prowling the nation's capital for special tax breaks
- Surface and tax the "underground economy" for the first time; all current tax evaders, from illegal aliens to tourists to UN diplomats and the D.C. diplomatic corps to organized crime, would become taxpayers every time they spent a dollar

Foreign goods sold in the United States would carry the same sales tax as American goods. And eliminating U.S. corporate and personal income taxes from the sticker price of American-made products would strengthen the competitive position of U.S. goods in the world market.

The major argument against an NST has been that the poor and the elderly on fixed incomes, who pay no income tax, would get a tax hike, because all their income is spent, while the wealthiest Americans would get a tax cut. But under a modified NST, food, clothing, and shelter can be made exempt, and the poor and working poor made whole with rebates.

The U.S. income tax code does not need reform; it needs to be ripped out by the roots. No system will satisfy everyone, and none is perfect, but the NST seems among the best options. It eliminates the IRS. It ensures that everyone pays, but only when we consume, not when we earn, save, or invest. Imports would carry the same taxes as U.S.-made goods; exports would go untaxed. Everyone would contribute to the defense of the nation and the necessary duties of government, as all should. In a republic there should be no free riders.

What about the flat tax? Any flat tax that excludes all dividends, interest, and capital gains would allow Palm Beach trust fund babies, who live off inherited wealth, to avoid taxation altogether. Neither Congress nor the public would ever accept such a system. However, a 16 percent flat tax on all salaries and wages, starting at $35,000, yoked to a separate flat tax on all dividends, interest, and capital gains above the first $35,000, might just pass muster. Investment and savings would be encouraged and rewarded, but the rich living off inherited wealth would not escape.

A mix of these tax, trade, and capital-accumulation policies would shift much of the burden of taxation off work, savings, and investment and onto consumption of imported goods, the revenue of foreign corporations, and the incomes of the well-to-do. Ours would be the most attractive market for investment in the world.

None of these ideas is written in stone, but something is written on the wind: either we walk away from a global system that is looting America of its industrial capacity, robbing our workers of their best jobs, bleeding away our sovereignty, and corrupting our politics, or the nation will fail. Implement these or like ideas, and in half a decade:

- U.S. trade deficits will have disappeared.
- U.S. vulnerability to global financial crises will end.
- Factories will be springing up, not shutting down.
- Millions of manufacturing jobs will have been created.
- Downward pressure on U.S. wages will be replaced by rising demand for U.S. workers. *America will get that pay raise!*
- The tax burden on American families will be lighter.
- Americans will find themselves less dependent on foreign producers and more reliant on one another.

The ultimate goal: greater security for America's workers and greater stability for America's families. After all, who is an economy for, if not the people? And what is an economy for, if not to serve society?

As this book began, I wrote that, in traveling across America in the campaign of 1995–96, I found that we seemed to be losing the country we grew up in. We are ceasing to be a "band of brothers." We need to heal the divisions, to come together again, as one nation and one people. That is what the great Americans sought. As Christopher Lasch wrote in the year before his death:

Whatever its faults, middle-class nationalism provided a common ground, common standards, a common frame of reference without which society dissolves into nothing more than contending factions, as the Founding Fathers of America understood so well — a war of all against all.[58]

The ideas in this book have to do with closing the divisions and easing the tensions in society that emanate from the economic order. They do not address the stresses rooted in the divisions of religion, culture, and race. But re-creation of a just economic order is a prerequisite of the restoration of the moral order. When all members of society prosper together, when property and wealth are more equitably shared, when a man can raise a family again on the sweat of his own labor, when Americans begin anew to put their own country and countrymen first — as natural law teaches we must — those tensions will ease as well.

There are many who say there is no turning back, that the Global Economy is inevitable, that the death warrant of the nation-state has been signed, and that there is to be no reprieve. I do not believe this. It is vital that we not surrender this fortress of freedom, liberty, and human dignity that our ancestors died creating. I do not want to live in their brave new world; if it is coming, let us all stand our post. And if indeed, as James Fitzjames Stephens wrote, "The waters are out and no human force can turn them back . . . I do not see why as we go with the stream we need sing Hallelujah to the river god." [59]

We *can* take our country back; and, God willing, we shall.

ACKNOWLEDGMENTS

The Great Betrayal owes much to many, and my gratitude goes to them all: to Terry Jeffrey, a good friend and captain in the Buchanan Brigades of '92 and '96, now editor of *Human Events*, for his ideas and research on the Founding Fathers; to Brian Robertson, for his preparation of the charts and graphs; to Bill Hawkins, who provided insights and research and whose own writings are often cited; and to John Meroney, who spent hundreds of hours in libraries, digging up original citations and gathering new evidence for presentation to a national jury.

Half a dozen friends volunteered to review drafts of the book; all suggested surgeries, some of which were not minor, and a few of which were done without anesthesia and under duress.

For editing, special thanks to my old friend from the White House days of Nixon and Reagan, Lyndon K. "Mort" Allin; to Tom Piatak of the American Cause, and George Csatary and Tom Greenlee of *The American Protectionist* for their insights on the thought of Hamilton and Adam Smith; to Alan Tonelson and Kevin Kearns of U.S. Business and Industrial Council, a Washington pillar of economic nationalism; to Al Eckes, former chairman of the International Trade Commission, who saved Harley-Davidson with his critical vote, a historian whose *Opening America's Market* is cited more often here than any other work; to Gabor Boritt of the Civil War Institute at Gettysburg College, whose definitive writings on the economic ideas of Lincoln are the primary source for my chapter "The Great Protectionist"; to Gus Stelzer, friend and former GM executive whose *Nightmare of Camelot* inspired my chapter on the auto industry; to author Pat Choate, the Reform Party candidate for vice president in 1996; and to one of our country's great historians, Robert H. Ferrell, professor emeritus at Indiana, author of dozens of books, whom I came to know after fortuitously stumbling across his splendid *American Diplomacy: A History* in a Seattle bookstore during the campaign of 1996.

Others who reviewed early chapters are my friend, the syndicated columnist Sam Francis; Peter Brimelow of *National Review;* Bernard Way of Christendom College; Thomas DiLorenzo of Loyola; Steve Sniegoski, writer and ex-student of historian Wayne Cole; and Dr. Cole himself.

This book also owes a great debt to Fredrica Friedman. Fredi, the brilliant editorial director at Little, Brown, edited my memoir *Right from the Beginning* a decade ago, arranged for this new book to be published, set the parameters, rearranged and refocused the arguments, culled and cut the text, and chaperoned the final product to publication.

Finally, my thanks to others who have defended the legacy and kept alive the ideas of Hamilton and Clay in the halcyon days of the free traders and from whose writings I have benefited: Bill Gill, author of *Trade Wars Against America;* Jay Olnek, author of *The Invisible Hand;* and Sir James Goldsmith, author of *The Trap* and *The Response*, and founder of Great Britain's Referendum Party. A generous friend who passed away in 1997 and relished any fight against entrenched power, "Jimmy" Goldsmith did more than any man of his time to alert Britain and France to the terrible price that absorption into the European Union means for those nations. If the cause of enlightened nationalism prevails in the West, as it shall, the tragedy will be that Jimmy is not there to host our victory party.

NOTES

Book One
A TALE OF TWO NATIONS

Chapter 1
"THE TWO AMERICAS"

1. Hilaire Belloc, *The Servile State* (New York: Henry Holt and Co., 1946), pp. xix–xx.
2. This story is from my own recollections and materials I read before visiting Rayne. The quotations of the women at the Fruit of the Loom plant are from a story by Anne Hull in the *Houston Chronicle*, Nov. 30, 1995. Statistics and facts are from a March 19, 1995, article by Bobby Lamb in the *Baton Rouge Sunday Advocate*, p. 1G; a *Chicago Sun-Times* story by Francis Knowles, Oct. 31, 1995, p. 43; a piece the same day by Randy McClain of the *Baton Rouge Advocate*, p. 1C; and a July 31, 1996, piece by Joan McKinney, Washington bureau chief of the *Advocate*, p. 13A.
3. Robert J. Lampman, *The Share of Top Wealth-Holders in National Wealth, 1922–1956* (Princeton, N.J.: Princeton University Press, 1962), p. 204; Steven Sass, "Passing the Buck," *Federal Reserve Bank of Boston Regional Review*, summer 1995, p. 16; James D. Smith and Stephen D. Franklin, "The Concentration of Personal Wealth, 1922–1969," *American Economic Review*, May 1974, pp. 162–67.
4. Irwin M. Stelzer, "Are CEOs Overpaid?" *Public Interest*, Winter 1997, p. 33.
5. Table B-45, "Hours and Earnings in Private Nonagricultural Industries, 1959–94," *Economic Report of the President, February 1995* (Washington, D.C.: Government Printing Office, 1995), p. 326.
6. Charles J. Whalen, "The Anxious Society: A Middle Class Perspective," *Durrell Journal of Money and Banking*, spring 1996, p. 14.

7. Jeff Madrick, "In the Shadows of Prosperity," *New York Review of Books*, Aug. 14, 1997, p. 41.

8. Table B-34, "Civilian Employment and Unemployment by Sex and Age, 1947–94," *Economic Report of the President, February 1995*, p. 314.

9. News release, Bureau of Labor Statistics, U.S. Department of Labor, Dec. 17, 1996; "Prisoners in 1996," bulletin, Bureau of Justice Statistics, U.S. Department of Justice, June 1997.

10. Lawrence Mishel, Jared Bernstein, and John Schmitt, *The State of Working America 1996–1997* (Washington, D.C.: Economic Policy Institute, 1996), p. 42.

11. Charles W. McMillion, "Wages Finally Gain on Inflation, But Stagnation Hits Hyped Jobs," *Washington Times*, Aug. 4, 1997, p. D4.

12. Charles Murray, "Income Inequality and IQ," *AEI*, American Enterprise Institute for Public Policy Research, Aug. 1997.

13. Pat Choate and Charles McMillion, *The Mysterious US Trade Deficit* (Washington, D.C.: Manufacturing Policy Project, 1997), pp. 6–7.

14. John B. Judis, "Dollar Foolish," *New Republic*, Dec. 9, 1996, p. 23.

15. Charles W. McMillion, testimony to the U.S. Senate Committee on Commerce, Science, and Transportation, Subcommittee on Manufacturing and Competitiveness, Apr. 13, 1997.

16. Ibid.

17. Table B-44, "Employees on Nonagricultural Payrolls, by Major Industry, 1946–94," *Economic Report of the President, February 1995*, pp. 324–25.

18. McMillion testimony.

19. Donald L. Barlett and James B. Steele, "America: Who Stole the Dream?" *Indianapolis Star*, Sept. 22, 1996 and Sept. 24, 1996.

20. Peter Coy, "Why Foreign Capital Won't Dry Up," *Business Week*, July 29, 1997, p. 71.

21. Ibid.

22. Choate and McMillion, *The Mysterious US Trade Deficit*, p. 1.

23. Mishel, Bernstein, and Schmitt, *The State of Working America*, p. 169.

24. William Branigin, "Illegal Immigrant Population Grows to 5 Million," *Washington Post*, Feb. 8, 1997, p. A3.

25. Medea Benjamin, "Nike in Asia: Is This Prosperity?" *Wall Street Journal*, June 4, 1997, p. A19; Bob Herbert, "Nike's Pyramid Scheme," *New York Times*, June 10, 1996, p. A17.

26. John Maynard Keynes, *The Economic Consequences of the Peace* (New York: Macmillan, 1920), p. 2.

Chapter 2
"Triumph of the Free Traders"

1. Cordell Hull, *The Memoirs of Cordell Hull*, vol. 1 (New York: Macmillan, 1948), p. 83.
2. Ibid, p. 76.
3. Ibid, p. 81.
4. Ravi Batra, *The Great American Deception: What Politicians Won't Tell You About Our Economy and Your Future* (New York: John Wiley & Sons, 1996), p. 80.
5. Hull, *Memoirs*, p. 81.
6. William Henry Chamberlin, *America's Second Crusade* (Chicago: Henry Regnery Co., 1950), p. 184.
7. Ibid.
8. U.S. Senate Committee on Finance, *Extending Authority to Negotiate Trade Agreements: Hearings Before the Committee on Finance, United States Senate, June 1–5, 1948* (Washington, D.C.: Government Printing Office, 1948), pp. 175–98.
9. "Cotton & King," *Time*, Aug. 17, 1936, p. 62.
10. Steve Dryden, *Trade Warriors: USTR and the American Crusade for World Trade* (New York: Oxford University Press, 1995), p. 10.
11. Ibid, p. 13.
12. Ibid, p. 11.
13. Ibid., p. 14.
14. Alfred E. Eckes, Jr., *Opening America's Market: U.S. Foreign Trade Policy Since 1776* (Chapel Hill: University of North Carolina Press, 1995), p. 157.
15. *A Trade and Tariff Policy in the National Interest* (Washington, D.C.: Public Advisory Board for Mutual Security, 1953) pp. 19–20.
16. Eckes, *Opening America's Market*, p. 167.
17. Dwight D. Eisenhower, *Public Papers of the Presidents of the United States: Dwight D. Eisenhower, 1954* (Washington, D.C.: Government Printing Office, 1960), p. 587.
18. Ibid.
19. Robert H. Ferrell, ed., *The Eisenhower Diaries* (New York: W. W. Norton, 1981), p. 242.
20. Eckes, *Opening America's Market*, p. 237.
21. Ibid., p. 238.
22. Ibid., 168.
23. Ibid.
24. Ibid.
25. Ibid.

26. Ibid., p. 170.

27. Ibid., p. 171.

28. Ibid., p. 172.

29. Ibid.

30. Ibid.

31. Jacob M. Schlesinger, *Shadow Shoguns: The Rise and Fall of Japan's Postwar Political Machine* (New York: Simon & Schuster, 1997), p. 48.

32. Eckes, *Opening America's Market*, p. 172.

33. William R. Hawkins, Director of the Economic Security Action Center, U.S. Business and Industrial Council, "The World's Best Educated Fast Food Cooks," Washington D.C., KRTN Forum.

34. Eckes, *Opening America's Market*, p. 175.

35. Ibid., p. 177.

36. Geir Lundestad, *The American "Empire"* (New York: Oxford University Press, 1990), pp. 70–72.

37. Wesley T. Wooley, *Alternatives to Anarchy: American Supranationalism Since World War II* (Bloomington: Indiana University Press, 1988), p. 169.

38. George W. Ball, *The Past Has Another Pattern* (New York: W. W. Norton, 1982), pp. 190–91.

39. Ibid., p. 191.

40. Editorial, "Cold War Weapon," *St. Louis Globe-Democrat*, Oct. 5, 1962.

41. John F. Kennedy, *Public Papers of the Presidents of the United States: John F. Kennedy, 1963* (Washington, D.C.: Government Printing Office, 1964), pp. 518–19.

42. Eckes, *Opening America's Market*, p. 193.

43. Ibid.

44. Ibid.

45. Ibid., p. 196.

46. Ibid., p. 199.

47. Ibid.

48. Thomas W. Zeiler, *American Trade and Power in the Sixties* (New York: Columbia University Press, 1992), p. 239.

49. Ibid., p. 240.

50. Ibid.

51. Eckes, *Opening America's Market*, pp. 202–03.

52. Milton Friedman, *There's No Such Thing as a Free Lunch* (LaSalle, Ill.: Open Court Publishing, 1975).

53. Herbert Stein, *Presidential Economics: The Making of Economic Policy from Roosevelt to Reagan and Beyond* (New York: Simon & Schuster, 1984), p. 167.

54. Eckes, *Opening America's Market*, p. 217.

55. "No. 687. U.S. Membership in AFL-CIO Unions, by Selected Union: 1979 to

1991," *Statistical Abstract of the United States: 1993* (Washington, D.C.: Government Printing Office, 1993), p. 435.

56. Ronald Reagan, *Public Papers of the Presidents of the United States: Ronald Reagan, 1985*, Book 2 (Washington, D.C.: Government Printing Office, 1988), p. 1015.

57. Eckes, *Opening America's Market*, p. 247.

58. Sidney Hook, *Out of Step: An Unquiet Life in the Twentieth Century* (New York: Harper & Row, 1987), pp. 598–99.

59. Ronald Reagan, *Public Papers of the Presidents of the United States: Ronald Reagan, 1987*, Book 1 (Washington, D.C.: Government Printing Office, 1989), p. 476.

60. Ibid., p. 478.

61. "U.S. Car Imports Number Nearly 5 Million," *Facts and Figures '85*, Motor Vehicle Manufacturers Association of the United States, p. 31.

62. Alan Tonelson, "Beating Back Predatory Trade," *Foreign Affairs*, July/Aug. 1994, p. 125.

63. Eckes, *Opening America's Market*, p. 260.

64. Clyde Prestowitz, "America Without Tools: Are We Turning Into a Nation That Can't Make Anything?" *Washington Post*, January 12, 1992, pp. C1–C2.

65. Patrick J. Buchanan, "Death of the American Heartland," *New York Post*, Oct. 31, 1994; *Denver Post*, Nov. 3, 1994.

66. Newt Gingrich, *To Renew America* (New York: HarperCollins, 1995), p. 7.

67. Dani Rodrik, *Has Globalization Gone Too Far?* (Washington, D.C.: Institute for International Economics, 1997), p. 7.

Chapter 3
"How Free Trade Is Killing America"

1. "Amalgamated Clothing and Textile Workers Union Press Conference Transcript," *News from the AFL-CIO*, Oct. 31, 1977, pp. 1, 6.

2. Adam Smith, *An Inquiry into the Nature and Causes of the Wealth of Nations* (New York: Modern Library, 1937), p. 424.

3. Milton and Rose Friedman, "The Tyranny of Controls," *Free to Choose: A Personal Statement* (New York: Harcourt Brace Jovanovich, 1980), p. 38.

4. Edward N. Luttwak, *The Endangered American Dream: How to Stop the United States from Becoming a Third-World Country and How to Win the Geo-Economic Struggle for Industrial Supremacy* (New York: Simon & Schuster, 1993), pp. 28, 31.

5. Terry Jeffrey, "Bye, Bye, Birdie," *Human Events*, Nov. 8, 1996, p. 7.

6. William R. Hawkins, "The Anti-History of Free Trade Ideology," *America*

Asleep: The Free Trade Syndrome and the Global Economic Challenge (Washington, D.C.: United States Industrial Council Educational Foundation, 1991), p. 68.

7. Bill Gertz, "Seoul Spies Take Aim at U.S. High-Tech Secrets," *Washington Times*, Oct. 2, 1996, p. A7; Murray Weiss and Andy Geller, "New Breed of Spies Target U.S. High-tech Firms," *New York Post*, Apr. 7, 1997.

8. Percy L. Greaves, Jr., *Mises Made Easier: A Glossary for Ludwig von Mises' Human Action* (Dobbs Ferry, N.Y.: Free Market Books, 1974), p. 85.

9. "Is Corruption an Asian Value?" *Wall Street Journal*, May 6, 1996, p. A14.

10. Dani Rodrik, *Has Globalization Gone Too Far* (Washington, D.C.: Institute for International Economics, 1997), p. 47.

11. Smith, *Wealth of Nations*, p. 461.

12. John C. Fitzpatrick, ed., *The Writings of George Washington*, vol. 30 (Washington, D.C.: Government Printing Office, 1939), pp. 491–92.

13. Smith, *Wealth of Nations*, pp. 422–23.

14. Piero Sraffa, ed., *On the Principles of Political Economy and Taxation*, vol. 1, *The Works and Correspondence of David Ricardo* (Cambridge: University Press, 1951), pp. 136–37.

15. Arthur Hendrick Vandenberg, *The Greatest American: Alexander Hamilton* (New York: G. P. Putnam's Sons, 1921), p. 198.

16. Julie Salamon, "To Some Bankers with Loans to Poland, Military Crackdown Isn't All Bad News," *Wall Street Journal*, Dec. 21, 1981, p. 10.

17. H. A. Washington, ed., *The Writings of Thomas Jefferson*, vol. 6 (New York: Derby & Jackson, 1859), p. 334.

18. T. R. Fehrenbach, *Greatness to Spare* (Princeton, N.J.: Van Nostrand, 1968), p. 220.

19. George Washington Parke Custis, *Recollections and Private Memoirs of Washington* (Washington, D.C.: W. H. Moore, 1859), pp. 336–37; Henry P. Johnston, *The Yorktown Campaign and the Surrender of Cornwallis, 1781* (New York: Harper & Brothers, 1881), pp. 139–40; Nell Moore Lee, *Patriot Above Profit: A Portrait of Thomas Nelson, Jr., Who Supported the American Revolution with His Purse and Sword* (Nashville, Tenn.: Rutledge Hill Press, 1988), p. 474.

20. Lester C. Thurow, "Free Market Fallacies," *Foreign Policy* 92 (Fall 1993), p. 187; Michael Schrage, "Two Kinds of Chips, One Kind of Challenge," *Los Angeles Times*, Jan. 21, 1993, p. D1.

21. Ibid., pp. 23–24.

22. J. A. Hobson, *Richard Cobden: The International Man* (New York: Henry Holt and Co., 1919), p. 37.

23. Jacob G. Hornberger, "What President Clinton Should Have Said to the Japanese," *The Case for Open Immigration and Free Trade* (Fairfax, Va.: Future of Freedom Foundation, 1995), p. 60.

24. Cordell Hull, *The Memoirs of Cordell Hull*, vol. 1 (New York: Macmillan, 1948), p. 81.

25. Joan Kennedy Taylor, ed., *Free Trade: The Necessary Foundation for World Peace* (Irvington on Hudson, N.Y.: Foundation for Economic Education, 1986), p. 137.

26. William Jefferson Clinton, "1997 State of the Union Address," *Vital Speeches of the Day*, Mar. 1, 1997, p. 294.

27. *Speeches on Questions of Public Policy by Richard Cobden, M.P.*, ed. John Bright and James E. Thorold Rogers (London, 1880), p. 40, cited in *Western Liberalism: A History in Documents from Locke to Croce*, ed. E. K. Bramsted and K. J. Melhuish (New York: Longman, 1978), p. 254.

28. Rodrik, *Has Globalization Gone Too Far*, p. 16.

29. Ludwig von Mises, *Human Action: A Treatise on Economics*, 3d rev. ed. (Chicago: Contemporary Books, 1966), p. 164.

30. David Morris, "Free Trade: The Great Destroyer," *The Case Against the Global Economy — And for a Turn to the Local*, Jerry Mander and Edward Goldsmith, eds. (San Francisco: Sierra Club Books, 1996), p. 222.

31. Louis Uchitelle, "More Work, Less Play Make Jack Look Better Off," Week in Review, *New York Times*, Oct. 5, 1997, p. 4.

32. Robert Gilpin, *U.S. Power and the Multinational Corporation: The Political Economy of Foreign Direct Investment* (New York: Basic Books, 1975), pp. 25–29.

33. Ibid., p. 34.

34. Paul Kennedy, *The Rise and Fall of the Great Powers: Economic Change and Military Conflict from 1500 to 2000* (New York: Random House, 1987), p. xxii.

35. Alfred E. Eckes, Jr., *Opening America's Market: U.S. Foreign Trade Policy Since 1776* (Chapel Hill: University of North Carolina Press, 1995), p. 133.

36. "The International Monetary Fund: Outdated, Ineffective, and Unnecessary," *Backgrounder*, Heritage Foundation, May 6, 1996, p. 8.

37. George F. Will, "Buchanan's Nonsense," *Washington Post*, Nov. 5, 1995, p. C7.

38. Sir James Goldsmith, *The Response* (self-published, 1995), p. 96.

39. Samuel Crowther, *America Self-Contained* (Garden City, N.Y.: Doubleday, Devon & Co., 1933), p. 9.

40. Lewis D. Eigen and Jonathan P. Siegel, eds., *Macmillan Dictionary of Political Quotations* (New York: Macmillan, 1993), p. 238.

41. Ibid., pp. 240–41.

Chapter 4
"ANATOMY OF A MURDER"

1. George F. Will, "Capitalism's Sublime Chaos," *Washington Post*, Mar. 3, 1996, p. C7.
2. David Halberstam, *The Reckoning* (New York: Morrow, 1986) p. 91.
3. V. Dennis Wrynn, *Detroit Goes to War: The American Automobile Industry in World War II* (Osceola, Wisc.: Motorbooks International, 1993).
4. Gus Stelzer, *The Nightmare of Camelot: An Expose of the Free Trade Trojan Horse* (Seattle, Wash.: PB Publishing, 1994), pp. 287–88.
5. Halberstam, *The Reckoning*, pp. 30, 50.
6. Maryann Keller, *Collision: GM, Toyota, Volkswagen and the Race to Own the 21st Century* (New York: Currency, 1993), p. 106.
7. Ibid., p. 109.
8. Ibid.
9. Walter Henry Nelson, *Small Wonder: The Amazing Story of the Volkswagen* (Boston: Little, Brown and Co., 1965), p. 52.
10. Ibid., p. 60.
11. Keller, *Collision*, p. 110.
12. Alan Cowell, "Volkswagen's History: The Darker Side Is Revisited," *New York Times*, Nov. 7, 1996, p. A14.
13. Halberstam, *The Reckoning*, p. 462.
14. Ibid.
15. Stelzer, *Nightmare of Camelot*, p. 290.
16. U.S. Department of Commerce, *The U.S. Industrial Outlook for 1964, Industry by Industry* (Washington, D.C.: Government Printing Office, 1964), p. ER-39.
17. Keller, *Collision*, p. 105.
18. Michael A. Cusamano, *The Japanese Auto Industry: And Management and Toyota*, published by the Council on East Asian Studies, Harvard University (Cambridge: Harvard University Press, 1985), p. 4.
19. Stelzer, *Nightmare of Camelot*, p. 290
20. Lawrence Martin, *The Presidents and the Prime Ministers, Washington and Ottawa Face to Face: The Myth of Bilateral Bliss, 1867–1982* (Garden City, N.Y.: Doubleday, 1982), p. 219.
21. Alfred E. Eckes, Jr., *Opening America's Market: U.S. Foreign Trade Policy Since 1776* (Chapel Hill: University of North Carolina Press, 1995), p. 193.
22. Mark Heinzl, "Made in Canada: Car Makers Head North: GM Strike Highlights Country's Growing Role in Sector," *Wall Street Journal*, Oct. 14, 1996, p. A2.
23. Ibid., p. A5.

24. Stelzer, *Nightmare of Camelot*, pp. 292-93.

25. Keith Bradsher, "GM to Regain American Market Share, Executives Say," *New York Times*, Jan. 9, 1997, p. D4.

26. Rebecca Blumenstein, "GM Is Building Plants in Developing Nations to Woo New Markets," *Wall Street Journal*, Aug. 4, 1997, p. 1.

27. Bradsher, "GM to Regain American Market Share," p. D4.

28. "Trade Route," *Business Week*, Dec. 9, 1996, p. 55.

29. Stelzer, *Nightmare of Camelot*, p. 295.

30. George Bush, *Public Papers of the Presidents of the United States: George Bush*, Book 1 (Washington, D.C.: Government Printing Office, 1993), p. 53.

31. Halberstam, *The Reckoning*, p. 684.

32. American Automobile Manufacturers Association, "Economic Indicators: The Motor Vehicle's Role in the U.S. Economy," Third Quarter 1996, p. 8.

33. "Car Crash Ahead," *Economist*, May 10, 1997, p. 13.

34. Ibid.

35. Ernest F. Hollings, "Protectionist and Proud of It," *Washington Post*, Mar. 17, 1996, p. C4.

Chapter 5

"MASTERS OF THE UNIVERSE"

1. As quoted in Peter Brimelow, *Alien Nation: Common Sense About America's Immigration Disaster* (New York: Harper Perennial, 1996), p. 293.

2. Robert B. Reich, "Who Is Them?" *Harvard Business Review*, Mar.–Apr., 1991, p. 78.

3. Henry Ford in collaboration with Samuel Crowther, *My Life and Work* (Garden City, N.Y.: Garden City Publishing, 1922), p. 123.

4. Sources for this section on the Milliken plant in La Grange include recollections from two visits to the plant; David Greising, "A Company That Knows How to Put Out a Fire," *Business Week*, Feb. 27, 1995, p. 50; Howard B. Stussman, "A Bias for Action," *Engineering News-Record*, Sept. 18, 1995, p. 28.

5. Greising, "A Company That Knows," p. 50.

6. Stussman, "A Bias for Action," p. 28.

7. E. Michael Myers, "Textile Workers Embrace Hopeful; Buchanan Rails at 'Country Club,' " *Washington Times*, Mar. 5, 1996, p. A6.

8. Michael Ryan, "They Call Their Boss a Hero," *Parade*, Sept. 8, 1996, p. 4.

9. Ibid.

10. Ibid., p. 5.

11. Ibid.

12. David Morris, "Free Trade: The Great Destroyer," *The Case Against the Global*

Economy — And for a Turn to the Local, Jerry Mander and Edward Goldsmith, eds. (San Francisco: Sierra Club Books, 1996), p. 221.

13. Reich, "Who Is Them?" p. 78.
14. Erle Norton, "Global Makeover: Ten years ago, Alcoa was a thoroughly American company. No longer," *Wall Street Journal,* Sept. 26, 1996, p. R14.
15. Reich, "Who Is Them?" p. 77.
16. John B. Judis, "America the Divided," *Washington Post Book World,* Jan. 15, 1995, p. 11.
17. Anthony Harrigan, "The Corporate Citizen, National vs. Transnational Economic Strategies," *Chronicles,* Jan. 1990, p. 25.
18. Christopher Lasch, *The Revolt of the Elites and the Betrayal of Democracy* (New York: W. W. Norton, 1995), pp. 34–35, 46.
19. William Greider, "The Ex-Im Files: How the Taxpayer-funded Export-Import Bank Helps Shift Jobs Overseas," *Rolling Stone,* Aug. 8, 1996, p. 70.
20. Harrigan, "The Corporate Citizen," p. 25.
21. Greider, "The Ex-Im Files," pp. 54, 70.
22. Ibid., p. 70.
23. Michael Skapinker, "Boeing Keen for New Joint Ventures with BAe," *Financial Times,* Mar. 12, 1997, p. 18.
24. Michael Skapinker, "Flight Plan From Seattle," *Financial Times,* Mar. 12, 1997, p. 13.
25. Ibid.
26. Ibid.
27. "The Appease China Sweepstakes (Cont.)," *Weekly Standard,* Sept. 8, 1997, p. 4.
28. "Investment Pact," *Financial Times,* Oct. 17, 1996, p. 13.
29. "U.S. Goods Trade: Imports & Exports by Related Parties, 1995," U.S. Department of Commerce, Sept. 10, 1996.
30. Helen V. Milner, *Resisting Protectionism: Global Industries and the Politics of International Trade* (Princeton, N.J.: Princeton University Press, 1988), p. 249.
31. Ibid., p. 253.
32. Donald Bruce Johnson and Kirk H. Porter, compilers, *National Party Platforms 1840–1972* (Urbana: University of Illinois Press, 1973), p. 859.
33. Jeff Gerten, "Business and Foreign Policy," *Foreign Affairs,* May/June 1997, pp. 70–71.
34. A. W. Clausen, "The International Corporation: An Executive View," *The Annals of the American Academy of Political and Social Science,* Sept. 1972, p. 21.
35. Richard J. Barnet and Ronald E. Müller, *Global Reach: The Power of the Multinational Corporations* (New York: Simon & Schuster, 1974), pp. 18–19.
36. Ibid., p. 16.
37. Ibid.

38. Zbigniew Brzezinski, *Between Two Ages: America's Role in the Technetronic Age* (New York: Viking, 1970), p. 58.

39. Ibid., p. 59.

40. Ibid.

41. Barnet and Müller, *Global Reach*, p. 14.

42. Ibid., p. 55.

43. Wesley T. Wooley, *Alternatives to Anarchy: American Supranationalism Since World War II* (Bloomington: Indiana University Press, 1988), p. 169.

44. Ibid, p. 168.

45. Strobe Talbott, "The Birth of the Global Nation," *Time*, July 20, 1992, p. 70.

46. Ibid., p. 71.

47. Richard N. Gardner, "The Hard Road to World Order" *Foreign Affairs*, Apr. 1974, p. 558.

48. Walter Wriston, *The Twilight of Sovereignty* (New York: Scribner's, 1992), p. 4.

49. William R. Hawkins, "The Surrender of Political and Military Sovereignty," *Chronicles*, Oct. 1995, p. 19.

50. E. Christian Kopff, "The Future Belongs to Us," *Chronicles*, Oct. 1995, p. 34.

51. Richard Cobden, "England, Ireland, and America," *Free Trade and Other Fundamental Doctrines of the Manchester School*, ed. Francis W. Hurst (New York: Augustus M. Kelly, 1958), p. 22.

Book Two
WHERE AND HOW WE LOST THE WAY

Chapter 6
"WHAT OUR FATHERS BELIEVED"

1. *Japan Economic Journal*, 1981, cited by Pat Choate, *Agents of Influence* (New York: Knopf, 1990), p. vii.

Chapter 7
"THE RISE OF AMERICAN NATIONALISM"

1. John A. Logan, *The Great Conspiracy: Its Origin and History* (New York: A. R. Hart & Co., 1886), pp. 13–14.

2. James Thomas Flexner, *George Washington: The Forge of Experience (1732–1775)* (Boston: Little, Brown and Co., 1965), p. 277.

3. Ibid, p. 278.
4. Ibid.
5. Ibid., p. 282.
6. Ibid.
7. Ibid., pp. 287–88.
8. John C. Miller, *Origins of the American Revolution* (Boston: Little, Brown and Co., 1943), p. 15.
9. Ibid., p. 273.
10. Ibid., p. 274.
11. Ibid., p. 8.
12. William J. Gill, *Trade Wars Against America: A History of United States Trade and Monetary Policy* (New York: Praeger, 1990), p. 13.
13. Clarence Walworth Alvord, *The Mississippi Valley in British Politics: A Study of the Trade, Land Speculation, and Experiments in Imperialism Culminating in the American Revolution* (New York: Russell & Russell, 1959), pp. 50–51.
14. Thomas A. Bailey, *A Diplomatic History of the American People*, 7th ed. (New York: Meredith Publishing Co., 1964), p. 26.
15. Oscar Theodore Barck, Jr., and Hugh Talmage Lefler, *Colonial America*, 2d ed. (New York: Macmillan, 1968), pp. 490–91.
16. Richard M. Ketchum, ed., *The American Heritage Book of the Revolution* (New York: American Heritage Publishing, 1971), p. 56.
17. Barck and Lefler, *Colonial America*, p. 493.
18. Michael Kraus, *The United States to 1865* (Ann Arbor: University of Michigan Press, 1959), p. 190.
19. Peter D. G. Thomas, *The Townshend Duties Crisis: The Second Phase of the American Revolution 1767–1773* (Oxford: Clarendon Press, 1987), p. 3.
20. Alvord, *Mississippi Valley in British Politics*, p. 51.
21. William MacDonald, ed., *Documentary Source Book of American History 1606–1926*, 3d ed. (New York: Macmillan, 1926), p. 140.
22. Sir Lewis Namier and John Brooke, *Charles Townshend*, (New York: St. Martin's Press, 1964), p. 90.
23. Samuel Eliot Morison and Henry Steele Commager, *Growth of the American Republic*, 5th ed., vol. 1 (New York: Oxford University Press, 1962), p. 165.
24. Robert H. Ferrell, *American Diplomacy: A History* (New York: W. W. Norton, 1959), p. 6.
25. Peter Cunningham, ed., *The Letters of Horace Walpole, Fourth Earl of Oxford*, vol. 5 (Edinburgh: John Grant, 1906), p. 64.
26. Barck and Lefler, *Colonial America*, p. 520.
27. Morison and Commager, *Growth of the American Republic*, p. 167.
28. Kraus, *United States to 1865*, p. 202.
29. Morison and Commager, *Growth of the American Republic*, p. 176.

30. Ketchum, *Revolution*, p. 71.

31. James Thomas Flexner, *George Washington and the New Nation (1783–1793)* (Boston: Little, Brown and Co., 1970), p. 69.

32. Flexner, *New Nation*, p. 73.

33. John Z. Fitzpatrick, ed., *The Writings of George Washington from the Original Manuscript Sources 1745–1799*, vol. 27 (Washington, D.C.: Government Printing Office, 1938) p. 475.

34. Flexner, *New Nation*, p. 73.

35. Ibid., p. 81.

36. Morison and Commager, *Growth of the American Republic*, p. 266.

37. Ibid., pp. 274–75.

38. William B. Willcox, ed., *The Papers of Benjamin Franklin*, vol. 21 (New Haven, Conn.: Yale University Press, 1978), p. 175.

39. Merrill D. Peterson, *Thomas Jefferson and the New Nation: A Biography* (New York: Oxford University Press, 1970), p. 290.

40. William Hawkins, "The Anti-History of Free Trade Ideology," *America Asleep: The Free Trade Syndrome and the Global Economic Challenge* (Washington, D.C.: U.S. Industrial Council Education Foundation, 1991), p. 62.

41. Dumas Malone, *Jefferson the Virginian: Jefferson and His Time* (Boston, Little, Brown and Co., 1948), p. 384.

42. *The Constitution of the United States with Index and the Declaration of Independence* (Washington, D.C.: Commission on the Bicentennial of the United States Constitution, 1991), p. 8.

43. *Documentary History of the Constitution of the United States of America*, vol. 2 (Washington, D.C.: Department of State, 1894), p. 1.

44. James Thomas Flexner, *Washington, the Indispensable Man* (Boston: Little, Brown and Co., 1974), p. 387.

45. Ibid., pp. 385–86.

46. Charles F. Hobson and Robert A. Rutland, eds., *The Papers of James Madison*, vol. 12 (Charlottesville: University Press of Virginia, 1979), pp. 64–65.

47. John M. Dobson, *Two Centuries of Tariffs: The Background and Emergence of the U.S. Trade Commission* (Washington, D.C.: Government Printing Office, 1976), pp. 6–7.

48. W. W. Abbot and Dorothy Twohig, eds., *The Papers of George Washington*, Presidential Series, vol. 4 (Charlottesville: University Press of Virginia, 1993), p. 544.

49. John Steele Gordon, *Hamilton's Blessing: The Extraordinary Life and Times of Our National Debt* (New York: Walker and Co., 1997), pp. 18–19.

50. Morton J. Frisch, ed., *Selected Writings and Speeches of Alexander Hamilton* (Washington, D.C.: American Enterprise Institute for Public Policy Research, 1985), pp. 313–14.

51. Arthur Hendrick Vandenberg, *The Greatest American* (New York: G. P. Putnam's Sons, 1921), p. 200.

52. Douglas Southall Freeman, *Patriot and President*, vol. 6 of *George Washington: A Biography* (New York: Charles Scribner's Sons, 1954), p. 195; Stephen Decatur, Jr., *Private Affairs of George Washington* (Boston: Houghton Mifflin, 1933), p. 7.

53. Freeman, *Patriot and President*, p. 188.

54. Decatur, *Private Affairs of George Washington*, pp. 10-11.

55. Ibid., pp. 8–9. (The Wadsworth letter may be the first time the phrase "infant Manufactures" was used.)

56. Ibid., p. 9.

57. Ibid.

Chapter 8

"JEFFERSON TO JACKSON"

1. Julian P. Boyd, ed., *The Papers of Thomas Jefferson*, vol. 8 (Princeton, N.J.: Princeton University Press, 1953), p. 427.

2. Edwin P. Whipple, ed., *The Great Speeches and Orations of Daniel Webster* (Boston: Little, Brown and Co., 1879), p. 428.

3. Thomas A. Bailey, *A Diplomatic History of the American People*, 7th ed. (New York: Meredith Publishing Co., 1964), p. 108.

4. Samuel Eliot Morison and Henry Steele Commager, *The Growth of the American Republic*, vol. 1 (New York: Oxford University Press, 1962), pp. 377–78.

5. Alexander De Conde, *A History of American Foreign Policy* (New York: Charles Scribner's Sons, 1963), p. 86.

6. *Dictionary of American History*, rev. ed. vol. 2 (New York: Charles Scribner's Sons), p. 16.

7. H. A. Washington, ed., *The Writings of Thomas Jefferson: Being His Autobiography, Correspondence, Reports, Messages, Addresses, and Other Writings, Official and Private*, vol. 5 (New York: Derby & Jackson, 1859), p. 127; De Conde, *American Foreign Policy*, p. 92; Bailey, *Diplomatic History*, p. 124.

8. Paul Leicester Ford, ed., *The Works of Thomas Jefferson*, vol. 9 (New York: G. P. Putnam's Sons, 1905), p. 220.

9. John Steele Gordon, *Hamilton's Blessing: The Extraordinary Life and Times of Our National Debt* (New York, Walker and Co., 1997), pp. 44–45.

10. Ibid. p. 45.

11. *Papers of Thomas Jefferson*, vol. 8, p. 332

12. Robert J. Taylor, ed., *Papers of John Adams*, vol. 5 (Cambridge: Harvard University Press, 1983), p. 145.

13. *Writings of Thomas Jefferson*, vol. 6, p. 431.

14. *Works of Thomas Jefferson*, vol. 11, pp. 502, 504–05.

15. Ibid., p. 505.

16. J. B. Condliffe, *The Commerce of Nations* (New York: W. W. Norton, 1950), p. 247.

17. Ravi Batra, *The Great American Deception: What Politicians Won't Tell You About Our Economy and Your Future* (New York: John Wiley & Sons, 1996), pp. 117–19.

18. Emory R. Johnson et. al., *History of Domestic and Foreign Commerce of the United States*, vol. 2 (Washington, D.C.: Carnegie Institute of Washington, 1915), p. 35; Jacob Viner, *Dumping: A Problem in International Trade* (New York: Augustus M. Kelley, 1966), p. 42.

19. William J. Gill, *Trade Wars Against America: A History of United States Trade and Monetary Policy* (New York: Praeger, 1991), p. 20.

20. Ibid.

21. Charles Francis Adams, *The Works of John Adams, Second President of the United States: With a Life of the Author, Notes and Illustrations*, vol. X (New York: AMS Press, 1971), p. 384.

22. John A. Logan, *The Great Conspiracy: Its Origin and History* (New York: Books for Libraries Press, 1971), p. 16; Gill, *Trade Wars Against America*, p. 21.

23. Batra, *Great American Deception*, p. 119.

24. Morison and Commager, *Growth of the American Republic*, vol. 1, p. 439.

25. John Spencer Bassett, ed., *Correspondence of Andrew Jackson*, vol. 3 (Washington, D.C.: Carnegie Institute of Washington, 1928), pp. 249–50.

26. James F. Hopkins, ed., *The Papers of Henry Clay*, vol. 3 (Lexington: University of Kentucky Press, 1963), p.

27. Burton J. Hendrick, *Bulwark of the Republic: A Biography of the Constitution* (Boston: Little, Brown and Co., 1937), p. 221.

28. Ibid., pp. 217, 219.

29. James A. Hamilton, *Reminiscences of James A. Hamilton; Of Men and Events, At Home and Abroad, During Three Quarters of a Century* (New York: Charles Scribner & Co., 1869), p. 62.

30. Hendrick, *Bulwark of the Republic*, p. 220.

31. *Papers of John Adams*, vol. 5, p. 79.

32. Ibid.

33. Morison and Commager, *Growth of the American Republic*, vol. 1, p. 475.

34. Henrick, *Bulwark of the Republic*, p. 222.

35. Robert A. Rutland, *James Madison and the Search for Nationhood* (Washington, D.C.: Library of Congress, 1981), p. 71.

36. Morison and Commager, *Growth of the American Republic*, vol. 1, p. 477.

37. Hendrick, *Bulwark of the Republic*, p. 138.

38. *Correspondence of Andrew Jackson*, vol. 3, p. 250.
39. Morison and Commager, *Growth of the American Republic*, vol. 1, pp. 480–81.
40. Marquis James, *Andrew Jackson: Portrait of a President* (Indianapolis: Bobbs-Merrill, 1940), p. 235
41. Morison and Commager, *Growth of the American Republic*, vol. 1, pp. 480–81.
42. Hendrick, *Bulwark of the Republic*, p. 251.
43. Morison and Commager, *Growth of the American Republic*, vol. 1, p. 481.
44. Ibid, p. 482; Logan, *The Great Conspiracy*, p. 25.
45. Marquis James, *The Life of Andrew Jackson* (Indianapolis: Bobbs-Merrill, 1939), pp. 611–12.
46. Ibid. p. 612.
47. Michael Kraus, *The United States to 1865* (Ann Arbor: University of Michigan Press, 1959), p. 360.
48. Gill, *Trade Wars Against America*, p. 26.
49. *Correspondence of Andrew Jackson*, vol. 4 (1929), p. 506.
50. Augustus C. Buell, *History of Andrew Jackson: Pioneer, Patriot, Soldier, Politician, President*, vol. 2 (New York: Charles Scribner's Sons, 1904), p. 245.
51. Ibid., p. 246.
52. James, *The Life of Andrew Jackson*, p. 153.
53. Calvin Colton, ed., *The Works of Henry Clay: Comprising His Life, Correspondence and Speeches*, vol. 7 (New York: G. P. Putnam's Sons, 1904), p. 543.
54. James, *The Life of Andrew Jackson*, p. 621.
55. Ibid.
56. Ibid., p. 617.
57. Ibid.
58. Logan, *The Great Conspiracy*, p. 30

Chapter 9

THE GREAT PROTECTIONIST

1. Alfred E. Eckes, Jr., *Opening America's Market: U.S. Foreign Trade Policy Since 1776* (Chapel Hill: University of North Carolina Press, 1995), p. 28.
2. W. Hayden Boyers and George B. deHuszar, trans. and ed., *Economic Harmonies by Frédéric Bastiat* (Princeton, N.J.: Van Nostrand Co., 1964), p. 463.
3. Gabor S. Boritt, *Lincoln and the Economics of the American Dream* (Chicago: University of Illinois Press, 1994), p. 94.
4. Ibid., p. 101.
5. Ibid., p. 130.
6. Ibid., p. 107.
7. Eckes, *Opening America's Market*, p. 25.

8. William H. Herndon and Jesse W. Weik, *Life of Lincoln* (Cleveland: Word Publishing Co., 1949), p. 86.

9. Roy P. Basler, *The Collected Works of Abraham Lincoln*, vol. 3 (New Brunswick, N.J.: Rutgers University Press, 1953), p. 29.

10. Gabor S. Boritt, "Old Wine Into New Bottles: Abraham Lincoln and the Tariff Reconsidered," *The Historian* 28 (1966), p. 299.

11. Ibid., p. 300.

12. Ibid., p. 294.

13. Ibid., p. 617.

14. *Illinois Gazette*, July 25, 1846, cited in Roy P. Basler, ed., *The Collected Works of Abraham Lincoln*, vol. 1 (New Brunswick, N.J.: Rutgers University Press, 1953), p. 382.

15. Ibid.

16. Boritt, "Old Wine Into New Bottles," p. 298.

17. Ibid, p. 299.

18. *Collected Works of Abraham Lincoln*, vol. 1, p. 313.

19. *Collected Works of Abraham Lincoln*, vol. 2, p. 158.

20. Boritt, *Lincoln and the Economics of the American Dream*, p. 118.

21. Reinhard H. Luthin, "Abraham Lincoln and the Tariff," *American Historical Review* 49, no. 4 (July 1944), p. 615.

22. Ibid., p. 613.

23. *Collected Works of Abraham Lincoln*, vol. 3, pp. 486–87.

24. Shelby Foote, *The Civil War: A Narrative*, vol. 1 (New York: Random House, 1958), p. 20.

25. *Collected Works of Abraham Lincoln*, vol. 3, p. 487.

26. Luthin, "Lincoln and the Tariff," p. 614.

27. Ibid., p. 612.

28. *Collected Works of Abraham Lincoln*, vol. 4, p. 49.

29. Luthin, "Lincoln and the Tariff," p. 615.

30. Boritt, "Old Wine Into New Bottles," p. 309.

31. Luthin, "Lincoln and the Tariff," p. 617.

32. Ibid., p. 618.

33. Ibid., p. 614.

34. *Collected Works of Abraham Lincoln*, vol. 4, p. 125.

35. Boritt, "Old Wine Into New Bottles," p. 310.

36. Luthin, "Lincoln and the Tariff," p. 621.

37. Ibid., pp. 621–26.

38. Ibid., pp. 623–24.

39. Boritt, "Old Wine Into New Bottles," p. 311n.

40. *Collected Works of Abraham Lincoln*, vol. 4, p. 214.

41. Ibid., p. 213.

42. Boritt, "Old Wine Into New Bottles," p. 313.

43. Luthin, "Lincoln and the Tariff," p. 626.

44. Samuel Crowther, *America Self-Contained* (Garden City, N.Y.: Doubleday, Doran & Co., 1933), p. 39.

45. Luthin, "Lincoln and the Tariff," pp. 628–29.

46. Boritt, "Old Wine Into New Bottles," p. 315.

47. Luthin, "Lincoln and the Tariff," p. 629.

48. Charles Adams, *For Good and Evil: The Impact of Taxes on the Course of Civilization* (Lanham, Md.: Madison Books, 1993), p. 330.

49. Marshall L. DeRosa, *The Confederate Constitution of 1861: An Inquiry into American Constitutionalism* (Columbia: University of Missouri Press), p. 139.

50. Kenneth M. Stamp, ed., *The Causes of the Civil War*, rev. ed. (Englewood Cliffs, N.J.: Prentice-Hall, 1974), pp. 69–70.

51. Adams, *For Good and Evil*, p. 332.

52. Ibid., p. 334.

53. Ibid., p. 332.

54. Ibid.

55. John Steele Gordon, *Hamilton's Blessing: The Extraordinary Life and Times of Our National Debt* (New York: Walker and Co., 1997), p. 56.

56. Murray N. Rothbard, "Our Two Just Wars," *Southern Partisan*, third quarter 1995, p. 23.

Chapter 10

"Free Markets vs. Free Trade"

1. Nassau William Senior, *Three Lectures on the Transmission of the Precious Metals from Country to Country and the Mercantile Theory of Wealth* (London: John Murray, 1828), p. 88.

2. Philip Schaff, ed., *Saint Augustine: Exposition on the Book of Psalms*, vol. 7 of *A Select Library of the Nicene and Post-Nicene Fathers of the Christian Church* (New York: Brown Brothers, 1888), p. 320.

3. Saint Thomas Aquinas, trans. Gerald B. Phelan, *On the Governance of Rulers (De Regimine Principum)*, rev. ed. (London: Sheed & Ward, 1938), pp. 118–19.

4. J. D. Condliffe, *The Commerce of Nations* (New York: W. W. Norton & Co., 1950), p. 99; Norman McCord, *Free Trade: Theory and Prac-tice from Adam Smith to Keynes* (New York: Barnes & Noble, 1970), p. 30.

5. Jay I. Olnek, *The Invisible Hand: How Free Trade Is Choking the Life Out of America* (Greenwich, Conn.: North Stonington Press, 1982), pp. 72–73.

6. Adam Smith, *An Inquiry into the Nature and Causes of the Wealth of Nations* (New York: Modern Library, 1937), p. 429.

7. Ibid., pp. 429–30.

8. Ibid., pp. 431–32.

9. Ibid., pp. 433–35.

10. Ibid., pp. 435–36.

11. Ian Simpson Ross, *The Life of Adam Smith* (Oxford: Clarendon Press, 1995), pp. 327–28, 320.

12. William R. Hawkins, "The Anti-History of Free-Trade Ideology," *America Asleep: The Free Trade Syndrome and the Global Economic Challenge* (Washington, D.C.: U.S. Industrial Council Education Foundation, 1991), p. 46.

13. Ibid.

14. Ibid.

15. Immanuel Kant, *Perpetual Peace: A Philosophical Essay*, trans. M. Campbell Smith (Bristol, England: Thoemmes Press, 1992), p. 136.

16. John C. Fitzpatrick, ed., *The Writings of George Washington from the Original Manuscript Source 1745–1799*, vol. 36 (Washington, D.C.: Government Printing Office, 1941), pp. 460–61.

17. Arthur Harrison Cole, *Industrial and Commercial Correspondence of Alexander Hamilton, Anticipating His Report on Manufactures* (New York: Augustus M. Kelley, 1968), p. 233.

18. Smith, *Wealth of Nations*, p. 349.

19. Morton J. Frisch, ed., *Selected Writings and Speeches of Alexander Hamilton* (Washington, D.C.: American Enterprise Institute, 1985), p. 314.

20. *Commercial Correspondence of Alexander Hamilton*, pp. 231–32.

21. Condliffe, *Commerce of Nations*, p. 246.

22. *Writings of Alexander Hamilton*, pp. 459–60.

23. Ibid.

24. Arthur Hendrick Vandenberg, *The Greatest American* (New York: G. P. Putnam's Sons, 1921), p. 347.

25. Condliffe, *Commerce of Nations*, p. 240.

26. James Mill, *Elements of Political Economy*, 3d ed., rev. and corrected (New York: Augustus M. Kelley, 1965), p. 123.

27. David Ricardo, *The Principles of Political Economy and Taxation* (London: J. M. Dent & Sons, 1960) p. 81.

28. John Stuart Mill, *The Subjection of Women* (Cambridge: M.I.T. Press, 1970), pp. 22, 28–29, 36–37, 48; cited by Allan Carlson, *The Family in America*, vol. 11, no. 13 (Rockford, Ill.: Howard Center for Family, Religion & Society, 1997), p. 2.

29. John Stuart Mill, *The Philosophy of John Stuart Mill: Ethical, Political and Religious* (New York: Modern Library), pp. ix, xii, xx, xxxv–xxxvi.

30. Douglas A. Irwin, *Against the Tide: An Intellectual History of Free Trade* (Princeton, N.J.: Princeton University Press, 1996), p. 128.

31. John Stuart Mill, *Principles of Political Economy with Some of Their Applications to Social Philosophy* (Fairfield, N.J.: Augustus M. Kelley, 1976), p. 581.

32. Richard Ebeling, "Free Trade, Managed Trade, and the State," *The Case for Free Trade and Open Immigration* (Fairfax, Va.: Future of Freedom Foundation, 1995), p.11.

33. Genesis II: 1–9, Authorized King James Version.

34. Irwin, *Against the Tide*, pp. 128–29.

35. Richard Cobden, as quoted in Alfred E. Eckes, Jr., *Opening America's Market: U.S. Foreign Trade Policy Since 1776* (Chapel Hill: University of North Carolina Press, 1995), p. 1.

36. John Bright and James E. Thorold Rogers, eds., *Speeches on Questions of Public Policy by Richard Cobden, M. P., in Two Volumes*, vol. 1 (London: MacMillan and Co., 1870), pp. 362–63.

37. Eckes, *Opening America's Market*, p. 24.

38. Bright and Rogers, *Speeches by Richard Cobden*, p. 363.

39. Arthur Goddard, trans. and ed., *Economic Sophisms, by Frédéric Bastiat* (Princeton, N.J.: Van Nostrand Co., 1964), p. 271.

40. Hawkins, "Anti-History of Free-Trade Ideology," p. 57.

41. Ibid.

42. Ibid.

43. Ibid.

44. Ibid., p. 45.

45. Ibid., pp. 55, 43.

46. Ibid.

47. *The Constitution of the United States and the Declaration of Independence*, 15th ed. (Washington, D.C.: Commission on the Bicentennial of the United States Constitution), p. 35.

48. Rt. Hon. Thomas Babington Macaulay, M.P., *Speeches in Two Volumes*, vol. 2 (New York: Redfield, 1853), p. 71.

49. Michael Lind, "The Op-Ed History of America," *National Interest*, fall 1994, p. 19.

50. W. Stanley Jevons, *The Coal Question: An Inquiry Concerning the Progress of the Nation, and the Probable Exhaustion of our Coal-Mines*, 3d ed. rev. (New York: Augustus M. Kelley, 1965), p. 411.

51. Samuel Crowther, *America Self-Contained* (Garden City, N.Y.: Doubleday, Doran & Co., 1933), pp. 30–31.

52. Condliffe, *Commerce of Nations*, p. 276.

53. Friedrich List, *The National System of Political Economy 1885* (New York: Augustus M. Kelley, 1966), p. 147.

54. Richard Ebeling, "The Ghost of Protectionism Past," *The Case for Free Trade and Open Immigration*, op. cit., p. 73.

55. List, *Political Economy 1885*, pp. 174–75.

56. Ibid., p. 144.

57. Hawkins, "Anti-History of Free-Trade Ideology," p. 54; List, *Political Economy 1885*, p. 133.

58. List, *Political Economy 1885*, p. 144

59. Karl Marx and Frederick Engels, *Collected Works*, vol. 6 (New York: International Publishers, 1976), p. 465.

60. Richard Cobden, "England, Ireland, and America," *Free Trade and Other Fundamental Doctrines of the Manchester School*, ed. Francis W. Hurst (New York: Augustus M. Kelly, 1958), p. 20.

61. Ebeling, "Free Trade, Managed Trade, and the State," p. 24.

62. William L. Law, "A Capitalist Looks at Free Trade," *The Case for Free Trade and Open Immigration*, op. cit., p. 39.

63. Milton and Rose Friedman, *Free to Choose: A Personal Statement* (New York: Harcourt Brace Jovanovich, 1980), p. 45.

64. James F. Hopkins, ed., *The Papers of Henry Clay* (Lexington: University of Kentucky Press, 1961), vol. 2, pp. 826–47; cited by Alfred E. Eckes, "Reviving the Grand Old Paradigm," *America Asleep: The Free Trade Syndrome and the Global Economic Challenge* (Washington, D.C.: U.S. Industrial Council Education Foundation, 1991), p. 77.

65. Ebeling, "Free Trade, Managed Trade, and the State," p. 9.

66. Ludwig von Mises, *Omnipotent Government: The Rise of the Total State and Total War* (New York: Yale University Press, 1944), pp. 91–92.

67. Bertrand Russell, *A History of Western Philosophy and Its Connections with Political and Social Circumstances from the Earliest Times to the Present Day* (New York: Simon & Schuster, 1945), p. 251.

68. Lind, "The Op-Ed History of America," p. 23.

69. Elizabeth John, ed., *The Collected Writings of John Maynard Keynes*, vol. 17 (London: MacMillan, 1977), p. 451.

70. Donald Moggridge, ed., *The Collected Writings of John Maynard Keynes*, vol. 19 (London: MacMillan, 1981), pp. 151–52, 156.

71. *The Collected Writings of John Maynard Keynes*, vol. 9 (London: MacMillan, 1972), p. 237.

72. Ibid.

73. Donald Moggridge, ed., *The Collected Writings of John Maynard Keynes*, vol. 20 (London: MacMillan, 1980), p. 508.

74. Ibid., p. 379.

75. Donald Moggridge, ed., *The Collected Writings of John Maynard Keynes*, vol. 21 (London: MacMillan, 1982), pp. 233–34.

76. Olnek, *The Invisible Hand*, p. 55.
77. Herman St. John-Stevas, ed., *The Collected Works of Walter Bagehot*, vol. 11 (London: The Economist, 1978), p. 224.
78. Irwin, *Against the Tide*, p. 227.
79. Friedman, *Free to Choose*, p. 39.

Chapter 11
"THE TIME OF THE PROTECTIONISTS"

1. Alfred E. Eckes, Jr., *Opening America's Market: U.S. Foreign Trade Policy Since 1776* (Chapel Hill: University of North Carolina Press, 1995), p. 30.
2. *The Congressional Globe: Containing Speeches, Important State Papers, Laws, Etc., of the Third Session, Thirty-Fourth Congress*, Appendix (Washington, D.C.: John C. Rives, 1857), p. 226.
3. *The Congressional Globe: Containing Speeches, Important State Papers, Laws, Etc., of the First Session of the Thirty-Sixth Congress*, Apr. 25, 1860, issue (Washington, D.C.: John C. Rives, 1860), p. 1832.
4. Charles W. Calhoun, "Political Economy in the Gilded Age: The Republican Party's Industrial Policy," *Journal of Political History* 8, no. 3 (1996), p. 293.
5. Edmund Morris, *The Rise of Theodore Roosevelt* (New York: Coward, McCann & Geoghegan, 1979), p. 386.
6. Calhoun, "Political Economy in the Gilded Age," p. 295.
7. Margaret Leech, *In the Days of McKinley* (New York: Harper & Brothers, 1959), p. 40.
8. Calhoun, "Political Economy in the Gilded Age," p. 295.
9. Ibid.
10. Thomas A. Bailey, *A Diplomatic History of the American People*, 7th ed. (New York: Meredith Publishing Co., 1964), p. 405.
11. Leech, *In the Days of McKinley*, p. 36–37.
12. Ibid., p. 7.
13. Bailey, *Diplomatic History*, p. 460.
14. Eckes, *Opening America's Market*, p. 31.
15. Ibid.
16. Ralph K. Andrist, ed., *The American Heritage History of the Confident Years* (New York: American Heritage Publishing Co., 1969), p. 252.
17. Ibid., pp. 252–53.
18. Ibid., p. 253.
19. Leech, *In the Days of McKinley*, p. 48.
20. Eckes, *Opening America's Market*, p. 33.

21. Alfred E. Eckes, Jr., "Cobden's Pyhrric Victory," *Chronicles*, Oct. 15, 1995, p. 16.
22. John Steele Gordon, *Hamilton's Blessing: The Extraordinary Life and Times of Our National Debt* (New York: Walker and Co., 1997), p. 86.
23. Ibid., pp. 76, 82.
24. Andrist, *The Confident Years*, p. 251.
25. Leech, *In the Days of McKinley*, p. 62.
26. Foster Rhea Dulles, *The United States Since 1865* (Ann Arbor: University of Michigan Press, 1959), p. 152.
27. David Ward Wood, *History of the Republican Party and Biographies of Its Supporters* (Chicago: Lincoln Engraving and Publishing Company, 1895), p. 6.
28. Ibid., p. 10
29. Ibid.
30. Calhoun, "Political Economy in the Gilded Age," pp. 303–04.
31. Leech, *In the Days of McKinley*, p. 89.
32. Genevieve Forbes Herrick and John Origen Herrick, *The Life of William Jennings Bryan* (Chicago: Buxton Publishing House, 1925), pp. 123–24.
33. Leech, *In the Days of McKinley*, p. 92.
34. Dulles, *United States Since 1865*, p. 153.
35. Eckes, *Opening America's Market*, p. 34.
36. Ibid.
37. Ibid.
38. Ibid.
39. W. Ross Yates, *Joseph Wharton: Quaker Industrial Pioneer* (Bethlehem, Pa.: Lehigh University Press, 1987), p. 182.
40. Ibid.
41. Ibid., p. 191.
42. Michael Lind, "The Op-Ed History of America," *National Interest*, fall 1994, pp. 20–21.
43. Dulles, *United States Since 1865*, p. 56.
44. Ibid., p. 64.
45. Ravi Batra, *The Myth of Free Trade: A Plan for America's Economic Revival* (New York: Charles Scribner's Sons, 1993), p. 136. (As source, Batra used the *Historical Statistics of the United States, 1975*.)
46. Gordon, *Hamilton's Blessing*, p. 90.
47. Eckes, *Opening America's Market*, p. 55.
48. "Average Annual and Daily Earnings of Nonfarm Employees: 1860 to 1900," U.S. Census Bureau, *Historical Statistics of the United States Bicentennial Edition*, p. 165.
49. Eckes, *Opening America's Market*, p. 50.

50. Ibid., p. 52.

51. Ibid., p. 51.

52. Ibid., p. 55.

53. Ibid., p. 53.

54. Henry Kissinger, *Diplomacy* (New York: Simon & Schuster, 1994), p. 37.

55. Samuel Eliot Morison and Henry Steele Commager, *The Growth of the American Republic*, vol. 2 (New York: Oxford University Press, 1962), pp. 440–41.

56. Samuel Eliot Morison, *The Oxford History of the American People* (New York: Oxford University Press, 1965), p. 789.

57. Alfred E. Eckes, Jr., "William McKinley: A Leader for the Next Century," An Address to the McKinley Centennial Conference, Ohio Historical Society, March 15, 1997.

58. Ibid. (*Washington Post*, Nov. 7, 1900, p. 6.)

59. Ibid. (*New York Times*, Nov. 7, 1900, p. 8.)

60. Batra, *Myth of Free Trade*, p. 132.

61. Paul Bairoch, *Economics and World History: Myths and Paradoxes* (Chicago: University of Chicago Press, 1993), p. 170.

62. Ibid., pp. 170–71.

63. Eckes, *Opening America's Market*, p. 51.

64. Peter Clarke, *Hope and Glory: Britain 1900–1990* (London: Penguin Press, 1996), p. 9.

65. Eckes, *Opening America's Market*, pp. 59–60.

66. Joseph Chamberlain, preface to *The Case Against Free Trade*, by John Murray (London, 1911), cited by William Gill, *Trade Wars Against America: A History of United States Trade and Monetary Policy* (New York: Praeger, 1991), p. vii.

67. Sidney Pollard and Colin Holmes, eds., *National Power and Industrial Rivalry 1870–1914*, vol. 2 of *Documents of European Economic History* (New York: St. Martin's Press, 1972), p. 196.

68. Otto Scott, *Otto Scott's Compass* 6, issue 69 (May 1, 1996), p. 11.

69. Charles S. Olcott, *William McKinley*, vol. 2 (Boston: Houghton Mifflin, 1916) pp. 379–82.

Chapter 12

"The Great Smoot-Hawley Myth"

1. James Bennet, "In Denver for Economic Talks, Clinton Calls for Freer Trade," *New York Times*, June 20, 1997, p. A10.

2. Elting E. Morison, ed., *The Letters of Theodore Roosevelt*, vol. 1 (Cambridge: Harvard University Press, 1951), p. 504.

3. Ibid.

4. Elting E. Morison, ed., *The Letters of Theodore Roosevelt*, vol. 14 (Cambridge: Harvard University Press, 1951), p. 934.

5. Ibid., p. 932.

6. Ibid., p. 933.

7. Thomas Hudson McKee, *The National Conventions and Platforms of All Political Parties, 1789–1905* (Baltimore, Md.: Friedenwald Co., 1906), p. 369.

8. *The Public Papers and Addresses of Franklin D. Roosevelt*, vol. 1 (New York: Random House, 1938), p. 766.

9. William J. Gill, *Trade Wars Against America: A History of United States Trade and Monetary Policy* (New York: Praeger, 1990), p. 48.

10. John Steele Gordon, *Hamilton's Blessing: The Extraordinary Life and Times of Our National Debt* (New York: Walker and Co., 1997), pp. 96–98.

11. Albert Bushnell Hart and Herbert Ronald Ferleger, eds., *Theodore Roosevelt Cyclopedia* (Westport, Conn.: Meckler Corp., 1989), p. 599.

12. Arthur S. Link, ed., *The Papers of Woodrow Wilson*, vol. 23 (Princeton, N.J.: Princeton University Press, 1977), p. 649.

13. Alfred E. Eckes, Jr., *Opening America's Market: U.S. Foreign Trade Policy Since 1776* (Chapel Hill: University of North Carolina Press, 1995), p. 35.

14. John M. Dobson, *Two Centuries of Tariffs: The Background and Emergence of the U.S. International Trade Commission* (Washington, D.C.: U.S. International Trade Commission, 1976), p. 31.

15. Thomas A. Bailey, *A Diplomatic History of the American People*, 7th ed. (New York: Meredith Publishing Co., 1964), p. 615.

16. Gordon, *Hamilton's Blessing*, p. 103.

17. Eckes, *Opening America's Market*, p. 43.

18. Rudyard Kipling, *Rudyard Kipling's Verse: Inclusive Edition 1885–1926* (Garden City, N.Y.: Doubleday, Doran & Co., 1936), pp. 830–31.

19. James West Davidson, William E. Gienapp, Christine Leigh Heyrman et al., *Nation of Nations* (New York: Knopf, 1991), p. 906.

20. Derek Alderoft, *From Versailles to Wall Street, 1919–1929* (Berkeley: University of California Press, 1981), pp. 298–300.

21. Gordon, *Hamilton's Blessing*, p. 111.

22. Eckes, *Opening America's Market*, p. 31.

23. Donald Bruce Johnson and Kirk H. Porter, compilers, *National Party Platforms, 1840–1972* (Urbana: University of Illinois Press, 1973), pp. 271–72.

24. Samuel I. Rosenman, compiler, *The Public Papers and Addresses of Franklin D. Roosevelt*, vol. 1 (New York: Random House, 1938), p. 724.

25. *Papers of Franklin D. Roosevelt*, vol. 1, p. 767.

26. *Public Papers of the Presidents of the United States: Herbert Hoover, January 1, 1932–March 4, 1933* (Washington, D.C.: Government Printing Office, 1977), p. 366.

27. Ibid., p. 476.

28. Ibid., p. 534.

29. *Papers of Franklin D. Roosevelt*, vol. 1, p. 853.

30. *Ferris Bueller's Day Off* (Paramount Pictures, 1986).

31. "Excerpts From the Free Trade Debate Between Gore and Perot," *New York Times*, Nov. 10, 1993, p. B16.

32. "Al Gore's Big Knockout," *Wall Street Journal*, Nov. 11, 1993, p. A14.

33. "NAFTA: A Defining Moment for America," *Business Week*, Nov. 22, 1993, p. 146.

34. The following section is based almost entirely on the documentary evidence in Eckes's Chapter 4, pp. 100–39.

35. Ravi Batra, *The Great American Deception: What Politicians Won't Tell You About Our Economy and Your Future* (New York: John Wiley & Sons, 1996), p. 76.

36. Gordon, *Hamilton's Blessing*, pp. 116–17.

37. A. G. Kenwood and A. L. Lougheed, *The Growth of the International Economy 1820–1960* (London: Allen and Unwin, 1971), p. 186.

38. Correli Barnett, *The Collapse of British Power* (New York: Morrow, 1971), p. 120.

39. Paul Bairoch, *Economics and World History: Myths and Paradoxes* (Chicago: University of Chicago Press, 1993), p. 4.

40. Cordell Hull, *The Memoirs of Cordell Hull*, vol. 1 (New York: Macmillan, 1948), p. 355.

41. Eckes, *Opening America's Market*, p. 31.

42. Alfred E. Eckes, Jr., "Cobden's Pyrrhic Victory," *Chronicles*, May 1995, p. 16.

Book Three

THE COUNTERREVOLUTION AND THE COMING OF A NEW POPULISM

Chapter 13

"1933–93"

1. Sam Crowther, *America Self-Contained* (Garden City, N.Y.: Doubleday, Doran & Co., 1933), pp. 4–5.

2. Alfred E. Eckes, Jr., *Opening America's Market: U.S. Foreign Trade Policy Since 1776* (Chapel Hill: University of North Carolina Press, 1995), p. 177.

Chapter 14
"COUNTERREVOLUTION"

1. John J. Sweeney, *America Needs a Raise* (New York: Houghton Mifflin, 1996), p. 98.
2. Kevin Goldman, "NAFTA Friends, Foes Blitz Public With Ads," *Wall Street Journal*, Sept. 16, 1992, p. B6.
3. Henry A. Kissinger, "The Trade Route; NAFTA a Step Toward a Prosperous World Order," *Cleveland Plain Dealer*, July 18, 1993, p. 1C.
4. Ronald A. Taylor, "Clinton Brings Out Big Trade Guns: Bush, Carter, Ford, Turn Out at White House for NAFTA," *Washington Times*, Sept. 15, 1993, p. A1.
5. Gwen Ifill, "Clinton Recruits 3 Presidents to Promote Trade Pact," *New York Times*, Sept. 15, 1993, p. B12.
6. Ibid.
7. Ann Devroy, "Clinton Enlists Predecessors in Fight for Trade Agreement," *Washington Post*, Sept. 15, 1993, p. A1.
8. Kissinger, "The Trade Route," p. 1C.
9. Paul Gigot, "GOP NAFTA Choice: Reagan or Smoot-Perot?" *Wall Street Journal*, Sept. 17, 1993, p. A10.
10. "For NAFTA," *New Republic*, Oct. 11, 1993, p. 8.
11. Patrick J. Buchanan, "Why Elites Show Teeth for NAFTA," *Washington Times*, Sept. 22, 1993, p. A21.
12. Patrick J. Buchanan, "Taste of Victory for an Unlikely Coalition, *Washington Times*, Nov. 19, 1993, p. A20.
13. "How Can Gingrich Support the WTO?" *Human Events*, Dec. 2, 1994, p. 3.
14. Lew Rockwell, *Free Market Letter* (Auburn, Ala.: Ludwig von Mises Institute, 1994), quoted by Patrick J. Buchanan, "Bill Swipes a GOP Issue," *New York Post*, Feb. 19, 1994.
15. William Drozdiak, "Historic Trade Pact Signed, But Global Tensions Persist," *Washington Post*, Apr. 16, 1994, p. A12.
16. Peter Brimelow, *Alien Nation: Common Sense About America's Immigration Disaster, with a New Afterword by the Author* (New York: Harper Perennial, 1995), p. 74.
17. Chris Whalen, *Financial Times*, Jan. 14, 1997, op-ed pg.
18. Pat Choate and Charles McMillion, *The Mysterious US Trade Deficit*, (Washington, D.C.: Manufacturing Policy Project, 1997), p. 7; Marcy Kaptur, testimony before the House Committee on International Relations, Subcommittee on the Western Hemisphere, Subcommittee on International Economic Policy and Trade, March 5, 1997.

19. Joel Millman, "Asian Investment Floods Into Mexican Border Region," *Wall Street Journal*, Sept. 6, 1996, p. A10.
20. "Halloween for NAFTA," *Wall Street Journal*, Sept. 9, 1993, p. A20.
21. "ABC Nightline Reveals DEA Hid Information on Mexican Drug Smuggling During 1993 NAFTA Debate," News from the New Teamsters, May 8, 1997.
22. Kissinger, "The Trade Route," p. 1C.
23. Alan Tonelson, "NAFTA Backers' Flawed Excuses," *Washington Times*, Mar. 28, 1997.
24. Sam Dillon, "Peso Crisis Bites Into Mexico's Long-Ruling Party," *New York Times*, July 4, 1997, p. A3.
25. Mark Falcoff, "Mexico's Midterm Elections: A Major Turning Point?" *American Enterprise Institute*, July–Aug. 1997, p. 1.
26. Brimelow, *Alien Nation*, p. 282.
27. Lorraine Woellert, "Tainted Strawberries Case Revives Battle over Free Trade," *Washington Times*, June 22, 1997, p. A5.
28. Brooke A. Masters, "Food Poisoning Is Linked to Basil Products; 126 Fell Ill After Eating Dishes from Sutton Place, Officials Say," *Washington Post*, July 19, 1997, pp. B1, B6.
29. Sandra G. Boodman, "Forbidding Fruit: How Safe Is Our Produce?" *Washington Post*, July 8, 1997, p. Z10.
30. Reuters, *Washington Post*, June 22, 1977, p. A4.
31. Wendy Lin, "How Safe Is Your Food?" *Newsday*, Aug. 13, 1997, p. B21.
32. Marian Burros, "Safety in Numbers? Hardly; Debate Fires Up for Merger of U.S. Food Inspection Agencies," *Pittsburgh Post-Gazette*, Apr. 17, 1997, p. F1.
33. "Fare Trade," *The Economist*, May 17, 1997, p. 20.
34. "Free Trade Gets an Unfriendly Reception," *Business Week*, Sept. 29, 1997, p. 34.
35. Arthur Schlesinger, Jr., "Bye, Bye, Woodrow," *Wall Street Journal*, Oct. 27, 1993, p. A16.
36. Debora Wiley, "The Little Toy Firm That Could," Gannett News Service, Sept. 29, 1992.
37. Ibid.
38. "Ertl Named to Farm Toy Hall of Fame," *Playthings*, Jan. 1993, p. 14.
39. Steve Webber, "Lawmakers Say State Can Do Little to Help," *Dubuque Telegraph Herald*, Oct. 11, 1995, p. A3.
40. Jean T. Levine, "Two Lords Master the Art of Running Firms on Both Sides of the Pond," *Business for Central New Jersey*, Apr. 28, 1993, p. 5.
41. "Ertl to Lay Off 300 in Iowa," Reuters Financial Service, Oct. 5, 1995.

Chapter 15
"A NEW NATIONALISM"

1. *The Works of Daniel Webster*, vol. 4 (Boston: Little and Brown, 1851), p. 310.
2. Samuel Crowther, *America Self-Contained* (Garden City, N.Y.: Doubleday, Doran & Co., 1933), p. 16.
3. *The Economic Report of the President, 1995*.
4. Ludwig von Mises, *Human Action: A Treatise on Economics* (New Haven, Conn.: Yale University Press, 1949), p. 195.
5. Ambrose Bierce, *The Devil's Dictionary* (New York: Sagamore Press, 1957), p. 189.
6. Ernest Renan, *The Poetry of the Celtic Races, and Other Studies* (Port Washington, N.Y.: Kennikat Press, 1970), pp. 80–81.
7. E. Christian Kopff, "The Future Belongs to Us," *Chronicles*, Oct. 1995, p. 33.
8. Renan, *Poetry of the Celtic Races*, p. 79.
9. Kopff, "The Future Belongs to Us," p. 33.
10. Andrew Gowers and David Buchan, "Balladur Calls for EU Action Against 'Unfair' Trade," *Financial Times*, Dec. 31, 1993, p. 1.
11. Will Carrington Heath, "Mises, Roëpke and the Fact/Value Distinction," *Roëpke Review*, winter/spring 1997, p. 13.
12. Wilhelm Roëpke, *A Humane Economy: The Social Framework of the Free Market* (Chicago: Henry Regnery Co., 1960), p. 91.
13. Ibid., p. 12.
14. Louis R. Harlan, ed., *The Booker T. Washington Papers*, vol. 1 (Urbana: University of Illinois Press, 1972), p. 331.
15. Ibid., p. 332.
16. Ibid.
17. Vernon M. Briggs, Jr., *Mass Immigration and the National Interest* (Armonk, N.Y.: M. E. Sharpe, 1992), pp. 91–92.
18. James Fallows, "How the World Works," *Atlantic*, Dec. 1993, p. 82.
19. John P. Cregan, "Free Trade Syndrome and America's Economic Disarmament," *America Asleep: The Free Trade Syndrome and the Global Economic Challenge* (Washington, D.C.: United States Industrial Council Educational Foundation, 1991), p. 28.
20. Greg McDonald, "White House Dream Is Over; Gramm Rips Buchanan, etc.," *Houston Chronicle*, Feb. 15, 1996, p. 1.
21. Lori Stahl, "Gramm Reflects on Presidential Bid, Says Louisiana Loss Marked the End," *Dallas Morning News*, Feb. 17, 1996, p. 35A.
22. Gerald F. Seib and John Harwood, "Disparate Groups on Right Join Forces to

Make Opposition to China's Trade Status a Key Issue," *Wall Street Journal*, June 10, 1997, p. A20.

23. Ibid.

24. James A. Dorn, "Trade and Human Rights: The Case of China," *Freedom to Trade: Refuting the New Protectionism* (Washington, D.C.: Cato Institute, 1997), p. 70.

25. Jacob G. Hornberger, preface to *The Case for Free Trade and Open Immigration* (Fairfax, Va.: Future of Freedom Foundation, 1995), p. viii.

26. Francis A. Walker, *Political Economy* (New York: Henry Holt and Co., 1888), p. 520.

27. Richard M. Ebeling, ed., *Money, Method, and the Market Process: Essays by Ludwig von Mises* (Norwell, Mass.: Kluwer Academic Publishers, 1990), p. 145.

28. Roy P. Basler, ed., *The Collected Works of Abraham Lincoln*, vol. 1 (New Brunswick, N.J.: Rutgers University Press, 1953), p. 312.

29. Ibid., p. 311.

30. Sidney Pollard and Colin Holmes, eds., *National Power and Industrial Rivalry 1870–1914*, vol. 2 of *Documents from European Economic History* (New York: St. Martin's Press, 1972), pp. 191–92.

31. Ibid., p. 194.

32. Paul Kennedy, *The Rise and Fall of the Great Powers: Economic Change and Military Conflict from 1500 to 2000* (New York: Random House, 1987), p. 202.

33. Jay Olnek, *The Invisible Hand: How Free Trade Is Choking the Life Out of America*, 2d ed. (Riverdale, N.Y.: North Stonington Press, 1984), p. 24.

34. Herman Hagedorn, ed., *The Works of Theodore Roosevelt*, vol. 17 (New York: Charles Scribner's Sons, 1925), pp. 501–02.

35. "Canada's Trade Surplus Set Record in August," *Wall Street Journal*, Oct. 21, 1996, p. A4.

36. *International Trade Reporter* 14, January 15, 1997, p. 76.

37. Greg Mastel, "The Art of the Steal," *Washington Post*, Feb. 19, 1995, p. C3.

38. Pat Choate and Charles McMillion, *The Mysterious US Trade Deficit* (Washington, D.C.: Manufacturing Policy Project, 1997), p. 10.

39. Richard Holman, compiler, "World Wire: China Snaps Up U.S. Bonds," *Wall Street Journal*, Oct. 18, 1996, p. A14.

40. David Wessel, "Rubin Presses China to Buy U.S. Goods, Trim Reserves," *Wall Street Journal*, Sept. 29, 1997, p. A19.

41. Choate and McMillion, *Mysterious US Trade Deficit*, p. 11.

42. Ravi Batra, *The Myth of Free Trade: A Plan for America's Economic Revival* (New York: Charles Scribner's Sons, 1993), p. 97.

43. "Down, But Not Out: Japanese Investment in Mexico Plans to Stay," *Business Mexico*, Aug. 1995, p. 9.

44. "Amalgamated Clothing and Textile Workers Union Press Conference Tran-

script," *News from the AFL-CIO* (Washington, D.C.: AFL-CIO, October 31, 1977), p. 6.

45. Ludwig von Mises, *Planning for Freedom*, 4th ed. (South Holland, Ill.: Libertarian Press, 1980), p. 207.

46. Ibid., pp. 196, 208.

47. Sir James Goldsmith, *The Response* (self-published, 1995), p. 19.

48. Von Mises, *Planning for Freedom*, p. 214.

49. Adam Smith, *An Inquiry into the Nature and Causes of the Wealth of Nations* (New York: Modern Library, 1937), p. 485.

50. Erik R. Pages, *Responding to Defense Dependence: Policy Ideas and the American Defense Industrial Base* (Westport, Conn.: Praeger, 1996), p. 11.

51. William J. Crowe, Jr., "Strategic Supplies Depend on U.S. Industries," *Washington Post*, Dec. 19, 1991, p. A20.

52. Pages, *Responding to Defense Dependence*, p. 17.

53. "Defense Industrial Security: Weaknesses in U.S. Security Arrangements with Foreign-owned Defense Contractors," GAO/NSIAD (Washington, D.C.: General Accounting Office, February 1996), p. 21.

54. Pages, *Responding to Defense Dependence*, p. 150.

55. Smith, *Wealth of Nations*, p. 352.

56. Bill Archer, "Would It Be a Good Idea to Replace the Income Tax with a Consumption Tax?" *Insight*, Sept. 23, 1996, p. 26.

57. Choate and McMillion, *Mysterious US Trade Deficit*, p. 9.

58. Christopher Lasch, *The Revolt of the Elites and the Betrayal of Democracy* (New York: W. W. Norton, 1995), pp. 48–49.

59. Jeffrey O. Nelson, "Missionary of Culture," *Intercollegiate Review*, fall 1996, p. 18.

INDEX